Lecture Notes in Computer Science 15403

Founding Editors

Gerhard Goos
Juris Hartmanis

Editorial Board Members

Elisa Bertino, *Purdue University, West Lafayette, IN, USA*
Wen Gao, *Peking University, Beijing, China*
Bernhard Steffen , *TU Dortmund University, Dortmund, Germany*
Moti Yung , *Columbia University, New York, NY, USA*

The series Lecture Notes in Computer Science (LNCS), including its subseries Lecture Notes in Artificial Intelligence (LNAI) and Lecture Notes in Bioinformatics (LNBI), has established itself as a medium for the publication of new developments in computer science and information technology research, teaching, and education.

LNCS enjoys close cooperation with the computer science R & D community, the series counts many renowned academics among its volume editors and paper authors, and collaborates with prestigious societies. Its mission is to serve this international community by providing an invaluable service, mainly focused on the publication of conference and workshop proceedings and postproceedings. LNCS commenced publication in 1973.

Sidney C. Nogueira · Ciprian Teodorov
Editors

Formal Methods: Foundations and Applications

27th Brazilian Symposium, SBMF 2024
Vitória, Brazil, December 4–6, 2024
Proceedings

 Springer

Editors
Sidney C. Nogueira 📵
Federal Rural University of Pernambuco
Recife, Pernambuco, Brazil

Ciprian Teodorov 📵
ENSTA Bretagne
Brest, France

ISSN 0302-9743 ISSN 1611-3349 (electronic)
Lecture Notes in Computer Science
ISBN 978-3-031-78115-5 ISBN 978-3-031-78116-2 (eBook)
https://doi.org/10.1007/978-3-031-78116-2

© The Editor(s) (if applicable) and The Author(s), under exclusive license to Springer Nature Switzerland AG 2025

This work is subject to copyright. All rights are solely and exclusively licensed by the Publisher, whether the whole or part of the material is concerned, specifically the rights of translation, reprinting, reuse of illustrations, recitation, broadcasting, reproduction on microfilms or in any other physical way, and transmission or information storage and retrieval, electronic adaptation, computer software, or by similar or dissimilar methodology now known or hereafter developed.
The use of general descriptive names, registered names, trademarks, service marks, etc. in this publication does not imply, even in the absence of a specific statement, that such names are exempt from the relevant protective laws and regulations and therefore free for general use.
The publisher, the authors and the editors are safe to assume that the advice and information in this book are believed to be true and accurate at the date of publication. Neither the publisher nor the authors or the editors give a warranty, expressed or implied, with respect to the material contained herein or for any errors or omissions that may have been made. The publisher remains neutral with regard to jurisdictional claims in published maps and institutional affiliations.

This Springer imprint is published by the registered company Springer Nature Switzerland AG
The registered company address is: Gewerbestrasse 11, 6330 Cham, Switzerland

If disposing of this product, please recycle the paper.

Preface

This volume contains the papers presented at the 27th Brazilian Symposium on Formal Methods (SBMF 2024). The conference was held in Vitória, Brazil, from December 4 to December 6, 2024, and was preceded by the 9th School of Theoretical Computer Science and Formal Methods (ETMF 2024) on December 3, 2024, in Serra, Brazil. SBMF was organized by the Instituto Federal do Espírito Santo and promoted by the Brazilian Computer Society (SBC).

The Brazilian Symposium on Formal Methods is dedicated to developing, disseminating, and applying formal methods to construct high-quality computational systems. It aims to promote opportunities for researchers and practitioners to discuss the latest advances in the field. SBMF is a well-established scientific and technical event in the software domain. Its first edition was in 1998, and we celebrated its 25th jubilee edition in 2022. Proceedings from recent editions have been published mostly in Springer's Lecture Notes in Computer Science series, including volumes 5902 (2009), 6527 (2010), 7021 (2011), 7498 (2012), 8195 (2013), 8941 (2014), 9526 (2015), 10090 (2016), 10623 (2017), 11254 (2018), 12475 (2020), 13130 (2021), 13768 (2022), and 14414 (2023).

The conference featured three invited talks, by Marcel Oliveira (Federal University of Rio Grande do Norte, Brazil), Julien Deantoni (Université Côte d'Azur, France), and Philipp Rümmer (University of Regensburg, Germany). A total of 12 papers were presented at the conference and included in this volume: 8 regular papers and 4 short papers, selected from 18 submissions (13 regular, 5 short) from 7 countries: Australia, Brazil, Denmark, Germany, Netherlands, UK, and USA. The selected papers were presented across four technical sessions, which form the sections of this volume: Formal Analysis and Verification in Temporal and Symbolic Systems, Formal Semantics and Verification of UML Models, Formal Verification and Proof Techniques in Algorithms and Logics, and Formal Methods for Security and Privacy. The PC comprised 33 members from the national and international formal methods community. Each submission was reviewed by three Program Committee members in a single-blind review process. Submissions, reviews, deliberations, and decisions were handled via EasyChair.

We thank the Program Committee for their dedication in evaluating submissions and suggesting improvements. Special thanks to the general chair of SBMF 2024, Jefferson Andrade (Instituto Federal do Espírito Santo, Brazil), whose efforts ensured the smooth running of the conference. We would like to thank SBC for their sponsorship and Springer for agreeing to publish the proceedings as part of the Lecture Notes in Computer Science series.

October 2024

Sidney C. Nogueira
Ciprian Teodorov

Organization

General Chair

Jefferson Andrade — Federal Institute of Espírito Santo, Brazil

Program Committee Chairs

Sidney Nogueira — Federal Rural University of Pernambuco, Brazil
Ciprian Teodorov — ENSTA Bretagne, France

Steering Committee

Haniel Barbosa — Universidade Federal de Minas Gerais, Brazil
Sérgio Campos — Universidade Federal de Minas Gerais, Brazil
Lucas Lima — Universidade Federal Rural de Pernambuco, Brazil
Marius Minea — University of Massachusetts Amherst, USA
Vince Molnár — Budapest University of Technology and Economics, Hungary
Yoni Zohar — Bar-Ilan University, Israel

Program Committee

Haniel Barbosa — Universidade Federal de Minas Gerais, Brazil
Luís Soares Barbosa — University of Minho, Portugal
Armin Biere — University of Freiburg, Germany
Sergio Campos — Universidade Federal de Minas Gerais, Brazil
Gustavo Carvalho — Universidade Federal de Pernambuco, Brazil
Márcio Cornélio — Universidade Federal de Pernambuco, Brazil
Katalin Fazekas — TU Wien, Austria
Mathias Fleury — University of Freiburg, Germany
Rohit Gheyi — Universidade Federal de Campina Grande, Brazil
Ahmed Irfan — SRI International, USA
Juliano Iyoda — Universidade Federal de Pernambuco, Brazil
Daniela Kaufmann — TU Wien, Austria

Thierry Lecomte	CLEARSY, France
Michael Leuschel	University of Düsseldorf, Germany
Lucas Lima	Universidade Federal Rural de Pernambuco, Brazil
Tiago Massoni	Universidade Federal de Campina Grande, Brazil
Marius Minea	Politehnica University Timișoara, Romania
Alvaro Miyazawa	University of York, UK
Vince Molnár	Budapest University of Technology and Economics, Hungary
Marianela Morales	IMDEA Software Institute, Spain
Alexandre Mota	Universidade Federal de Pernambuco, Brazil
Edjard Mota	Federal University of Amazonas, Brazil
Marcel Oliveira	Universidade Federal do Rio Grande do Norte, Brazil
Pedro Ribeiro	University of York, UK
Philipp Rümmer	University of Regensburg, Germany
Augusto Sampaio	Universidade Federal de Pernambuco, Brazil
Hans-Jörg Schurr	University of Iowa, USA
Volker Stolz	Høgskulen på Vestlandet, Norway
Leopoldo Teixeira	Universidade Federal de Pernambuco, Brazil
Nils Timm	University of Pretoria, South Africa
Maurice ter Beek	CNR, Italy
Jim Woodcock	University of York, UK
Yoni Zohar	Bar-Ilan University, Israel

Additional Reviewers

Ulises Torrella
Ármin Zavada
Bertalan Zoltán

Evanesco: Hiding Formal Methods from Muggles while Ensuring System Correctness

Marcel Vinícius Medeiros Oliveira

Department of Informatics and Applied Mathematics, Federal University of Rio Grande do Norte, Natal, 59078970 Brazil
marcel@dimap.ufrn.br

Keywords: Software Architecture · Relay-Based Railway Interlocking Systems · CSP · Model Checking · Formal Verification

1 Abstract

This talk will explore two distinct examples of integrating formal methods into software development and system design, emphasizing how these rigorous techniques can be hidden from the "Muggles"- those who do not know about the magic of formal methods—while still ensuring system reliability and safety. By embedding formal verification into user-friendly tools, these examples show how software engineers and system designers can benefit from advanced formal methods without requiring expertise in the underlying "spells" (i.e., mathematical models).

The first example, **project FormAr**, demonstrates how software architects can be assisted in performing formal verification using a SysML-based language like SysADL. But no need to be a wizard! This is achieved through the automatic transformation of SysADL architecture descriptions into formal specifications in the Communicating Sequential Processes (CSP) process algebra, on which the formal semantics of SysADL has been defined. This transformation allows software architects to verify critical architectural properties, such as deadlock-freedom, model consistency, safety, and compliance between different architectural viewpoints, without even knowing CSP or the FDR4 model checker exist. The SysADL Studio tool, now enhanced to seamlessly handle this "magic", lets architects focus on design and analysis while the hard work of translating the SysADL architecture description into CSP and interacting with FDR4 to achieve formal verification happens invisibly in the background. The results of the formal verification are presented in a comprehensible format, highlighting issues directly within the SysADL architectural models and offering diagnostics to assist in quickly locating and resolving architectural problems—no wand required! This work demonstrates the power of formal methods to improve software architecture analysis without imposing additional complexity on the non-magical architect.

The second example ventures into the safety-critical world of **Relay-Based Railway Interlocking Systems (RIS)**—a space where a little bit of "magic" could save the day. This work provides a method to model Relay-based RIS in CSP, allowing the automatic verification of key properties such as deadlock detection, the presence of short circuits, and the identification of infinite activation/deactivation cycles (the so-called "Ring-bell Effect"). By abstracting the general behavior of each type of relay component and instantiating these into a full system, the approach allows for system specifications to be generated directly from the relay diagrams and connections. Engineers do not need to don a wizard's hat, though: the tool developed for this approach enables them to build RIS diagrams, select circuits and properties for verification, and receive visual feedback in case of failures, with problematic components or paths highlighted on the relay diagram itself. This approach ensures that engineers can address safety-critical concerns in RIS design without needing to understand the "magic" happening under the hood with CSP models and formal verification techniques.

Through these two examples, we illustrate how formal methods can be embedded in tools to support software architects and engineers, enabling them to reach higher levels of assurance in their designs while remaining focused on their domain-specific "Muggle" concerns. Both examples show that the benefits of formal verification—improved safety, reliability, and correctness—can be delivered without exposing users to the "magical" intricacies of formal methods themselves.

Software Language Engineering Towards Formal Systems Engineering: A Journey

Julien Deantoni

Université Côte d'Azur, CNRS/I3S/Inria Kairos, France
julien.deantoni@univ-cotedazur.fr

The development of software-intensive systems such as smartphones, robots, and vehicles has become increasingly complex. These systems, defined by interactions between heterogeneous models require interdisciplinary collaboration across various domains [2]. In order to manage this complexity, over the past decade, the Kairos team's research has focused on addressing the possibility to use Software Language Engineering to formalize *model-based systems engineering* [9].

One challenge to enable V&V of software intensive systems is ensuring behavioral consistency between the heterogeneous models used to represent different aspects of the system; each of them being specified by using a specific domain-specific modeling language. However, the behavioral semantics of these models are often described ambiguously, making formal analysis difficult. The Kairos team worked on developing formal, language-agnostic methods to specify model behaviors, facilitating consistent interpretation and reasoning across heterogeneous models [4, 13, 12, 8, 11, 3].

Another challenge is understanding and managing the semantics underlying *correspondences* between models in order to ensure that decisions made in one model propagate accurately to others. Kairos contributed to formalizing these correspondences, enabling more effective coordination of models in complex systems [15, 14, 16, 10].

Additionally, the lack of robust *metalanguages* for specifying behavioral semantics, particularly regarding concurrency and non-determinism, presents a barrier to tool automation. While syntax-driven tools like Xtext provide useful functionality for model syntax, there are few options for generating time and concurrency aware interpreters or compilers from a behavioral semantics specification. In collaboration with people from the GEMOC initiative, Kairos focused on creating new metalanguages to address these gaps and enable automatic tool generation [7, 5, 6, 19].

Lastly, automating the coordination between heterogeneous models remains a challenge. Existing methods are limited in flexibility and often require manual intervention, which is error-prone and inefficient. I have worked on formal approaches to automate the generation of coordination patterns, reducing the manual effort required and improving the accuracy of multi-model systems development [20, 21, 1, 22, 17, 18].

In this talk, I propose to give a journey in the research activity realized in the last 15 years by the Kairos team.

References

1. Centomo, S., Deantoni, J., de Simone, R.: Using systemc cyber models in an FMI co-simulation environment: results and proposed FMI enhancements. In: Kitsos, P. (ed.) 2016 Euromicro Conference on Digital System Design, DSD 2016, Limassol, Cyprus, August 31 – September 2, 2016, pp. 318–325. IEEE Computer Society (2016)
2. Combemale, B., Deantoni, J., Baudry, B., France, R.B., Jezequel, J.-M., Gray, J.: Globalizing modeling languages. Computer **47**(6), 68–71 (2014)
3. Deantoni, J., André, C., Gascon, R.: CCSL denotational semantics. Research Report RR-8628 (2014)
4. Deantoni, J., Cambeiro, J., Bateni, S., Lin, S., Lohstroh, M.: Debugging and verification tools for lingua franca in gemoc studio. In: 24th Forum on specification & Design Languages, FDL 2021, Antibes, France, September 8–10, 2021, pp. 1–8. IEEE (2021)
5. Deantoni, J., Diallo, P.I., Champeau, J., Combemale, B., Teodorov, C.: Operational semantics of the model of concurrency and communication language. Research Report RR-8584, INRIA (2014)
6. Deantoni, J., Diallo, I.P., Teodorov, C., Champeau, J., Combemale, B.: Towards a meta-language for the concurrency concern in DSLs. In: *Design, Automation and Test in Europe Conference and Exhibition (DATE)*, Grenoble, France (2015).
7. Deantoni, J., Mallet, F.: ECL: the event constraint language, an extension of OCL with events. Research Report RR-8031, INRIA (2012)
8. DeAntoni, J., Mallet, F.: Timesquare: treat your models with logical time. In: Furia, C.A., Nanz, S. (eds.) Objects, Models, Components, Patterns. TOOLS 2012. Lecture Notes in Computer Science, vol. 7304, pp. 34–41. Springer, Heidelberg (2012). https://doi.org/10.1007/978-3-642-30561-0_4
9. Deantoni, J.: Towards Formal System Modeling: Making Explicit and Formal the Concurrent and Timed Operational Semantics to Better Understand Heterogeneous Models. Habilitation à diriger des recherches, Université Côte d'Azur, CNRS, I3S, France (2019)
10. Garcés, K., Deantoni, J., Mallet, F.: A model-based approach for reconciliation of polychronous execution traces. In: 37th EUROMICRO Conference on Software Engineering and Advanced Applications, SEAA 2011, Oulu, Finland, August 30 – September 2, 2011, pp. 259–266. IEEE Computer Society (2011)
11. Gascon, R., Mallet, F., Deantoni, J.: Logical time and temporal logics: comparing UML MARTE/CCSL and PSL. In: Combi, C., Leucker, M., Wolter, F. (eds.) Eighteenth International Symposium on Temporal Representation and Reasoning, TIME 2011, Lübeck, Germany, September 12–14, 2011, pp. 141–148. IEEE (2011)
12. Glitia, C., DeAntoni, J., Mallet, F., Millo, J. V., Boulet, P., Gamatié, A.: Progressive and explicit refinement of scheduling for multidimensional data-flow applications using UML MARTE. Design Autom. Emb. Sys. **19**(1-2), 1–33 (2015)
13. Glitia, C., DeAntoni, J., Mallet, F.: Logical time at work: capturing data dependencies and platform constraints. In: Morawiec, A., Hinderscheit, J. (eds.) Proceedings of

the 2010 Forum on Specification & Design Languages, FDL 2010, September 14–16, 2010, Southampton, UK, p. 241. ECSI, Electronic Chips & Systems design Initiative (2010)
14. Gomez, C., Deantoni, J., Mallet, F.: Multi-view power modeling based on UML, MARTE and SysML. In: Software Engineering and Advanced Applications (SEAA), pp. 17–20 (2012)
15. Gomez, C., DeAntoni, J., Mallet, F.: Power consumption analysis using multi-view modeling. power and timing modeling, optimization and simulation (PATMOS), pp. 235–238 (2013)
16. Khecharem, A., Gomez, C., DeAntoni, J., Mallet, F., De Simone, R.: Execution of heterogeneous models for thermal analysis with a multi-view approach. In: FDL 2014: Forum on specification and Design Languages, Munich, Germany, IEEE (2014)
17. Larsen, M.E.V., Deantoni, J., Combemale, B., Mallet, F.: A behavioral coordination operator language (BCOOL). In: Lethbridge, T., Cabot, J., Egyed, A. (eds.) 18th ACM/IEEE International Conference on Model Driven Engineering Languages and Systems, MoDELS 2015, Ottawa, ON, Canada, September 30 – October 2, 2015, pp. 186–195. IEEE Computer Society (2015)
18. Larsen, M.E.V., Deantoni, J., Combemale, B., Mallet, F.: A model-driven based environment for automatic model coordination. In: Kulkarni, V., Badreddin, O. (eds.), Proceedings of the MoDELS 2015 Demo and Poster Session co-located with ACM/IEEE 18th International Conference on Model Driven Engineering Languages and Systems (MoDELS 2015), Ottawa, Canada, September 27, 2015, vol. 1554 CEUR Workshop Proceedings, pp. 44–47. CEUR-WS.org (2015)
19. Latombe, F., Crégut, X., Combemale, B., Deantoni, J., Pantel, M.: Weaving concurrency in executable domain-specific modeling languages. In: Paige, R.F., Ruscio, D.D., Völter, M. (eds.) Proceedings of the 2015 ACM SIGPLAN International Conference on Software Language Engineering, SLE 2015, Pittsburgh, PA, USA, October 25–27, 2015, pp. 125–136. ACM, (2015)
20. Liboni, G., Deantoni, J., Portaluri, A., Quaglia, D., De Simone, R.: Beyond time-triggered co-simulation of cyber-physical systems for performance and accuracy improvements. In: Chillet, D. (ed.) Proceedings of the RAPIDO 2018 Workshop on Rapid Simulation and Performance Evaluation: Methods and Tools, Manchester, UK, January 22–24, 2018, pp. 2:1–2:8. ACM (2018)
21. Liboni, G., Deantoni, J.: WIP on a coordination language to automate the generation of co-simulations. In: Kazmierski, T.J., von Hanxleden, R., Mak, T.S.T. (eds.), 2019 Forum for Specification and Design Languages, FDL 2019, Southampton, United Kingdom, September 2–4, 2019, pp. 1–4. IEEE (2019)
22. Thule, C., Gomes, C., Deantoni, J., Larsen, P.G., Brauer, J., Vangheluwe, H.: Towards the verification of hybrid co-simulation algorithms. In: Mazzara, M., Ober, I., Salaün, G. (eds.) Software Technologies: Applications and Foundations. STAF 2018. Lecture Notes in Computer Science, vol. 11176, pp. 5–20. Springer, Cham (2018). https://doi.org/10.1007/978-3-030-04771-9_1

Verification by Program Transformation

Philipp Rümmer

In deductive verification and software model checking, dealing with certain language constructs can be problematic when the back-end solver is not sufficiently powerful or lacks the required theories. This applies, in particular, to the concept of extended quantifiers found in specification languages like JML and ACSL. Extended quantifiers can be used to compute, among others, the maximum element or the sum of elements of an array and are frequently used in specifications, but tend to be difficult to support in verification tools. In the talk, I will present our ongoing research on how to automatically transform programs with such complicated operators to equivalent programs not containing the operators, and to reason about the correctness of those simpler programs instead. We apply our framework to cover the different kinds of extended quantifiers, which we formalize as monoid homomorphisms. Our approach is generic, however, and can be applied to describe a wide range of program transformations.

The presentation is based on joint work with Jesper Amilon, Zafer Esen, Dilian Gurov, Christian Lidström, Marten Voorberg.

Contents

Formal Analysis and Verification in Temporal and Symbolic Systems

On the Existence of Unions of Timed Scenarios 3
   Neda Saeedloei

SMTQuery: Analysing SMT-LIB String Benchmarks 22
   Mitja Kulczynski, Kevin Lotz, Florin Manea,
   Danny Bøgsted Poulsen, and Paul Sarnighausen-Cahn

Autonomous Vehicles Path Planning Under Temporal Logic Specifications 35
   Akshay Dhonthi, Nicolas Schischka, Ernst Moritz Hahn,
   and Vahid Hashemi

Formal Semantics and Verification of UML Models

A CSP Semantics for UML State Machines Aiming at Hidden Formal
Methods Verification 49
   Diego Ferreira and Lucas Lima

Verifying Integrated Designs of UML State Machines and Activities Using
CSP 68
   Diego Ferreira and Lucas Lima

An Integrated Framework for Analysing, Simulating and Testing UML
Models 86
   Gustavo Carvalho, José Dihego, and Augusto Sampaio

Formal Verification and Proof Techniques in Algorithms and Logics

Brzozowski's Algorithm for Automata Minimization Verified in Coq 107
   Filipe Ramos, Karina Girardi Roggia, and Rafael Castro G. Silva

Soundness-Preserving Fusion of Modal Logics in Coq 120
   Miguel Alfredo Nunes, Karina Girardi Roggia,
   and Paulo Henrique Torrens

Formally Verified Implementation of the K-Nearest Neighbors
Classification Algorithm 139
   Bernny Velasquez, Jessica Herring, and Nadeem Abdul Hamid

Formal Methods for Security and Privacy

Formal Verification of Forward Secrecy and Post-Compromise Security for TreeKEM 155
   Alex J. Washburn and Subash Shankar

Formal Privacy Analyses for Open Banking 171
   Luigi D. C. Soares, Mário S. Alvim, Di Bu, Natasha Fernandes, and Yin Liao

Trusted Deployer: A Tool for Safe Creation and Upgrade of Ethereum Smart Contracts 194
   Juliandson Ferreira, Pedro Antonino, Augusto Sampaio, A. W. Roscoe, and Filipe Arruda

Author Index 205

Formal Analysis and Verification in Temporal and Symbolic Systems

On the Existence of Unions of Timed Scenarios

Neda Saeedloei[(✉)]

Towson University, Towson, USA
nsaeedloei@towson.edu

Abstract. In earlier work it was shown that, given two consistent timed scenarios, there might not exist a scenario whose semantics is the union of those of the two. A sufficient condition for the non-existence of such a union was also identified. In this paper we report on a comprehensive study of the union operation for scenarios. We identify a new sufficient condition that provides a syntactic criterion for the existence of a scenario that is the union of two given scenarios. We also prove that the condition is necessary.

1 Introduction

Using scenarios for specifying complex systems (including real time systems and distributed systems [1,2]), and synthesizing formal models of systems from scenarios have been active areas of research for several decades [3–10].

In our earlier work [11] we developed a formal, yet simple notation for timed scenarios. Intuitively, a scenario is a sequence of events along with a set of constraints between the times of these events, which can be used to specify the partial behaviours of a system or a component of a system (see Sect. 2 for more details). We defined the semantics of a timed scenario as the set of all behaviours that are "allowed" by the scenario. All such behaviours must satisfy the same set of constraints. We developed the notion of "stable distance table", as a *canonical* representation of the set of constraints of a scenario: it captures the tightest set of constraints of the scenario. We used stable distance tables as the foundation for various algorithms for determining the consistency and equivalence of scenarios, as well as for optimizing scenarios [11,12]. More recently, we used them for developing the notions of intersection, union and subsumption for scenarios [13]. In particular, we studied the conditions under which the union of the behaviours allowed by two scenarios can be represented by a single scenario, and presented a sufficient condition for the non-existence of the union [13]. The problem of whether the condition is also necessary was left open [13].

The operations on scenarios—the union, in particular—are directly relevant to the problem of synthesizing timed automata from a set of scenarios [14]. Assume a set Ξ of scenarios includes ξ and η such that $\gamma = \xi \cup \eta$. Then replacing both ξ and η in Ξ with γ, before synthesis, always results in fewer locations, and often in fewer clocks in the synthesized automaton [14].

These operations are, in general, also relevant to model-checking timed automata [15]. Model-checking [16] is an automatic technique based on exhaustive exploration of the reachable state space of a system: given a model of a system and some property p, the goal is to determine whether there exists a state reachable from the initial state in which p holds. A major obstacle to using model-checking in practice is the state explosion problem. For real-time systems modeled as timed automata the state space is infinite due to clock variables, therefore a complete search of the state space is impossible. However, the reachability problem for timed automata is decidable [15], thanks to various abstraction techniques that have been developed to overcome the state space explosion problem [17]. One such abstraction is using clock zones, as symbolic representations of the states of timed automata. A clock zone is a set of constraints, each of which puts a bound on the difference between the values of two clocks. Each location of a timed automaton is associated with a zone, and the reachability analysis involves manipulating clock zones along various paths of the automaton. A location, in general, can be associated with more than one zone, for example when it can be reached via different paths. In that case, the union of all these zones must be taken, in order to get the zone corresponding to the location. However, the union of zones, in general, cannot be represented by a zone, and therefore, it is often approximated [17,18]. One such approximation is obtained by taking the convex hull of the zones [17].

Various data structures for representing zones, and a variety of reachability algorithms utilizing these data structures have been introduced [17,19,20]. Examples include using difference bound matrices (DBMs) [21], binary decision diagrams (BDDs) [18], clock difference diagrams (CDDs) [19] and Numerical decision digrams (NDDs) [20,22].

As part of an earlier work [12,23] we showed how—in the case of a timed automaton that corresponds to a single timed scenario—our distance tables can be used to represent time zones similarly to DBMs. So the next natural step for us is to investigate the necessary conditions under which it is possible to form the union of two timed scenarios represented by two distance tables. More specifically, we make the following contributions:

- We introduce the notion of z_pairs between two different constraints α and β of two scenarios ξ and η, respectively. Intuitively, α and β form a z_pair, if there exist behaviours whose times do not satisfy constraints α and β, but satify the constraints of the "quasi-union" of ξ and η (see Sect. 2.1 for details). That is, they do not belong to the semantics of either ξ or η, but belong to the semantics of the "quasi-union" of ξ and η. We call such behaviours "zigzagging behaviours". We show that if there is no z_pair between scenarios ξ and η, then $\xi \cup \eta$ exists. This will be a new sufficient condition for the existence of the union of two scenarios, but stronger than our previous condition [13].
- We prove that the existence of z_pairs is also a necessary condition for the existence of zigzagging behaviours, and therefore the non-existence of the union of ξ and η. This will address the problem that was previously left open [13].

0 : a ;	
1 : b {$\tau_{0,1} \geq 3$} ;	
2 : c {$\tau_{0,2} \leq 7$} .	

	1	2
0	$(3,\infty)$	$(0,7)$
1		$(0,\infty)$

	1	2
0	$(3,7)$	$(3,7)$
1		$(0,4)$

Fig. 1. ξ, its initial table and its stable table

2 Timed Scenarios

This section briefly recounts our earlier work [11–13].

Let Σ be a finite set of symbols called *events*. A *behaviour*[1] over Σ is a sequence $(e_0, t_0)(e_1, t_1)(e_2, t_2)\ldots$, such that $e_i \in \Sigma$, $t_i \in \mathbb{R}^{\geq 0}$ and $t_{i-1} \leq t_i$ for $i \in \{1, 2 \ldots\}$.

For a finite behaviour $\mathcal{B} = (e_0, t_0)(e_1, t_1)\ldots(e_{n-1}, t_{n-1})$ of length n, and for any $0 \leq i < j < n$, the *distance*, in time units, of event j from event i in $\mathcal{B}$ is denoted by $t_{ij}^{\mathcal{B}}$. That is, $t_{ij}^{\mathcal{B}} = t_j - t_i$.

A *timed scenario* (scenario for short) of length $n \in \mathbb{N}$ over Σ is a pair $(\mathcal{E}, \mathcal{C})$, where $\mathcal{E} = e_0 e_1 \ldots e_{n-1}$ is a sequence of events, and $\mathcal{C} \subset \Phi(n)$ is a finite set of constraints. Each constraint in $\Phi(n)$ is of the form $b \sim a$, where b is the symbol $\tau_{i,j}$ (for some integers $0 \leq i < j < n$), $\sim \in \{\leq, \geq\}$ and a is a constant in the set of rational numbers, $\mathbb{Q}$. The interpretation is that $\tau_{i,j}$ is the time distance between the i-th and the j-th events in the behaviours described by a scenario. The constraints $\tau_{i,j} \geq 0$ and $\tau_{i,j} \leq \infty$ are called *default constraints*.

A behaviour $\mathcal{B} = (e_0, t_0)(e_1, t_1)\ldots(e_{n-1}, t_{n-1})$ over Σ is *allowed* by scenario $\xi = (\mathcal{E}, \mathcal{C})$ iff $\mathcal{E} = e_0 \ldots e_{n-1}$ and every $\tau_{i,j} \sim a$ in $\mathcal{C}$ evaluates to true after $\tau_{i,j}$ is replaced by $t_{ij}^{\mathcal{B}}$. The *semantics* of scenario ξ, denoted by $[\![\xi]\!]$, is the set of behaviours that are allowed by ξ.

Figure 1 shows the "external representation" of scenario $\xi = (abc, \{\tau_{0,1} \geq 3, \tau_{0,2} \leq 7\})$, $[\![\xi]\!] = \{(a, t_0)(b, t_1)(c, t_2) \mid t_0 \leq t_1 \leq t_2 \wedge t_1 - t_0 \geq 3 \wedge t_2 - t_0 \leq 7\}$. A scenario ξ is *consistent* iff $[\![\xi]\!] \neq \emptyset$. It is *inconsistent* iff $[\![\xi]\!] = \emptyset$.

For a consistent scenario ξ of length n, and for $0 \leq i < j < n$, $m_{ij}^{\xi} = min\{t_{ij}^{\mathcal{B}} \mid \mathcal{B} \in [\![\xi]\!]\}$ and $M_{ij}^{\xi} = max\{t_{ij}^{\mathcal{B}} \mid \mathcal{B} \in [\![\xi]\!]\}$. The absence of an upper bound for some i and j will be denoted by $M_{ij}^{\xi} = \infty$. We will write just m_{ij} and M_{ij} when ξ is understood. For any behaviour $\mathcal{B}$ in $[\![\xi]\!]$, $0 \leq m_{ij} \leq t_{ij}^{\mathcal{B}} \leq M_{ij} \leq \infty$.

For a consistent scenario ξ of length n, and for any $0 \leq i < j < k < n$ the following inequations hold [11]:

$$m_{ij} + m_{jk} \leq m_{ik} \leq \begin{cases} m_{ij} + M_{jk} \\ M_{ij} + m_{jk} \end{cases} \leq M_{ik} \leq M_{ij} + M_{jk} \qquad (1)$$

Let $\xi = (\mathcal{E}, \mathcal{C})$ be a scenario of length n, such that, for any $0 \leq i < j < n$, $\mathcal{C}$ contains at most one constraint of the form $\tau_{i,j} \geq c$ and at most one of the form $\tau_{i,j} \leq c$. A *distance table* for ξ is a representation of $\mathcal{C}$ in the form of a triangular matrix $\mathcal{D}^{\xi}$. For $0 \leq i < j < n$, $\mathcal{D}^{\xi}[i, j] = (l_{ij}^{\xi}, h_{ij}^{\xi})$, where l_{ij}^{ξ} and h_{ij}^{ξ} are rational

---

[1] The notion of "behaviour" is equivalent to that of Alur's "timed word" [15].

numbers. If $\tau_{i,j} \geq c \in \mathcal{C}$ then $l_{ij}^\xi = c$, otherwise $l_{ij}^\xi = 0$; if $\tau_{i,j} \leq c \in \mathcal{C}$ then $h_{ij}^\xi = c$, otherwise $h_{ij}^\xi = \infty$. We will write just l_{ij} and h_{ij} when ξ is understood. A distance table for ξ of Fig. 1 is shown in the middle of the figure.

A distance table for a scenario of size n is *valid* iff $l_{ij} \leq h_{ij}$, for all $0 \leq i < j < n$. A table that is not valid is *invalid*. If $\mathcal{D}^\xi$ is invalid, then ξ is inconsistent.

A valid distance table for a scenario of size n is *stable* iff, for all $0 \leq i < j < k < n$, the inequations in (1) hold when m_{ij}, m_{jk}, m_{ik} are replaced by l_{ij}, l_{jk}, l_{ik} and M_{ij}, M_{jk}, M_{ik} are replaced by h_{ij}, h_{jk}, h_{ik}. If $\mathcal{D}^\xi$ is stable then ξ is consistent. The table of a consistent scenario ξ can be stabilized by applying the following six rules:

$$l_{ij} + l_{jk} > l_{ik} \longrightarrow l_{ik} := l_{ij} + l_{jk} \qquad l_{ik} > l_{ij} + h_{jk} \longrightarrow l_{ij} := l_{ik} - h_{jk}$$
$$l_{ik} > h_{ij} + l_{jk} \longrightarrow l_{jk} := l_{ik} - h_{ij} \qquad l_{ij} + h_{jk} > h_{ik} \longrightarrow h_{jk} := h_{ik} - l_{ij}$$
$$h_{ij} + l_{jk} > h_{ik} \longrightarrow h_{ij} := h_{ik} - l_{jk} \qquad h_{ik} > h_{ij} + h_{jk} \longrightarrow h_{ik} := h_{ij} + h_{jk}$$

At least one rule is applicable if and only if some inequation in (1) does not hold. The purpose of each rule is to tighten a constraint (i.e., increase a lower bound or decrease an upper bound) just enough to establish a particular inequation. If none of the rules is applicable, and the table is valid, then it is stable. The table on the right of Fig. 1 is the stable distance table of ξ in that figure.

If ξ is a scenario of length n and $\mathcal{D}_s^\xi$ is its stable table, then for every $0 \leq i < j < n$, $l_{ij}^\xi = m_{ij}^\xi$ and $h_{ij}^\xi = M_{ij}^\xi$, that is, $\mathcal{D}_s^\xi[i,j] = (m_{ij}^\xi, M_{ij}^\xi)$. Intuitively, $\mathcal{D}_s^\xi[i,j]$ corresponds to a pair of constraints: the time distance between events i and j in every behaviour in $[\![\xi]\!]$ must be at least m_{ij}^ξ and at most M_{ij}^ξ. We use $\mathcal{C}(\mathcal{D}_s^\xi)$ to denote the set of constraints represented by $\mathcal{D}_s^\xi$. All the constraints in $\mathcal{C}(\mathcal{D}_s^\xi)$ are as *tight* as possible. Moreover, $\mathcal{C}(\mathcal{D}_s^\xi)$ includes all the constraints that are implied [12] by the initial set of constraints.

A scenario ξ can be transformed to an equivalent scenario η by *optimizing* its set of constraints [23], so that η has a minimal set of constraints[2]. We call η the *optimized* form of ξ. For an optimized scenario $\xi = (\mathcal{E}, \mathcal{C})$ the members of $\mathcal{C}$ will be referred to as *explicit constraints*. We know that $\mathcal{D}_s^\xi$ also includes *implicit constraints*: default constraints and constraints that are implied by $\mathcal{C}$.

The stable table of Fig. 1 represents the set of constraints $\{\tau_{0,1} \geq 3, \tau_{0,1} \leq 7, \tau_{0,2} \geq 3, \tau_{0,2} \leq 7, \tau_{1,2} \geq 0, \tau_{1,2} \leq 4\}$. Observe that, for example, $\mathcal{D}_s^\xi[1,2] = (0,4)$: $m_{12}^\xi = 0$, which corresponds to a default constraint, and $M_{12}^\xi = 4$, which corresponds to an implied constraint. The set of explicit constraints of ξ, which is already in optimized form, is $\{\tau_{0,1} \geq 3, \tau_{0,2} \leq 7\}$, while $\{\tau_{0,1} \leq 7, \tau_{0,2} \geq 3, \tau_{1,2} \leq 4\}$ is the set of implicit constraints.

The *interval* I_{ij}^ξ is $\{a \in \mathbb{Q} \mid m_{ij}^\xi \leq a \leq M_{ij}^\xi\}$ where $\mathcal{D}_s^\xi[i,j] = (m_{ij}^\xi, M_{ij}^\xi)$. Intuitively, I_{ij}^ξ specifies the set of all the possible values of t_{ij} that can appear in the behaviours allowed by ξ. We will write just I_{ij} when ξ is understood.

If $i = j$, then by definition, $t_{ii} = 0$, so $m_{ii} = 0$, $M_{ii} = 0$ and $I_{ii} = [0,0]$.

---

[2] The aim of optimization which begins with the construction of a stable distance table, is to obtain a minimal set of constraints, i.e., removal of any of these constraints would change the semantics.

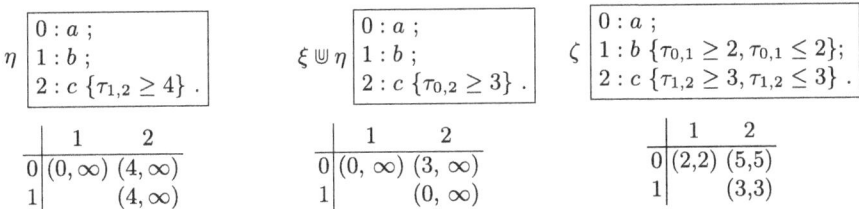

Fig. 2. η and its stable table

Fig. 3. The combination of ξ of Fig. 1 and η of Fig. 2, and ζ with its stable table

2.1 Combination of Two Timed Scenarios

If ξ and η are two consistent scenarios of length n with the same sequences of events, $\mathcal{E}$, such that $\forall_{0 \leq i < j < n} \ I^\xi_{ij} \cap I^\eta_{ij} \neq \emptyset$, then the *combination* (or the "quasi-union") of ξ and η, denoted by $\xi \uplus \eta$, is *defined*. In that case, $\xi \uplus \eta$ is a scenario whose sequence of events is $\mathcal{E}$ and whose constraints are given by $\mathcal{D}^{\xi \uplus \eta}$, where $\mathcal{D}^{\xi \uplus \eta}[i,j] = (\min(m^\xi_{ij}, m^\eta_{ij}), \max(M^\xi_{ij}, M^\eta_{ij}))$.

If $\xi \uplus \eta$ is defined, then $[\![\xi]\!] \cup [\![\eta]\!] \subseteq [\![\xi \uplus \eta]\!]$. But, in general, $[\![\xi \uplus \eta]\!] \not\subseteq [\![\xi]\!] \cup [\![\eta]\!]$. This is because table $\mathcal{D}^{\xi \uplus \eta}_s$ allows all the behaviours in $[\![\xi]\!] \cup [\![\eta]\!]$, but there is a possibility that it may also allow some extra behaviours, namely those that satisfy all the constraints of the combination, but do not satisfy some of the constraints in ξ and some of the constraints in η. That is, $[\![\xi \uplus \eta]\!] = [\![\xi]\!] \cup [\![\eta]\!] \cup \mathcal{Z}(\xi, \eta)$, where $[\![\xi]\!] \cap \mathcal{Z}(\xi, \eta) = \emptyset$ and $[\![\eta]\!] \cap \mathcal{Z}(\xi, \eta) = \emptyset$. We call members of $\mathcal{Z}(\xi, \eta)$ *zigzagging* behaviours.

As an example consider scenarios ξ of Fig. 1 and η of Fig. 2. Figure 3 shows $\xi \uplus \eta$ along with its stable table. Scenario ζ of Fig. 3 represents a set of behaviours in which the time distance between events a and b is exactly 2, and between events b and c is exactly 3 units of time. There is no behaviour in the semantics of ζ that is allowed by either ξ or η, yet $[\![\zeta]\!] \subset [\![\xi \uplus \eta]\!]$. That is, all behaviours in $[\![\zeta]\!]$ belong to $\mathcal{Z}(\xi, \eta)$. This indicates that the union of the sets of behaviours allowed by ξ and η cannot be represented by a single scenario.

Given two consistent scenarios ξ and η of length n with the same sequence of events, $\mathcal{E}$, such that $\xi \uplus \eta$ is defined, behaviour $\mathcal{B}^z$ with the sequence of events $\mathcal{E}$ belongs to $\mathcal{Z}(\xi, \eta)$ iff (1) For every $0 \leq i < j < n$, $t^{\mathcal{B}^z}_{ij} \in I^{\xi \uplus \eta}_{ij}$, (2) There exist $0 \leq i < j < n$ and $0 \leq k < l < n$ such that (a) $i \neq k$ or $j \neq l$, (b) $t^{\mathcal{B}^z}_{ij} \notin I^\xi_{ij}$, $t^{\mathcal{B}^z}_{ij} \in I^\eta_{ij}$, and (c) $t^{\mathcal{B}^z}_{kl} \in I^\xi_{kl}$, $t^{\mathcal{B}^z}_{kl} \notin I^\eta_{kl}$.

There is a sufficient condition for the non-existence of zigzagging behaviours [13]: if $\mathcal{Z}(\xi, \eta) \neq \emptyset$ then ξ and η each has at least one explicit constraint, such that the constraints are not between the same events i and j in both ξ and η.

Given ξ and η, if $\mathcal{Z}(\xi, \eta) = \emptyset$, $\xi \uplus \eta$ becomes their *union*, denoted by $\xi \cup \eta$. Then, scenario $\xi \cup \eta$ captures the union of the sets of behaviours allowed by ξ, η or both: $[\![\xi \cup \eta]\!] = [\![\xi]\!] \cup [\![\eta]\!]$. Figure 4 shows two scenarios and their union.

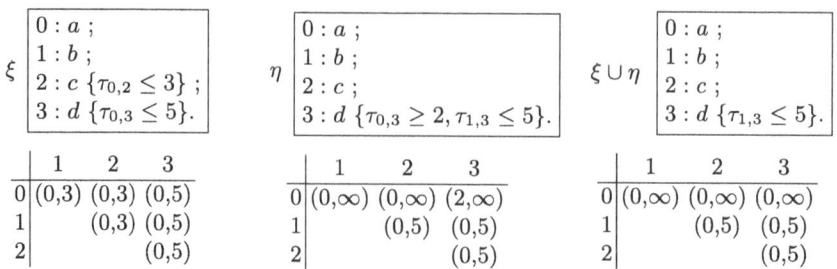

Fig. 4. Two scenarios and their union

3 Construction of Zigzagging Behaviours

In this section we develop a method for constructing zigzagging behaviours, along with the necessary definitions and theoretical foundations.

Definition 1 is a generalization of our previously-introduced notion of compatibility of a timed sequence with a stable distance table [11].

Definition 1. *Let ξ be a scenario of size n and $\mathcal{D}_s^\xi$ be its stable distance table. Let $0 \leq k < n$ and let $\mathcal{J} = \{b_0, b_1, \ldots, b_k\} \subseteq \{i \in \mathbb{N} \mid 0 \leq i < n\}$, where $b_0 < b_1 < \cdots < b_k$. The sequence of real numbers $S = t_{b_0} t_{b_1} \ldots t_{b_k}$ is compatible with $\mathcal{D}_s^\xi$ iff the following three conditions hold:*

1. $b_0 > 0 \Rightarrow t_{b_0} \geq m_{0 b_0}$,
2. $\forall i, l \in \mathcal{J} \ (i < l \Rightarrow t_i \leq t_l)$ and
3. $\forall i, l \in \mathcal{J} \ (i < l \Rightarrow t_{il} \in I_{il}^\xi)$.

Notice that if $k = 0$ then the sequence consists of one item. Conditions 2 and 3 are then trivially true. An empty sequence is not compatible with any stable table.

The sequence $t_1 t_2$, where $t_1 = 3$ and $t_2 = 4$, is compatible with the stable table for scenario ξ of Fig. 4: $t_1 \geq m_{01} = 0$, $t_1 \leq t_2$ and $t_{12} = t_2 - t_1 = 1 \in I_{12}^\xi$.

Observation 1. *Let ξ be a scenario of size n, let $\mathcal{D}_s^\xi$ be its stable distance table and let $e_o e_1 .. e_{n-1}$ be the events of ξ. The sequence $S = t_0 t_1 \ldots t_{n-1}$ is compatible with $\mathcal{D}_s^\xi$ iff $(e_o, t_o)(e_1, t_1) \ldots (e_{n-1}, t_{n-1}) \in [\![\xi]\!]$.*

Intuitively, a sequence that is compatible with a stable table of a scenario is the sequence of time values shared by the members of a set of behaviours allowed by the scenario. If the sequence has n elements, then the set is a singleton, i.e., the sequence represents one "complete" behaviour. If the sequence has less than n elements, it can be thought of as a behaviour that is only partially specified. Such a "partial" behaviour can always be extended to a complete behaviour, as shown in Theorem 1.

Theorem 1. *Let ξ be a scenario of size n and $\mathcal{D}_s^\xi$ be its stable distance table. Let $\mathcal{J} = \{b_0, b_1, \ldots, b_k\} \subseteq \{i \in \mathbb{N} \mid 0 \leq i < n\}$, $k \geq 0$, $b_0 < b_1 < \cdots < b_k$ and let $S = t_{b_0} t_{b_1} \ldots t_{b_k}$ be compatible with $\mathcal{D}_s^\xi$. Then, for any $r \in \{i \in \mathbb{N} \mid 0 \leq i < n\} \setminus \mathcal{J}$, there exists a real number t_r such that*

1. *if $b_k < r < n$, then $t_{b_0} \ldots t_{b_k} \ldots t_r$ is compatible with $\mathcal{D}_s^\xi$;*
2. *if $b_0 < r < b_k$, then $t_{b_0} \ldots t_r \ldots t_{b_k}$ is compatible with $\mathcal{D}_s^\xi$;*
3. *if $0 \leq r < b_0$, then $t_r \ldots t_{b_0} \ldots t_{b_k}$ is compatible with $\mathcal{D}_s^\xi$.*

Proof. (Figure 5 illustrates the three cases of the theorem.) We show the proof for Case 1. The complete proof is presented in the longer version of the paper [24]. **Case 1:** If $k = 0$, then let $i = b_0$ and $b_0 < r$. We must show that there exists a real number t_r such that $t_i \leq t_r$ and $m_{ir} \leq t_{ir} \leq M_{ir}$. But because $m_{ir} \leq M_{ir}$, it is always possible to find a t_{ir} that satisfies the inequations.

Let $k > 0$, $b_k < r$ and let $i = b_p$ and $j = b_q$, where $0 \leq p < q \leq k$. We must show that there exists a real number t_r such that $t_i \leq t_j \leq t_r$ and

$$m_{jr} \leq t_{jr} \leq M_{jr} \quad (2) \qquad m_{ir} \leq t_{ir} \leq M_{ir} \quad (3)$$

Inequation (2) is equivalent to $m_{jr} \leq t_{ir} - t_{ij} \leq M_{jr}$, which is equivalent to

$$t_{ij} + m_{jr} \leq t_{ir} \leq t_{ij} + M_{jr} \quad (4)$$

Clearly, $t_{ij} + m_{jr} \leq t_{ij} + M_{jr}$, because $m_{jr} \leq M_{jr}$. Moreover, $0 \leq t_{ij} + m_{jr}$, because neither of the terms is negative. So it is possible to find a t_{ir} that satisfies (4), therefore (2) can be satisfied.

Inequation (3) is equivalent to $m_{ir} \leq t_{ij} + t_{jr} \leq M_{ir}$ which is equivalent to

$$m_{ir} - t_{ij} \leq t_{jr} \leq M_{ir} - t_{ij} \quad (5)$$

Obviously, $m_{ir} - t_{ij} \leq M_{ir} - t_{ij}$, because $m_{ir} \leq M_{ir}$.

It is easy to show that $0 \leq M_{ir} - t_{ij}$:

$\mathcal{D}_s^\xi$ is stable, so $M_{ij} + m_{jr} \leq M_{ir}$, therefore $m_{jr} \leq M_{ir} - M_{ij}$. Since $t_{ij} \leq M_{ij}$, $M_{ir} - M_{ij} \leq M_{ir} - t_{ij}$. But $0 \leq m_{jr}$, therefore $0 \leq M_{ir} - t_{ij}$.

So it is possible to find a t_{jr} that satisfies (5), therefore (3) can be satisfied.

Next, we must show that the same value of t_r can simultaneously satisfy both (2) and (3), or—equivalently—both (2) and (5). We do so by showing that $m_{jr} \leq M_{ir} - t_{ij}$ and $m_{ir} - t_{ij} \leq M_{jr}$.

$\mathcal{D}_s^\xi$ is stable, so $M_{ij} + m_{jr} \leq M_{ir}$, therefore $m_{jr} \leq M_{ir} - M_{ij} \leq M_{ir} - t_{ij}$ (because $t_{ij} \leq M_{ij}$).

Similarly, $m_{ir} \leq m_{ij} + M_{jr}$, therefore $m_{ir} - m_{ij} \leq M_{jr}$. But $m_{ir} - t_{ij} \leq m_{ir} - m_{ij}$ (because $m_{ij} \leq t_{ij}$), so $m_{ir} - t_{ij} \leq M_{jr}$.

Intuitively, this means that none of the lower bounds on t_r imposed by (2) and (3) exceeds any of the upper bounds imposed by these inequations, for any choice of i and j that satisfies the assumptions. □

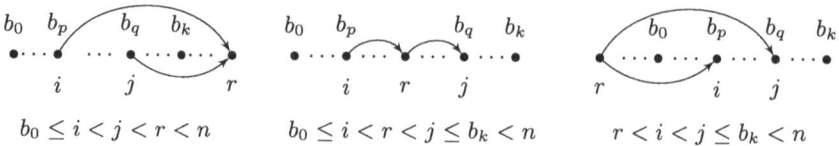

Fig. 5. Three cases of Theorem 1

For example, the sequence $t_1 t_2$, where $t_1 = 3$ and $t_2 = 4$, which is compatible with the stable table for scenario ξ of Fig. 4, can be extended to $t_0 t_1 t_2$, where $t_0 = 1$, or to $t_1 t_2 t_3$, where $t_3 = 6$, or to $t_0 t_1 t_2 t_3$. All of the extended sequences are compatible with the stable table for ξ. The last one corresponds to a complete behaviour allowed by ξ: $(a, 1)(b, 3)(c, 4)(d, 6) \in [\![\xi]\!]$.

Definition 2. Let $\mathcal{D}_s^\xi$ be the stable distance table for scenario ξ of length n. Let $0 \leq i < j < n$, $m_{ij} \neq M_{ij}$ and $v \in I_{ij}^\xi$. The action of setting both l_{ij} and h_{ij} in $\mathcal{D}_s^\xi$ to v is called *collapsing* I_{ij}^ξ *to* v. Then I_{ij}^ξ is a *collapsed* interval.

When an interval is collapsed to a value, the distance table may cease to be stable. Moreover, both the table and the interval are now associated with a different scenario, namely ξ augmented with the additional constraint $t_{ij} = v$.

Observation 2. *Let $\mathcal{D}_s^\xi$ be the stable distance table for scenario ξ of length n. After collapsing I_{ij}^ξ to a value in I_{ij}^ξ, $\mathcal{D}_s^\xi$ can be successfully stabilised (i.e., stabilisation does not make the table invalid).*

Proof. Let $v \in I_{ij}^\xi$. Collapsing I_{ij}^ξ to v is equivalent to imposing the additional constraints $t_{ij} \geq v, t_{ij} \leq v$. Consider the sequence $s = t_i t_j$, such that $t_i \geq m_{0i}^\xi$ and $t_j - t_i = v$. Clearly, s is compatible with $\mathcal{D}_s^\xi$. By Theorem 1, s can be extended to a complete behaviour $\mathcal{B} \in [\![\xi]\!]$. Behaviour $\mathcal{B}$ corresponds to a scenario, say η, such that for $0 \leq r < s < n$, if $t_{rs}^\mathcal{B} = u$, then $\mathcal{D}^\eta[r, s] = (u, u)$. That is, $m_{rs}^\eta = M_{rs}^\eta = u$. We show that $\mathcal{D}^\eta$ is stable:

For every $0 \leq i < j < k < n$: $m_{ij}^\eta = M_{ij}^\eta = t_{ij}^\mathcal{B}$, $m_{jk}^\eta = M_{jk}^\eta = t_{jk}^\mathcal{B}$, $m_{ik}^\eta = M_{ik}^\eta = t_{ik}^\mathcal{B}$. Inequation (1) becomes

$$t_{ij} + t_{jk} \leq t_{ik} \leq \begin{cases} t_{ij} + t_{jk} \\ t_{ij} + t_{jk} \end{cases} \leq t_{ik} \leq t_{ij} + t_{jk}$$

By definition, $t_{ij} + t_{jk} = (t_j - t_i) + (t_k - t_j) = t_k - t_i = t_{ik}$. So $\mathcal{D}^\eta$ satisfies all the inequations. That is, $\mathcal{D}^\eta$ is stable, which means that, after collapsing I_{ij}^ξ, stabilization could not have made $\mathcal{D}_s^\xi$ invalid, since every interval in the stabilized table must contain the corresponding interval of $\mathcal{D}^\eta$. □

It will sometimes be convenient to not annotate the symbols with the name of the scenario, i.e., to write I_{ij} and $\mathcal{D}$, instead of I_{ij}^ξ and $\mathcal{D}^\xi$.

Observation 3. *Let $\mathcal{D}$ be a stable distance table for a scenario of length n, $0 \leq i < j < n$, $0 \leq k < l < n$ and $i \neq k \vee j \neq l$. If I_{ij} and I_{kl} are collapsed intervals, then it is possible to construct a sequence $S = t_{b_0} t_{b_1} t_{b_2} t_{b_3}$ such that $\{b_0, b_1, b_2, b_3\} \subseteq \{i, j, k, l\}$ and S is compatible with $\mathcal{D}$.*

Proof. We show how to construct a compatible sequence for each of three[3] cases:

1. $0 \leq k \leq i < j \leq l < n$
2. $0 \leq i < k < j < l < n$
3. $0 \leq i < j \leq k < l < n$

We show the proof for Case 1. The complete proof is presented elsewhere [24].

Case 1: $0 \leq k \leq i < j \leq l < n$ (see the diagrams in Fig. 6)

Let $k = b_0, i = b_1, j = b_2$ and $l = b_3$. Let $t_k \geq m_{0k}$, $t_i = t_k + m_{ki}$, $t_j = t_i + m_{ij}$ and $t_l = t_k + m_{kl}$.

We must show that (a) $t_{ki} \in I_{ki}$, (b) $t_{kj} \in I_{kj}$, (c) $t_{il} \in I_{il}$ and (d) $t_{jl} \in I_{jl}$[4].

(a) By definition, $t_{ki} = t_i - t_k = t_k + m_{ki} - t_k = m_{ki} \in I_{ki}$.
(b) By definition, $t_{kj} = t_{ki} + t_{ij}$. Because I_{ij} is a collapsed interval, $t_{ij} = M_{ij}$. Therefore, $t_{kj} = m_{ki} + M_{ij}$. But $m_{kj} \leq m_{ki} + M_{ij} \leq M_{kj}$, so $t_{kj} \in I_{kj}$.
(c) By definition, $t_{kl} = t_{ki} + t_{il}$. So $t_{il} = t_{kl} - t_{ki}$. Because I_{kl} is a collapsed interval, $t_{kl} = m_{kl}$. Therefore, $t_{il} = m_{kl} - m_{ki}$.
We know $m_{ki} + m_{il} \leq m_{kl}$, so $m_{il} \leq m_{kl} - m_{ki}$. That is, $m_{il} \leq t_{il}$.
We know $m_{kl} \leq m_{ki} + M_{il}$, so $m_{kl} - m_{ki} \leq M_{il}$. Therefore, $t_{il} \leq M_{il}$.
(d) By definition, $t_{il} = t_{ij} + t_{jl}$, so $t_{jl} = t_{il} - t_{ij} = m_{kl} - m_{ki} - t_{ij}$.
I_{ij} is a collapsed interval: $t_{ij} = m_{ij}$. So $t_{jl} = m_{kl} - (m_{ki} + m_{ij})$.
We know $m_{ki} + m_{ij} \leq m_{kj}$, so, $t_{jl} \geq m_{kl} - m_{kj}$. But $m_{kj} + m_{jl} \leq m_{kl}$, so $m_{kl} - m_{kj} \geq m_{jl}$. Therefore, $t_{jl} \geq m_{jl}$.
I_{ij} is a collapsed interval: $t_{ij} = M_{ij}$. So $t_{jl} = m_{kl} - (m_{ki} + M_{ij})$.
We know $m_{kj} \leq m_{ki} + M_{ij}$, so, $t_{jl} \leq m_{kl} - m_{kj}$. But $m_{kl} \leq m_{kj} + M_{jl}$, so $m_{kl} - m_{kj} \leq M_{jl}$. Therefore, $t_{jl} \leq M_{jl}$. $\square$

4 z_pairs

In our earlier work [13] we proved that if $\xi = (\mathcal{E}, \mathcal{C}_1)$ and $\eta = (\mathcal{E}, \mathcal{C}_2)$ are two optimized scenarios of length n, such that $\mathcal{Z}(\xi, \eta) \neq \emptyset$, then there are constraints $\alpha = \tau_{i,j} \sim a \in \mathcal{C}_1$ and $\beta = \tau_{k,l} \sim b \in \mathcal{C}_2$ (for some $a, b \in \mathbb{Q}$, $0 \leq i < j < n$, $0 \leq k < l < n$), such that $\alpha \notin \mathcal{C}_2$, $\beta \notin \mathcal{C}_1$ and ($i \neq k$ or $j \neq l$). That is, the absence of such a pair of explicit constraints implies that there is no zigzagging.

---

[3] There are three other cases, which can be obtained from these by replacing i and j with k and l, and vice versa. The proofs can be obtained by interchanging i and k, as well as j and l.

[4] If $k = i$, then $t_{ki} = 0$, hence $t_{ki} \in I_{ki} = [0, 0]$. Similarly, if $j = l$, then $t_{jl} = 0$, hence $t_{jl} \in I_{jl} = [0, 0]$.

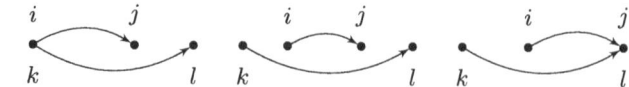

Fig. 6. case 1 of Observation 3 and of Definition 4

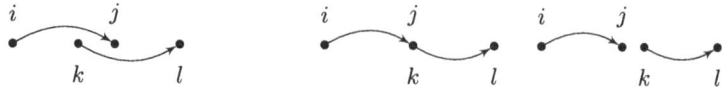

Fig. 7. cases 2, 3 of Observation 3 and of Definition 4

It turns out that in the presence of zigzagging behaviours the constraints of ξ and η are involved in some interesting relations, which depend on the positions of i, j, k and l with respect to each other. This will allow us to formulate a stronger condition: zigzagging is present if and only if the condition is satisfied (Theorems 2 and 3).

Definition 3. Let ξ and η be two scenarios of length n.
If behaviour $\mathcal{B}^z \in \mathcal{Z}(\xi,\eta)$ is such that $t_{ij}^{\mathcal{B}^z} \notin I_{ij}^{\xi}$, $t_{ij}^{\mathcal{B}^z} \in I_{ij}^{\eta}$, $t_{kl}^{\mathcal{B}^z} \in I_{kl}^{\xi}$, $t_{kl}^{\mathcal{B}^z} \notin I_{kl}^{\eta}$ and $i \neq k \vee j \neq l$ ($0 \leq i < j < n, 0 \leq k < l < n$), then we say $\mathcal{B}^z$ zigzags through ij and kl.

As an example consider ξ of Fig. 1 and η of Fig. 2. Behaviour $\mathcal{B}^z = (a,0)(b,2)(c,5)$ zigzags through 01 and 12: $t_{01}^{\mathcal{B}^z} \notin I_{01}^{\xi}$, $t_{01}^{\mathcal{B}^z} \in I_{01}^{\eta}$, $t_{12}^{\mathcal{B}^z} \notin I_{12}^{\eta}$ and $t_{12}^{\mathcal{B}^z} \in I_{12}^{\xi}$.

Definition 4. Let ξ and η be two scenarios of length n with the same sequences of events, such that $\xi \not\subseteq \eta$, $\eta \not\subseteq \xi$ and $\xi \uplus \eta$ is defined. Let $\alpha = \tau_{i,j} \sim a \in \mathcal{C}(\mathcal{D}_s^{\xi})$ and $\beta = \tau_{k,l} \sim b \in \mathcal{C}(\mathcal{D}_s^{\eta})$ ($a,b \in \mathbb{Q}$), such that $i \neq k \vee j \neq l$, $\alpha \notin \mathcal{C}(\mathcal{D}_s^{\eta})$ and $\beta \notin \mathcal{C}(\mathcal{D}_s^{\xi})$. Constraints α and β form a z_pair if one of the following conditions holds[5]:

(1) $0 \leq k \leq i < j \leq l < n$ and
  (a) $\alpha = \tau_{i,j} \geq a$, $\beta = \tau_{k,l} \geq b$, $m_{ij}^{\eta} < a$, $m_{kl}^{\xi} < b$, or
  (b) $\alpha = \tau_{i,j} \geq a$, $\beta = \tau_{k,l} \leq b$, $m_{ij}^{\eta} < a$, $b < M_{kl}^{\xi}$, and additionally $M_{ki}^{\xi \uplus \eta} + a + M_{jl}^{\xi \uplus \eta} > b$, or
  (c) $\alpha = \tau_{i,j} \leq a$, $\beta = \tau_{k,l} \geq b$, $a < M_{ij}^{\eta}$, $m_{kl}^{\xi} < b$, and additionally $m_{ki}^{\xi \uplus \eta} + a + m_{jl}^{\xi \uplus \eta} < b$, or
  (d) $\alpha = \tau_{i,j} \leq a$, $\beta = \tau_{k,l} \leq b$, $a < M_{ij}^{\eta}$, $b < M_{kl}^{\xi}$.
(2) $0 \leq i < k < j < l < n$ and
  (a) $\alpha = \tau_{i,j} \geq a$, $\beta = \tau_{k,l} \geq b$, $m_{ij}^{\eta} < a$, $m_{kl}^{\xi} < b$, and additionally $m_{il}^{\xi \uplus \eta} - a < b - m_{kj}^{\xi \uplus \eta}$, or
  (b) $\alpha = \tau_{i,j} \geq a$, $\beta = \tau_{k,l} \leq b$, $m_{ij}^{\eta} < a$, $b < M_{kl}^{\xi}$, and additionally $a + M_{jl}^{\xi \uplus \eta} > m_{ik}^{\xi \uplus \eta} + b$, or

---
[5] See the diagrams in Figs. 6 and 7.

$$I_{ij} \quad\quad \substack{a \\ m_{ij}^\eta} \frac{\quad\quad\quad}{\quad\quad\quad} \substack{M_{ij}^\xi \\ M_{ij}^\eta} \quad I_{kl} \quad \substack{m_{kl}^\xi \\ m_{kl}^\eta} \frac{\quad\quad\quad}{\quad\quad\quad b} \quad M_{kl}^\xi$$

Fig. 8. Definition 4 cases (1)(b), (2)(b) and (3)(b): $\tau_{i,j} \geq a$, $\tau_{k,l} \leq b$, $m_{ij}^\eta < a$, $b < M_{kl}^\xi$

(c) $\alpha = \tau_{i,j} \leq a$, $\beta = \tau_{k,l} \geq b$, $a < M_{ij}^\eta$, $m_{kl}^\xi < b$, and additionally $a + m_{jl}^{\xi \cup \eta} < M_{ik}^{\xi \cup \eta} + b$, or

(d) $\alpha = \tau_{i,j} \leq a$, $\beta = \tau_{k,l} \leq b$, $a < M_{ij}^\eta$, $b < M_{kl}^\xi$, and additionally $M_{il}^{\xi \cup \eta} - a > b - M_{kj}^{\xi \cup \eta}$.

(3) $0 \leq i < j \leq k < l < n$ and

  (a) $\alpha = \tau_{i,j} \geq a$, $\beta = \tau_{k,l} \geq b$, $m_{ij}^\eta < a$, $m_{kl}^\xi < b$, or

  (b) $\alpha = \tau_{i,j} \geq a$, $\beta = \tau_{k,l} \leq b$, $m_{ij}^\eta < a$, $b < M_{kl}^\xi$, or

  (c) $\alpha = \tau_{i,j} \leq a$, $\beta = \tau_{k,l} \geq b$, $a < M_{ij}^\eta$, $m_{kl}^\xi < b$, or

  (d) $\alpha = \tau_{i,j} \leq a$, $\beta = \tau_{k,l} \leq b$, $a < M_{ij}^\eta$, $b < M_{kl}^\xi$.

In each case there are four other subcases which can be obtained by interchanging ξ and η.

The three cases of Definition 4 cover all[6] the possibilities of the positions of i, j, k and l with respect to each other. The "main" subcases of each case cover all the possible combinations of the forms of α and β, and the relations between the minima and maxima of distances between events i and j and between events k and l in ξ and η. Intuitively, the conditions capture all the possibilities for $I_{ij}^\eta \setminus I_{ij}^\xi \neq \emptyset$ and $I_{kl}^\xi \setminus I_{kl}^\eta \neq \emptyset$, to guarantee "there is room" for behaviours to zigzag through ij and kl. But these are only half of the possibilities: The cases for $I_{ij}^\xi \setminus I_{ij}^\eta \neq \emptyset$ and $I_{kl}^\eta \setminus I_{kl}^\xi \neq \emptyset$ are obtained by exchanging ξ and η.

Figure 8 is a schematic illustration of the main conditions of cases (1)(b), (2)(b) and (3)(b): $\alpha = \tau_{i,j} \geq a$, $\beta = \tau_{k,l} \leq b$, $m_{ij}^\eta < a$, $b < M_{kl}^\xi$. Because of constraint α, $m_{ij}^\xi = a$ and because of constraint β, $M_{kl}^\eta = b$. Therefore, $I_{ij}^\eta \setminus I_{ij}^\xi = \{u \in \mathbb{Q}_{\geq 0} \mid m_{kl}^\eta \leq u < a\} \neq \emptyset$ and $I_{kl}^\xi \setminus I_{kl}^\eta = \{v \in \mathbb{Q}_{\geq 0} \mid b < v < M_{kl}^\xi\} \neq \emptyset$.

The *additional* conditions specify certain relations that must hold between various minima and maxima in ξ and η for there to be zigzagging behaviours.

It is worth mentioning that if α and β form a *z_pair*, then neither of them can be a default constraint.

In the rest of the paper we are going to prove theorems that will show the following relations between the existence of a *z_pair* and the existence of the union of two scenarios:

- no *z_pair* $\Rightarrow$ no zigzagging $\Rightarrow$ union (Theorem 2);
- *z_pair* $\Rightarrow$ zigzagging $\Rightarrow$ no union (Theorem 3).

---

[6] In the definition it is assumed that ij is within ξ and kl is within η. There are three other cases where ij is within η and kl is within ξ. Those cases are symmetric and can be obtained by interchanging ξ and η.

5 A Sufficient Condition for the Existence of Union

Theorem 2. *Let ξ and η be two scenarios of length n with the same sequences of events, such that $\xi \not\subseteq \eta$ and $\eta \not\subseteq \xi$. If $\mathcal{B}^z \in \mathcal{Z}(\xi, \eta)$ zigzags through ij and kl, then there exist $\alpha = \tau_{i,j} \sim a \in \mathcal{C}(\mathcal{D}_s^\xi)$ and $\beta = \tau_{k,l} \sim b \in \mathcal{C}(\mathcal{D}_s^\eta)$ $(a, b \in \mathbb{Q})$ such that α and β form a z_pair.*

Proof. We show the proof for case (1) of Definition 4: $0 \leq k \leq i < j \leq l < n$.

The complete proof is presented elsewhere [24].

Let $\mathcal{B}^z$ be a behaviour in $\mathcal{Z}(\xi, \eta)$ that zigzags through ij and kl. There are two cases to consider:

(1) $t_{ij}^{\mathcal{B}^z} \notin I_{ij}^\xi$, $t_{ij}^{\mathcal{B}^z} \in I_{ij}^\eta$, $t_{kl}^{\mathcal{B}^z} \notin I_{kl}^\eta$ and $t_{kl}^{\mathcal{B}^z} \in I_{kl}^\xi$.

Since $t_{ij}^{\mathcal{B}^z} \notin I_{ij}^\xi$, one of the following two cases must hold:

(a) $t_{ij}^{\mathcal{B}^z} < m_{ij}^\xi$. Since $t_{ij}^{\mathcal{B}^z} \in I_{ij}^\eta$, we must have $m_{ij}^\eta \leq t_{ij}^{\mathcal{B}^z}$. It follows that $m_{ij}^\eta < m_{ij}^\xi$. Therefore $m_{ij}^\xi > 0$: there exists a non-default constraint $\alpha = \tau_{i,j} \geq a$ in $\mathcal{C}(\mathcal{D}_s^\xi)$, where $a = m_{ij}^\xi$.

Since $t_{kl}^{\mathcal{B}^z} \notin I_{kl}^\eta$, one of the following two cases must hold:

– $t_{kl}^{\mathcal{B}^z} < m_{kl}^\eta$. Since $t_{kl}^{\mathcal{B}^z} \in I_{kl}^\xi$, we must have $m_{kl}^\xi \leq t_{kl}^{\mathcal{B}^z}$. It follows that $m_{kl}^\xi < m_{kl}^\eta$. Therefore $m_{kl}^\eta > 0$: there exists a non-default constraint $\beta = \tau_{k,l} \geq b \in \mathcal{C}(\mathcal{D}_s^\eta)$, where $b = m_{kl}^\eta$.
So α and β form a z_pair (case (1)(a) of Definition 4).

– $M_{kl}^\eta < t_{kl}^{\mathcal{B}^z}$. Since $t_{kl}^{\mathcal{B}^z} \in I_{kl}^\xi$, we must have $t_{kl}^{\mathcal{B}^z} \leq M_{kl}^\xi$. It follows that $M_{kl}^\eta < M_{kl}^\xi$. Therefore $M_{kl}^\eta < \infty$: there exists a non-default constraint $\beta = \tau_{k,l} \leq b \in \mathcal{C}(\mathcal{D}_s^\eta)$, where $b = M_{kl}^\eta$.
The constraints α and β fit case (1)(b) of Definition 4. We must show $M_{ki}^{\xi \uplus \eta} + a + M_{jl}^{\xi \uplus \eta} > b$.

Assume $M_{ki}^{\xi \uplus \eta} + a + M_{jl}^{\xi \uplus \eta} \leq b$.
By definition, $t_{kl}^{\mathcal{B}^z} = t_{ki}^{\mathcal{B}^z} + t_{ij}^{\mathcal{B}^z} + t_{jl}^{\mathcal{B}^z}$. Because $\mathcal{B}^z \in [\![\xi \uplus \eta]\!]$, we have $t_{ki}^{\mathcal{B}^z} \leq M_{ki}^{\xi \uplus \eta}$ and $t_{jl}^{\mathcal{B}^z} \leq M_{jl}^{\xi \uplus \eta}$. Therefore, $t_{kl}^{\mathcal{B}^z} \leq M_{ki}^{\xi \uplus \eta} + t_{ij}^{\mathcal{B}^z} + M_{jl}^{\xi \uplus \eta}$. Since $t_{ij}^{\mathcal{B}^z} < m_{ij}^\xi$ and $m_{ij}^\xi = a$, we have $t_{kl}^{\mathcal{B}^z} < M_{ki}^{\xi \uplus \eta} + a + M_{jl}^{\xi \uplus \eta}$. By the assumption, $M_{ki}^{\xi \uplus \eta} + a + M_{jl}^{\xi \uplus \eta} \leq b$. So it follows that $t_{kl}^{\mathcal{B}^z} < b$. But $M_{kl}^\eta < t_{kl}^{\mathcal{B}^z}$, so $M_{kl}^\eta < b$: a contradiction.
So α and β form a z_pair (case (1)(b) of Definition 4).

(b) $M_{ij}^\xi < t_{ij}^{\mathcal{B}^z}$. Since $t_{ij}^{\mathcal{B}^z} \in I_{ij}^\eta$, we must have $t_{ij}^{\mathcal{B}^z} \leq M_{ij}^\eta$. It follows that $M_{ij}^\xi < M_{ij}^\eta$. Therefore $M_{ij}^\xi < \infty$: there exists a non-default constraint $\alpha = \tau_{i,j} \leq a$ in $\mathcal{C}(\mathcal{D}_s^\xi)$, where $a = M_{ij}^\xi$.

Since $t_{kl}^{\mathcal{B}^z} \notin I_{kl}^\eta$, one of the following two cases must hold:

– $t_{kl}^{\mathcal{B}^z} < m_{kl}^\eta$. Since $t_{kl}^{\mathcal{B}^z} \in I_{kl}^\xi$, we must have $m_{kl}^\xi \leq t_{kl}^{\mathcal{B}^z}$. It follows that $m_{kl}^\xi < m_{kl}^\eta$. Therefore $m_{kl}^\eta > 0$: there exists a non-default constraint $\beta = \tau_{k,l} \geq b \in \mathcal{C}(\mathcal{D}_s^\eta)$, where $b = m_{kl}^\eta$.
The constraints α and β fit case (1)(c) of Definition 4. We must show $m_{ki}^{\xi \uplus \eta} + a + m_{jl}^{\xi \uplus \eta} < b$.

Assume $m_{ki}^{\xi \uplus \eta} + a + m_{jl}^{\xi \uplus \eta} \geq b$.
By definition, $t_{kl}^{\mathcal{B}^z} = t_{ki}^{\mathcal{B}^z} + t_{ij}^{\mathcal{B}^z} + t_{jl}^{\mathcal{B}^z}$. Because $\mathcal{B}^z \in [\![\xi \uplus \eta]\!]$, we have $t_{ki}^{\mathcal{B}^z} \geq m_{ki}^{\xi \uplus \eta}$ and $t_{jl}^{\mathcal{B}^z} \geq m_{jl}^{\xi \uplus \eta}$. Therefore, $t_{kl}^{\mathcal{B}^z} \geq m_{ki}^{\xi \uplus \eta} + t_{ij}^{\mathcal{B}^z} + m_{jl}^{\xi \uplus \eta}$. Since $t_{ij}^{\mathcal{B}^z} > M_{ij}^{\xi}$ and $M_{ij}^{\xi} = a$, we have $t_{kl}^{\mathcal{B}^z} > m_{ki}^{\xi \uplus \eta} + a + m_{jl}^{\xi \uplus \eta}$. By the assumption, $m_{ki}^{\xi \uplus \eta} + a + m_{jl}^{\xi \uplus \eta} \geq b$. So it follows that $t_{kl}^{\mathcal{B}^z} > b$. But $m_{kl}^{\eta} > t_{kl}^{\mathcal{B}^z}$, so $m_{kl}^{\eta} > b$: a contradiction.
So α and β form a z_pair (case (1)(c) of Definition 4).
- $M_{kl}^{\eta} < t_{kl}^{\mathcal{B}^z}$. Since $t_{kl}^{\mathcal{B}^z} \in I_{kl}^{\xi}$, we must have $t_{kl}^{\mathcal{B}^z} \leq M_{kl}^{\xi}$. It follows that $M_{kl}^{\eta} < M_{kl}^{\xi}$. Therefore $M_{kl}^{\eta} < \infty$: there exists a non-default constraint $\beta = \tau_{k,l} \leq b \in \mathcal{C}(\mathcal{D}_s^{\eta})$, where $b = M_{kl}^{\eta}$.
So α and β form a z_pair (case (1)(d) of Definition 4).
(2) $t_{ij}^{\mathcal{B}^z} \in I_{ij}^{\xi}, t_{ij}^{\mathcal{B}^z} \notin I_{ij}^{\eta}, t_{kl}^{\mathcal{B}^z} \in I_{kl}^{\eta}$ and $t_{kl}^{\mathcal{B}^z} \notin I_{kl}^{\xi}$.
The proof can be obtained by exchanging ξ and η in case (1). □

As an example consider ξ and η of Figs. 1 and 2 along with their stable distance tables once more. As we mentioned before, $\mathcal{Z}(\xi, \eta) \neq \emptyset$ and there is a behaviour that zigzags through 01 and 12. For example, $\mathcal{B}^z = (a, 0)(b, 1)(c, 4)$ is such a behaviour: $t_{01}^{\mathcal{B}^z} = 1 - 0 \notin I_{01}^{\xi}$ and $t_{12}^{\mathcal{B}^z} = 4 - 1 \notin I_{12}^{\eta}$. According to Theorem 2 at least one z_pair must exist between ξ and η. Indeed, constraints $\alpha = \tau_{0,1} \geq 3$ in ξ and $\beta = \tau_{1,2} \geq 4$ in η satisfy the requirements of Definition 4 (case 3.a), and therefore, form a z_pair: $i = 0, j = k = 1, l = 2, i < j = k < l, a = 3, b = 4$, $m_{01}^{\eta} = 0 < a = 3$ and $m_{12}^{\xi} = 0 < b = 4$.

As another example consider scenarios ξ and η of Fig. 4. Constraints $\tau_{0,2} \leq 3$ in ξ and $\tau_{0,3} \geq 2$ in η do not form a z_pair: $i = k = 0, j = 2, l = 3$, and $a = 3 < M_{02}^{\eta} = \infty$, $m_{03}^{\xi} = 0 < b = 2$ (case 1.c), but $m_{02}^{\xi \uplus \eta} + a + m_{23}^{\xi \uplus \eta} = 0 + 3 + 0 \not< b = 2$. Constraints $\tau_{0,3} \leq 5$ in ξ and $\tau_{1,3} \leq 5$ in η do not form a z_pair: $I_{13}^{\xi} = I_{13}^{\eta}$. Constraints $\tau_{0,2} \leq 3$ in ξ and $\tau_{1,3} \leq 5$ in η do not form a z_pair for the same reason. Of course, constraints $\tau_{0,3} \leq 5$ in ξ and $\tau_{0,3} \geq 2$ in η do not form a z_pair: $i = k = 0$, $j = l = 3$, so $i = k \wedge j = l$.

In fact, none of the constraints of ξ and η satisfy the conditions of any of the cases of Definition 4: there is no z_pair between constraints of ξ and η. This is in accordance with Theorem 2: as we mentioned before, $\mathcal{Z}(\xi, \eta) = \emptyset$.

The consequence of Theorem 2 is that if there is no z_pair between scenarios ξ and η, then $\mathcal{Z}(\xi, \eta) = \emptyset$, therefore $\xi \cup \eta$ exists. That is, the non-existence of z_pairs between two scenarios is a sufficient condition for the existence of the union between the two (provided $\xi \uplus \eta$ is defined).

In our earlier work [13] we identified another such condition: if scenarios ξ and η are optimized and $\mathcal{Z}(\xi, \eta) \neq \emptyset$, then ξ and η must each have at least one explicit constraint that the other does not have, such that the two constraints are not between the same events in both ξ and η. The absence of such a pair of explicit constraints is also a sufficient condition for the existence of $\xi \cup \eta$, but the pair need not be a z_pair.

0 : a ;		1	2	3
1 : b $\{\tau_{0,1} \geq 1\}$;	0	(1,2)	(1,2)	$(1,\infty)$
2 : c $\{\tau_{0,2} \leq 2\}$;	1		(0,1)	$(0,\infty)$
3 : d .	2			$(0,\infty)$

Fig. 9. ξ and its stable table

0 : a ;		1	2	3
1 : b $\{\tau_{0,1} \leq 1\}$;	0	(0,1)	(0,2)	$(4,\infty)$
2 : c $\{\tau_{1,2} \leq 1\}$;	1		(0,1)	$(4,\infty)$
3 : d $\{\tau_{1,3} \geq 4\}$.	2			$(3,\infty)$

Fig. 10. η and its stable table

The existence of a *z_pair* turns out to be not only a necessary, but also a sufficient condition for the existence of zigzagging behaviours (see Theorem 3).

Consider scenarios ξ of Fig. 9 and η of Fig. 10: $\mathcal{Z}(\xi, \eta) \neq \emptyset$. Indeed, constraints $\tau_{0,2} \leq 2$ of ξ and $\tau_{1,3} \geq 4$ of η are two different explicit constraints between different events, events 0 and 2, and events 1 and 3, respectively. However, the two constraints do not form a *z_pair*: their form fits case (2)(c) of Definition 4, however $a = 2 \not< M_{02}^{\eta} = 2$. But, of course, there must exist at least one *z_pair*. Constraint $\tau_{0,2} \geq 1$ of ξ, which is an implied constraint, and constraint $\tau_{1,3} \geq 4$ of η form a *z_pair*.

6 A Sufficient Condition for the Non-existence of Union

Our goal is to show that the existence of a *z_pair* between two scenarios ξ and η is a sufficient condition for the non-existence of $\xi \cup \eta$, because of the existence of zigzagging behaviours between the two scenarios. More precisely, if there is a *z_pair* between ξ and η, then there exist $0 \leq i < j < n$, $0 \leq k < l < n$, $u \in I_{ij}^{\xi \uplus \eta}$, $v \in I_{kl}^{\xi \uplus \eta}$ and behaviour $\mathcal{B}^z \in [\![\xi \uplus \eta]\!]$, such that $t_{ij}^{\mathcal{B}^z} = u \in I_{ij}^{\xi} \setminus I_{ij}^{\eta}$ and $t_{kl}^{\mathcal{B}^z} = v \in I_{kl}^{\eta} \setminus I_{kl}^{\xi}$.

Observation 4. *Let $\mathcal{D}$ be a stable distance table for a scenario of length n and let $0 \leq i \leq j \leq k < n$ be integers.*

Let t_{ij} satisfy $m_{ij} \leq t_{ij} \leq M_{ij}$. Then, after replacing m_{ij} and M_{ij} with t_{ij} and stabilising the table, if m_{ik} changes, it will increase to at most $t_{ij} + m_{jk}$.

Proof. The proof is presented in the longer version of the paper [24]. □

Observation 5. *Let $\mathcal{D}$ be a stable distance table for a scenario of length n and let $0 \leq i \leq j \leq k < n$ be integers. Let t_{ij} satisfy $m_{ij} \leq t_{ij} \leq M_{ij}$.*

Then, after replacing m_{ij} and M_{ij} with t_{ij}, if the inequation $t_{ij} + m_{jk} \leq m_{ik}$ holds, then during stabilisation m_{ik} will not change.

Proof. Assume m_{ik} will change during stabilisation. In that case, $m_{ik} < \boldsymbol{m}_{ik}$, and By Observation 4, $\boldsymbol{m}_{ik} \leq t_{ij} + m_{jk}$.

By the assumption, the inequation $t_{ij} + m_{jk} \leq m_{ik}$ holds. It follows that $\boldsymbol{m}_{ik} \leq m_{ik}$: a contradiction with $m_{ik} < \boldsymbol{m}_{ik}$. □

Theorem 3. *Let ξ and η be two scenarios of length n with the same sequences of events, such that $\xi \not\subseteq \eta$, $\eta \not\subseteq \xi$ and $\xi \uplus \eta$ is defined. If there are $\alpha = \tau_{i,j} \sim a \in \mathcal{C}(\mathcal{D}_s^{\xi})$ and $\beta = \tau_{k,l} \sim b \in \mathcal{C}(\mathcal{D}_s^{\eta})$ $(a, b \in \mathbb{Q})$, such that α and β form a z_pair, then there is a $\mathcal{B}^z \in \mathcal{Z}(\xi, \eta)$, such that $\mathcal{B}^z$ zigzags through ij and kl.*

Proof. Just as in Definition 4, there are three cases, determined by the relative positions of i, j, k and l. Each of these cases has four subcases, determined by the relations between the minima and maxima of the relevant intervals.

We show the proof for case (1)(a). The complete proof is presented elsewhere [24].

Case (1)(a): $0 \leq k \leq i < j \leq l < n$ ($i \neq k \vee j \neq l$)

$$\alpha = \tau_{i,j} \geq a, \ \beta = \tau_{k,l} \geq b, \ m_{ij}^\eta < a, \ m_{kl}^\xi < b$$

We show the proof for the case $0 \leq k < i < j < l < n$. The proofs for $k = i$ or $j = l$ are special cases of the proof shown below.

We must show that there is a behaviour $\mathcal{B}^z \in [\![\xi \uplus \eta]\!]$ such that $\mathcal{B}^z$ zigzags through ij and kl. Because ij is entirely within kl, i.e., $k < i < j < l$, we must have $t_{ij}^{\mathcal{B}^z} \leq t_{kl}^{\mathcal{B}^z}$.

Because of constraint α, $m_{ij}^\xi = a$ and because of constraint β, $m_{kl}^\eta = b$. $m_{ij}^{\xi \uplus \eta} = \min(m_{ij}^\xi, m_{ij}^\eta) = m_{ij}^\eta$ and $m_{kl}^{\xi \uplus \eta} = \min(m_{kl}^\xi, m_{kl}^\eta) = m_{kl}^\xi$.

Both $I_{ij}^{\xi \uplus \eta} \setminus I_{ij}^\xi = \{u \in \mathbb{Q}_{>0} \mid m_{ij}^\eta \leq u < a\}$ and $I_{kl}^{\xi \uplus \eta} \setminus I_{kl}^\eta = \{w \in \mathbb{Q}_{\geq 0} \mid m_{kl}^\xi \leq w < b\}$ are non-empty.

So it is possible to pick a value $t_{ij} = a - \delta$ ($\delta \in \mathbb{Q}_{>0}$) in the interval $I_{ij}^{\xi \uplus \eta} \setminus I_{ij}^\xi$.

Next we must show that after collapsing $I_{ij}^{\xi \uplus \eta}$ of $\mathcal{D}_s^{\xi \uplus \eta}$ to t_{ij} (i.e., setting $m_{ij}^{\xi \uplus \eta} = M_{ij}^{\xi \uplus \eta} = t_{ij}$ and stabilizing $\mathcal{D}_s^{\xi \uplus \eta}$), hence obtaining $\boldsymbol{D}_s^{\xi \uplus \eta}$, it is still possible to pick a value t_{kl} in the interval $\boldsymbol{I}_{kl}^{\xi \uplus \eta}$ of table $\boldsymbol{D}_s^{\xi \uplus \eta}$, such that t_{kl} belongs to I_{kl}^ξ, but does not belong to I_{kl}^η, and that $t_{ij} \leq t_{kl}$.

(We use bold font to distinguish items that are updated during stabilization.)

In $\mathcal{D}_s^{\xi \uplus \eta}$ we have $m_{ki}^{\xi \uplus \eta} + m_{ij}^{\xi \uplus \eta} \leq m_{kj}^{\xi \uplus \eta}$ and $m_{kj}^{\xi \uplus \eta} + m_{jl}^{\xi \uplus \eta} \leq m_{kl}^{\xi \uplus \eta}$.

We set $\boldsymbol{m}_{ij}^{\xi \uplus \eta} = \boldsymbol{M}_{ij}^{\xi \uplus \eta} = t_{ij}$ in interval $\boldsymbol{I}_{ij}^{\xi \uplus \eta}$ of $\mathcal{D}_s^{\xi \uplus \eta}$ stabilise it to obtain $\boldsymbol{D}_s^{\xi \uplus \eta}$. After this one of the following two things will happen:

(i) The inequation $m_{ki}^{\xi \uplus \eta} + t_{ij} \leq m_{kj}^{\xi \uplus \eta}$ holds, in which case, by Observation 5, $m_{kj}^{\xi \uplus \eta}$ will not change: $\boldsymbol{m}_{kj}^{\xi \uplus \eta} = m_{kj}^{\xi \uplus \eta}$. The inequation $m_{kj}^{\xi \uplus \eta} + m_{jl}^{\xi \uplus \eta} \leq m_{kl}^{\xi \uplus \eta}$ will then continue to hold. Therefore $m_{kl}^{\xi \uplus \eta}$ will not change: $\boldsymbol{m}_{kl}^{\xi \uplus \eta} = m_{kl}^{\xi \uplus \eta} = m_{kl}^\xi$. Hence, $\boldsymbol{I}_{kl}^{\xi \uplus \eta} \setminus I_{kl}^\eta = \{w \in \mathbb{Q}_{\geq 0} \mid m_{kl}^\xi \leq w < b\}$.

(ii) The inequation $m_{ki}^{\xi \uplus \eta} + t_{ij} \leq m_{kj}^{\xi \uplus \eta}$ does not hold. In that case, to restore the inequation, $m_{kj}^{\xi \uplus \eta}$ will be set to $m_{ki}^{\xi \uplus \eta} + t_{ij}$. By Observation 4, $m_{kj}^{\xi \uplus \eta}$ cannot further increase, therefore $\boldsymbol{m}_{kj}^{\xi \uplus \eta} = m_{ki}^{\xi \uplus \eta} + a - \delta$. But since $\boldsymbol{m}_{kj}^{\xi \uplus \eta}$ has changed, the inequation $\boldsymbol{m}_{kj}^{\xi \uplus \eta} + m_{jl}^{\xi \uplus \eta} \leq m_{kl}^{\xi \uplus \eta}$ might not hold. There are two cases to consider:

1. If the new value of $\boldsymbol{m}_{kj}^{\xi \uplus \eta}$ does not affect the satisfiability of the inequation $\boldsymbol{m}_{kj}^{\xi \uplus \eta} + m_{jl}^{\xi \uplus \eta} \leq m_{kl}^{\xi \uplus \eta}$, then $m_{kl}^{\xi \uplus \eta}$ will remain the same, so just as in case (i), $\boldsymbol{I}_{kl}^{\xi \uplus \eta} \setminus I_{kl}^\eta = \{w \in \mathbb{Q}_{\geq 0} \mid m_{kl}^\xi \leq w < b\}$.
2. If $\boldsymbol{m}_{kj}^{\xi \uplus \eta} + m_{jl}^{\xi \uplus \eta} \leq m_{kl}^{\xi \uplus \eta}$ is not satisfied, the inequation will be restored by setting $m_{kl}^{\xi \uplus \eta}$ to $\boldsymbol{m}_{kj}^{\xi \uplus \eta} + m_{jl}^{\xi \uplus \eta}$: $\boldsymbol{m}_{kl}^{\xi \uplus \eta} := \boldsymbol{m}_{kj}^{\xi \uplus \eta} + m_{jl}^{\xi \uplus \eta} = m_{ki}^{\xi \uplus \eta} + a - \delta + m_{jl}^{\xi \uplus \eta}$. Now the inequation $\boldsymbol{m}_{kj}^{\xi \uplus \eta} + m_{jl}^{\xi \uplus \eta} \leq \boldsymbol{m}_{kl}^{\xi \uplus \eta}$ holds, and by

Observation 5, $m_{kl}^{\xi \uplus \eta}$ cannot be further increased. Next, we show that $m_{kl}^{\xi \uplus \eta} < b$. For that, we show that $m_{ki}^{\xi \uplus \eta} + a + m_{jl}^{\xi \uplus \eta} < b$.
Assume $b \leq m_{ki}^{\xi \uplus \eta} + a + m_{jl}^{\xi \uplus \eta}$. Because $m_{kl}^{\xi} < b$, we will have $m_{kl}^{\xi} < m_{ki}^{\xi \uplus \eta} + a + m_{jl}^{\xi \uplus \eta}$. Since $m_{ki}^{\xi \uplus \eta} \leq m_{ki}^{\xi}$ and $m_{jl}^{\xi \uplus \eta} \leq m_{jl}^{\xi}$, we will have $m_{kl}^{\xi} < m_{ki}^{\xi} + a + m_{jl}^{\xi}$.
But $m_{ki}^{\xi} + m_{il}^{\xi} \leq m_{kl}^{\xi}$, so $m_{ki}^{\xi} + m_{il}^{\xi} < m_{ki}^{\xi} + a + m_{jl}^{\xi}$. Therefore $m_{il}^{\xi} < a + m_{jl}^{\xi}$. But $m_{ij}^{\xi} + m_{jl}^{\xi} \leq m_{il}^{\xi}$, and $m_{ij}^{\xi} = a$. So $a + m_{jl}^{\xi} < a + m_{jl}^{\xi}$: a contradiction.
Because $m_{ki}^{\xi \uplus \eta} + a + m_{jl}^{\xi \uplus \eta} < b$, we will have $\boldsymbol{m}_{kl}^{\xi \uplus \eta} < b$.
So $\boldsymbol{I}_{kl}^{\xi \uplus \eta} \setminus I_{kl}^{\eta} = \{w \in \mathbb{Q}_{\geq 0} \mid \boldsymbol{m}_{kl}^{\xi \uplus \eta} \leq w < b\}$ will be non-empty.

If (i) or (ii).1, because ξ is consistent, we have $m_{ij}^{\xi} \leq m_{kl}^{\xi}$. Since $t_{ij} = a - \delta$, any value that is picked for t_{kl} from $\boldsymbol{I}_{kl}^{\xi \uplus \eta} \setminus I_{kl}^{\eta}$ will satisfy $t_{ij} \leq t_{kl}$.
If (ii).2, since $\boldsymbol{m}_{kl}^{\xi \uplus \eta} = m_{ki}^{\xi \uplus \eta} + t_{ij} + m_{jl}^{\xi \uplus \eta}$, we have $t_{ij} \leq \boldsymbol{m}_{kl}^{\xi \uplus \eta}$. Then any value t_{kl} in $\boldsymbol{I}_{kl}^{\xi \uplus \eta} \setminus I_{kl}^{\eta} = \{w \in \mathbb{Q}_{\geq 0} \mid \boldsymbol{m}_{kl}^{\xi \uplus \eta} \leq w < b\}$ will satisfy $t_{ij} \leq t_{kl}$.
Obviously, $t_{ij} \in \boldsymbol{I}_{ij}^{\xi \uplus \eta}$ and $t_{kl} \in \boldsymbol{I}_{il}^{\xi \uplus \eta}$. Moreover, $0 \leq k < i < j < l < n$, so, by Observation 3, it is possible to form a sequence $t_k \leq t_i \leq t_j \leq t_l$ that is compatible with $\boldsymbol{D}_s^{\xi \uplus \eta}$. By Theorem 1, S can be extended to a behaviour, say $\mathcal{B}^z$, in $[\![\xi \uplus \eta]\!]$. Clearly, $t_{ij}^{\mathcal{B}^z} \notin I_{ij}^{\xi}$ and $t_{kl}^{\mathcal{B}^z} \notin I_{kl}^{\eta}$. Therefore, $\mathcal{B}^z$ zigzags through ij and kl. □

The consequence of Theorem 3 is that if ξ and η have constraints that form a z_pair, then $\xi \cup \eta$ does not exist.

7 Conclusions

In our earlier work [13] we had found a sufficient condition for the existence of the union of two optimized timed scenarios $\xi = (\mathcal{E}, \mathcal{C}_1)$ and $\eta = (\mathcal{E}, \mathcal{C}_2)$: if $\mathcal{C}_1$ and $\mathcal{C}_2$ do not contain a pair of constraints $\alpha = \tau_{i,j} \sim a$ and $\beta = \tau_{k,l} \sim b$, respectively, such that $i \neq k$ or $j \neq l$, $\alpha \notin \mathcal{C}_2$ and $\beta \notin \mathcal{C}_1$, then there will be no "zigzagging" behaviours between ξ and η, and therefore $\xi \cup \eta$ exists. Zigzagging behaviours belong neither to $[\![\xi]\!]$, nor to $[\![\eta]\!]$, even though they belong to $[\![\xi \uplus \eta]\!]$, i.e., the semantics of the combination (or the "quasi-union") of ξ and η.

In the current paper we investigate, in more depth, the conditions under which the union of the sets of behaviours allowed by two consistent scenarios, ξ and η, can be represented by a single scenario, namely the union $\xi \cup \eta$. Our investigation reveals that in the presence of zigzagging behaviours the constraints of ξ and η must satisfy certain additional criteria. Based on this observation we formulate a sufficient and necessary condition for the existence of the union (Theorems 2 and 3).

The union operation is directly relevant to the problem of synthesizing timed automata with minimal numbers of clocks from a set of scenarios [14]. It is also relevant to various model-checking techniques based on timed automata, if stable distance tables are used to capture zones corresponding to locations in the automata.

A detailed comparison of timed scenarios with other related work, in particular with Difference Bounds Matrices (DBMs) [25], can be found in our earlier work [10,12]. A union operation has been defined for DBMs, which are used for representing zones in timed automata. However, the union of two zones (represented by DBMs) is—in general—a non-convex set, and therefore cannot be represented by a DBM. So the union of two zones has to be approximated, e.g., by convex hulls [18], or some other safe abstraction [17]. Another method for checking whether the union of two DBMs is itself a DBM has been developed using convex hulls together with Clock Difference Diagrams (CDDs) [26].

Our necessary and sufficient condition provides a syntactic criterion for the existence of the union of two timed scenarios. So the exact union can be computed when it exists. Otherwise, the combination (i.e., the "quasi-union") provides an approximation for the exact union.

Acknowledgements. I am grateful to Feliks Kluźniak for long hours of discussion, contributing many constructive suggestions and corrections, and reading several drafts of the paper. The tool-set for timed scenarios that he has implemented over the past eight years made it possible to run many examples and helped tremendously with validating the results before they were formally proven. The proof of Observation 2 is an adaptation of his proof. I would also like to thank an anonymous referee of this paper for detailed and helpful comments.

References

1. Salah, A., Mizouni, R., Dssouli, R., Parreaux, B.: Formal composition of distributed scenarios. In: de Frutos-Escrig, D., Núñez, M. (eds.) Formal Techniques for Networked and Distributed Systems - FORTE 2004, pp. 213–228. Springer Berlin Heidelberg, Berlin, Heidelberg (2004)
2. Greenyer, J.: Scenario-based modeling and programming of distributed systems. In: Köhler-Bussmeier, M., Kindler, E., Rölke, H. (eds.) Proceedings of the International Workshop on Petri Nets and Software Engineering 2021 Co-located with the 42nd International Conference on Application and Theory of Petri Nets and Concurrency (PETRI NETS 2021), Paris, France, June 25th, 2021 (due to COVID-19: virtual conference), Vol. 2907 of CEUR Workshop Proceedings, CEUR-WS.org, pp. 241–252 (2021)
3. Somé, S., Dssouli, R., Vaucher, J.: From scenarios to timed automata: building specifications from users requirements. In: Proceedings of the Second Asia Pacific Software Engineering Conference, APSEC '95, IEEE Computer Society, pp. 48–57
4. Chandrasekaran, P., Mukund, M.: Matching scenarios with timing constraints. In: Asarin, E., Bouyer, P. (eds.) Formal Modeling and Analysis of Timed Systems, pp. 98–112. Springer, Berlin, Heidelberg (2006)
5. Harel, D., Kugler, H., Pnueli, A.: Synthesis Revisited: Generating Statechart Models from Scenario-Based Requirements, pp. 309–324. Springer, Berlin Heidelberg (2005)
6. Uchitel, S., Kramer, J., Magee, J.: Synthesis of behavioral models from scenarios. IEEE Trans. Softw. Eng. **29**(2), 99–115 (2003)

7. Akshay, S., Mukund, M., Kumar, K.N.: Checking coverage for infinite collections of timed scenarios. In: CONCUR 2007 - Concurrency Theory, 18th International Conference, CONCUR 2007, Proceedings, pp. 181–196
8. Bollig, B., Katoen, J., Kern, C., Leucker, M.: Replaying play in and play out: synthesis of design models from scenarios by learning. In: Proceedings of the 13th International Conference on Tools and Algorithms for the Construction and Analysis of Systems, TACAS, pp. 435–450 (2007)
9. Alur, R., Martin, M., Raghothaman, M., Stergiou, C., Tripakis, S., Udupa, A.: Synthesizing Finite-State Protocols from Scenarios and Requirements. In: Yahav, E. (ed.) Hardware and Software: Verification and Testing, pp. 75–91. Springer International Publishing, Cham (2014)
10. Saeedloei, N., Kluźniak, F.: From scenarios to timed automata. In: Formal Methods: Foundations and Applications - 20th Brazilian Symposium, SBMF 2017, Proceedings, pp. 33–51
11. Saeedloei, N., Kluźniak, F.: Timed scenarios: consistency, equivalence and optimization. In: Formal Methods: Foundations and Applications - 21st Brazilian Symposium, SBMF 2018, Proceedings, pp. 215–233
12. Saeedloei, N., Kluźniak, F.: Optimization of timed scenarios. In: Carvalho, G., Stolz, V. (eds.) Formal Methods: Foundations and Applications - 23rd Brazilian Symposium, SBMF 2020, Ouro Preto, Brazil, November 25–27, 2020, Proceedings. Lecture Notes in Computer Science, vol. 12475, pp. 119–136. Springer (2020)
13. Saeedloei, N., Kluźniak, F.: Operations on timed scenarios. In: Huisman, M., Ravara, A. (eds.) Formal Techniques for Distributed Objects, Components, and Systems - 43rd IFIP WG 6.1 International Conference, FORTE 2023, Held as Part of the 18th International Federated Conference on Distributed Computing Techniques, DisCoTec 2023, Lisbon, Portugal, June 19–23, 2023, Proceedings. Lecture Notes in Computer Science, Vol. 13910, pp. 97–114. Springer (2023). https://doi.org/10.1007/978-3-031-35355-0_7
14. Saeedloei, N., Kluźniak, F.: Synthesizing timed automata with minimal numbers of clocks from optimized timed scenarios. In: Formal Techniques for Distributed Objects, Components, and Systems - International Conference, FORTE 2024, Proceedings, To appear
15. Alur, R., Dill, D.L.: A theory of timed automata. Theor. Comput. Sci. **126**(2), 183–235 (1994)
16. Clarke, E.M., Jr., Grumberg, O., Peled, D.A.: Model Checking. MIT Press, Cambridge (1999)
17. Daws, C., Tripakis, S.: Model checking of real-time reachability properties using abstractions. In: Proceedings of the Fourth International Conference on Tools and Algorithms for the Construction and Analysis of Systems. Lecture Notes in Computer Science, vol. 1384, pp. 313–329. Springer-Verlag (1998). https://doi.org/10.1007/BFb0054180
18. Balarin, F.: Approximate reachability analysis of timed automata. In: 17th IEEE Real-Time Systems Symposium, pp. 52–61 (1996). https://doi.org/10.1109/REAL.1996.563700
19. Larsen, K.G., Larsson, F., Pettersson, P., Yi, W.: Efficient verification of real-time systems: compact data structure and state-space reduction. In: 18th IEEE Real-Time Systems Symposium, pp. 14–24 (1997)
20. Asarin, E., Bozga, M., Kerbrat, A., Maler, O., Pnueli, A., Rasse, A.: Datastructures for the verification of timed automata. In: Maler, O. (ed.) Hybrid and Real-Time Systems, pp. 346–360. Springer Berlin Heidelberg, Berlin, Heidelberg (1997)

21. Dill, D.L.: Timing assumptions and verification of finite-state concurrent systems. In: Proceedings of the International Workshop on Automatic Verification Methods for Finite State Systems, pp. 197–212. Springer-Verlag New York, Inc. (1990)
22. Bozga, M., Maler, O., Pnueli, A., Yovine, S.: Some progress in the symbolic verification of timed automata. In: Grumberg, O. (ed.) Computer Aided Verification, pp. 179–190. Springer Berlin Heidelberg, Berlin, Heidelberg (1997)
23. Saeedloei, N., Kluźniak, F.: Minimization of the number of clocks for timed scenarios. In: Campos, S., Minea, M. (eds.) Formal Methods: Foundations and Applications - 24th Brazilian Symposium, SBMF 2021 Proceedings. Lecture Notes in Computer Science, vol. 13130, pp. 122–139. Springer (2021)
24. Saeedloei, N.: On the Existence of Unions of Timed Scenarios. https://tigerweb.towson.edu/nsaeedloei/thech-report-union.pdf
25. Bengtsson, J., Yi, W.: Timed automata: semantics, algorithms and tools. In: Desel, J., Reisig, W., Rozenberg, G. (eds.) Lectures on Concurrency and Petri Nets: Advances in Petri Nets, pp. 87–124. Springer Berlin Heidelberg, Berlin, Heidelberg (2004)
26. Behrmann, G., Larsen, K.G., Pearson, J., Weise, C., Yi, W.: Efficient timed reachability analysis using clock difference diagrams. In: Halbwachs, N., Peled, D. (eds.) Computer Aided Verification, pp. 341–353. Springer Berlin Heidelberg, Berlin, Heidelberg (1999)

SMTQuery: Analysing SMT-LIB String Benchmarks

Mitja Kulczynski[1], Kevin Lotz[1], Florin Manea[2],
Danny Bøgsted Poulsen[3], and Paul Sarnighausen-Cahn[2](✉)

[1] Department of Computer Science, Kiel University, Kiel, Germany
{mku,kel}@informatik.uni-kiel.de
[2] Department of Computer Science, University of Göttingen, Göttingen, Germany
{florin.manea,paul.cahn}@cs.uni-goettingen.de
[3] Department of Computer Science, Aalborg University, Aalborg, Denmark
dannybpoulsen@cs.aau.dk

Abstract. Constraint satisfaction problems involving strings have been a subject of theoretical study for decades, but it is only in recent years that practical solving methods have begun to emerge. This increasing interest in solving string constraints led to the development of various techniques and solvers, often accompanied by specific benchmark sets. As a result, there is now a substantial corpus of publicly available, yet largely unclassified, such benchmarks. In this context, we present SMTQUERY, a framework for maintaining and analyzing benchmarks for SMT string problems. SMTQUERY enables the execution of user-defined queries to extract domain-specific information from these benchmarks, facilitating a deeper analysis of the underlying problems. We demonstrate its utility by analyzing over 100,000 benchmarks and training an algorithm selection model to match benchmarks with suitable solvers.

1 Introduction

The canonical problem of string solving is to decide the satisfiability of first-order formulas with predicates and functions on finite *strings* (containing constant letters and string-variables), often augmented with statements about string lengths. These predicates or functions, known as constraints, include word equations (equalities between strings with letters and variables), language membership predicates (asserting string membership in a formal language), and linear relations between string lengths. The main focus is on the satisfiability of quantifier-free formulas, determining if there exists a substitution mapping each string variable to a constant string, such that the formula evaluates to true under the given predicates' semantics. String constraint solving has been pivotal in enhancing web application security [1,20,28,31,32] and it has also been applied to formal verification through symbolic execution [19] and model checking [16]. Recently, it has been used to verify the security properties of cloud resource access policies [4]. Over the years, numerous dedicated string solvers, such as NORN [1], STRANGER [31], ABC [3], WOORPJE [11,13,21], OSTRICH [10],

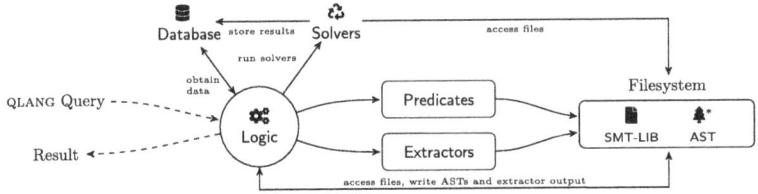

Fig. 1. The architecture of SMTQUERY.

CERTISTR [18], NFA2SAT [24], and NOODLER [9], have been developed. Additionally, general-purpose SMT-solvers like CVC5 [5] and Z3 [8,14,25,30] include integrated string-solving components. Efforts to improve the performance of these solvers are ongoing.

From a theoretical perspective, the satisfiability of many fragments within the SMT-LIB theory of strings is undecidable or has intractably high complexity [6,17,26], resulting in varied support and performance across different solvers: not all solvers can handle every input formula, and their performance can significantly differ depending on the specific input problem. Currently, a wide range of publicly available benchmarks is used to evaluate string solvers' performance (see [22] for an overview). However, these benchmarks are largely uncategorized w.r.t. the satisfiability of their instances and the logical fragments they belong to. This lack of classification makes it challenging to develop algorithms targeting string constraints that appear in practice, as it is difficult to determine the prevalent constraints and their structure, and match these to specific application areas.

We address this problem by introducing a novel tool, SMTQUERY, for extracting information from SMT-LIB benchmarks. This tool systematically analyzes and categorizes large collections of SMT-LIB string benchmarks, revealing, in this way, novel insights into the presence and importance of certain logical fragments within these benchmarks and suggesting them, e.g., as focal points for further theoretical studies. Additionally, we leverage SMTQUERY's capabilities to develop an algorithm selection model, which enhances our understanding of solvers, identifying the conditions under which they perform better or worse.

2 The SMTQUERY Framework

We introduce SMTQUERY[1], a framework designed for storing, analyzing, and querying extensive collections of SMT-LIB benchmarks. An overview of its architecture is depicted in Fig. 1. SMTQUERY stores structural properties of formulas and outcomes from user-defined solvers. Users submit *queries* to filter benchmarks based on specific predicates, which can examine structural properties of formulas or solver outcomes. The system compiles these benchmarks into user-chosen formats. The system supports combining multiple predicates using

---

[1] https://smtquery.github.io/.

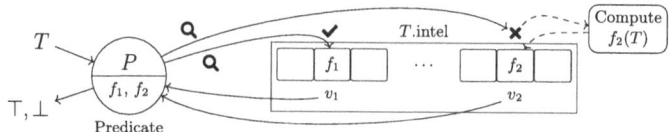

Fig. 2. Evaluation of a predicate P on a formula T. The predicate requires two properties $f_1(T)$ and $f_2(T)$, one of which already present in the INTELDICTIONARY. The other is missing and computed on demand.

Boolean logic for versatile information retrieval. All queries are formulated in QLANG, a query language inspired by SQL but tailored to address the unique requirements of the system, developed specifically for SMTQUERY. QLANG is inspired by SQL but is tailored to address the unique requirements of the system.

Maintaining Benchmarks. SMTQUERY processes collections of SMT-LIB benchmarks by registering each instance in a database. If configured, it executes a predefined set of solvers on each instance, storing the results alongside the benchmark in the database. Simultaneously, SMTQUERY constructs an internal data structure capturing the logical structure of the SMT formula and additional derived information. Thus, the storage layer comprises two primary components: a database recording all processed benchmarks along with metrics of the executed solvers, and an internal representation of each benchmark's logical formula, enhanced with metadata. The latter is maintained in the form of an *abstract syntax tree (AST)* that can be dynamically augmented with additional data. Each node in the AST is annotated with an INTELDICTIONARY, a key-value store containing arbitrary metadata about the node. Initially, when a new instance is presented to the system, its corresponding INTELDICTIONARY is empty. Whenever the answer to a query depends on a node's structural properties, SMTQUERY first checks if this information exists in the INTELDICTIONARY. If present, the result is retrieved directly; if not, SMTQUERY computes the property and stores it in the INTELDICTIONARY. This process is explained in more detail below.

Querying Information. SMTQUERY provides an interface for querying stored information. Each query is structured into two components: 1. a boolean combination of *predicates* $\mathcal{P}$, which filter stored instances, and 2. an *extractor* e, which specifies the desired output format. SMTQUERY selects the set of instances T' that fulfill $\mathcal{P}$. The query is then answered by evaluating the extractor e on resulting set T'. In its simplest form, extractors return the names of the instances or the instances themselves in SMT-LIB format. More complex extractors can generate plots from the data (e.g. the ones shown in Sect. 2). SMTQUERY provides a rich set of predicates and extractors out of the box, addressing a wide range of use cases. The architecture is flexible enough to be easily extended with more complex operations.

```
S       ::= Select Extractor From d F M
d       ::= * | Set | Set:Track | d, d
F       ::= ε | Where Pred
Pred    ::= P_R | P_ψ | (Pred And Pred) | (Pred Or Pred) | (Not Pred)
```

Fig. 3. Syntax of QLANG. P_R and P_ψ denote result and AST predicates, respectively.

Predicate Evaluation. Every predicate in $\mathcal{P}$ is either a *result predicate* or an *AST predicate*. Result predicates relate to the outcomes of running solvers. For example, SMTQUERY provides the isSAT(*solver*) result predicate, which filters instances that a given solver declared satisfiable. The required information is stored in the relational database; therefore, SMTQUERY evaluates result predicates using SQL queries. The second type, *AST predicates*, relate to the logical structure of the formulas. Defined as functions P_φ, these take an AST T of a formula as input and return a truth value based on whether T meets the specified condition. For instance, the in-built predicate hasWEQ(T) returns true if T contains a word equation. When a query includes an AST predicate P_φ, SMTQUERY retrieves the ASTs T from the storage layer and evaluates $P_\varphi(T)$ for each retrieved tree T. The evaluation amounts to comparing properties $f_1(T), \ldots, f_n(T)$ that are computed on the AST T. For example, consider the predicate isRegexHeavy(T), which checks whether T has more regular constraints than word equations. This predicate requires counting these elements (regular constraints and word equations, respectively) and comparing their totals. The evaluation process, outlined in Fig. 2, checks if a property $f(T)$ needed by P_φ is in the root node's INTELDICTIONARY. If absent, it is computed and stored in the INTELDICTIONARY. This method ensures that each value for an AST T is computed once, then cached for constant-time retrieval and reuse across different predicates. For example, if hasRegex(T), which returns true if the number of regular constraints in T is greater than 0, is evaluated after the execution of isRegexHeavy(T), the number of regular constraints is already available in the cache, so it is not computed again. Additionally, since every node—not just the root—has its own cache, the computation of a property can benefit from previously calculated properties: If the computation requires evaluation on a sub-tree, the computation can be shortcut, if a value is already available.

Extractors. After filtering the benchmark set using predicates, SMTQUERY employs an extractor to compile the information. In simple scenarios, it functions like a projection in relational algebra, retrieving details such as instance names or storage locations. It also supports basic aggregation, like counting instances, and can directly output the SMT-LIB formulas of the benchmarks. SMTQUERY also offers complex extraction capabilities, including various plots, such as cactus plots for visualizing solver runtimes across benchmarks to analyze performance trends (examples shown in Sect. 2). Additionally, feature sets—customized collections of benchmark metrics—can be extracted.

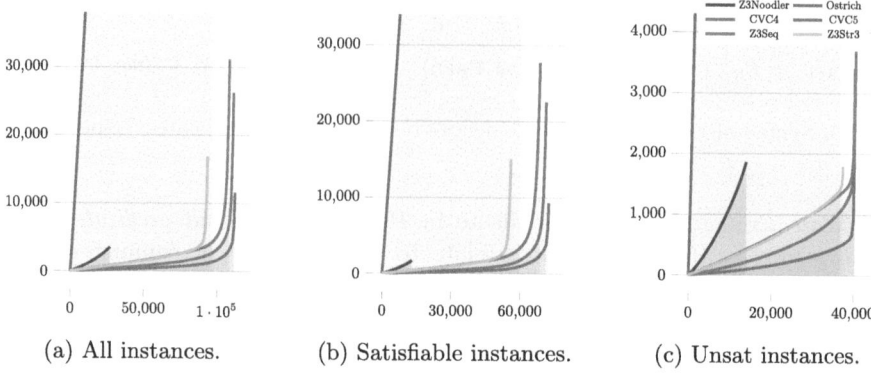

Fig. 4. Cactus plots showing solver results classified by satisfiability. The x-axis shows the number of solved instances and the y-axis the runtime in seconds.

The QLANG Query Language. All queries in SMTQUERY are composed using the SQL-inspired query language QLANG. The syntax is detailed in Fig. 3. A QLANG query consists at least of an extractor and a benchmark set, identified by a name or *, representing all benchmarks. For instance, **Select** Name **From** * retrieves the names of all benchmarks processed by SMTQUERY. To refine the selection, a **Where** clause can be added, specifying a combination of predicates $\mathcal{P}$, each referenced by an identifier. For example, to query benchmarks that CVC5 could not solve, one might use the following query: **Select** Name **From** * **Where** (Not isSAT(CVC5)) And (Not isUNSAT(CVC5)).

3 Analysis of SMT-LIB String Benchmarks

We use SMTQUERY to systematically analyze a collection of 114,468 SMT-LIB string benchmarks from [22], distributed across 19 sets from practical and academic applications. We classify these benchmarks based on satisfiability, the presence of operators, and the logical fragments they fall into. Additionally, we categorize the benchmarks by their decidability and the runtime performance of various solvers on these instances.

Setup and Initialisation. We initialize SMTQUERY on the benchmark set, using solvers CVC5 (1.1.2), CVC4 (1.8), Z3 (4.13.0) (including Z3STR3 and Z3SEQ), OSTRICH (#e386836), and Z3NOODLER (1.1.0). Each solver has a 20-second time-out. Initialization took 90 seconds and running the solvers took 324 minutes. We provide the database alongside the tool for ease of use. Experiments were conducted on a machine with 2 AMD 7742 64-core CPUs and 2 TB of memory, running Linux 5.4.0.

Classification by Satisfiability. We classify the benchmarks by their satisfiability status using two QLANG queries **Select** Count **From** * **Where** X, where X is, in the first case, a disjunction of the predicates isSAT(s) **and** isCorrect(s),

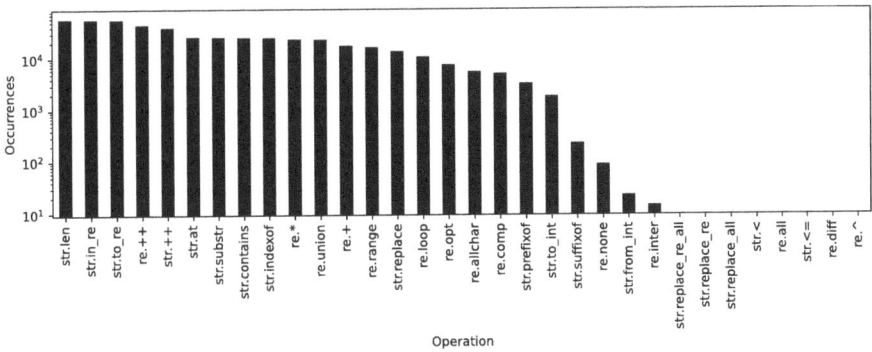

Fig. 5. Distribution of operators in the benchmarks in log-scale.

and, in the second case, of isUNSAT(s) and isCorrect(s), for all tested solvers s. As such, an instance is satisfiable (unsatisfiable) if at least one solver declared it as such, and the result was cross-validated, either by verifying the model or by majority vote. If no solver can solve the instance, it is considered unknown. Out of the 114,468 benchmarks, the majority (73,125) are satisfiable; 41,287 are unsatisfiable; only 56 of the benchmarks could not solved by any of our tested solvers.

We additionally query the runtime of the solvers for all, satisfiable, and unsatisfiable benchmarks to gain insights into solver performance across the different classes. The results are presented as cactus plots in Fig. 4. A cactus plot visually represents solver performance by plotting the number of solved instances against cumulative time. Each solver is depicted by a line showing the increasing number of solved instances over time, allowing easy comparison. Better-performing solvers appear further to the right and closer to the bottom of the plot. Moreover, we query the runtime of the solvers for all benchmarks, all satisfiable benchmarks, and all unsatisfiable benchmarks, to get insights into the performance of the solvers on the different classes of benchmarks. We obtained the cactus plots by posing the queries (a) **Select** CactusPlot **From** *, (b) **Select** CactusPlot **From** * **Where** (((isSAT(CVC5) **and** isVerified(CVC5)) **or** (isSAT(Z3Str3) **and** isVerified(Z3Str3))) **or** (isSAT(Z3Seq) **and** isVerified (Z3Seq))), and (c) **Select** CactusPlot **From** * **Where** ((isUNSAT(CVC5) **or** isUNSAT(Z3Str3)) **or** isUNSAT(Z3Seq)).

Relevancy of Operators. We investigate the significance of various operators defined within the SMT-LIB theory of strings by querying the number of instances containing each specific operator. Using the query **Select** OperatorPlot **From** *, we obtain the distribution of operators shown in Fig. 5. The plot highlights the prevalence of length constraints over string variables, concatenation, and regular constraints, and the absence of lexicographic orderings and most string-replace operations. This distribution suggests areas for solver optimization by targeting the most common operations in the benchmarks. We further analyze the frequency of combinations of operators (logical fragments) to identify common and rare occurrences.

Table 1. Number of instances within different fragments of the theory of strings.

Category	Fragments	Occurrences
Word Equations, Regular Constraints, and Length Constraints	WE	26,622
	REG	25,048
	WE+LEN	605
	REG+LEN	4,875
	WE+REG	2,786
	WE+REG+LEN	22,538
Substring and Indexing	WE+LEN+S	2,776
	WE+LEN+I	1
	REG+LEN+I	1
String-Replacement	WE+R	21
	WE+LEN+R	1
	WE+REG+R	3
String-Number Conversion	WE+LEN+SN	1
	REG+LEN+SN	881
	WE+REG+LEN+SN	936

Categorisation into Fragments. Based on the occurrence of operators, we classify benchmarks into several logical fragments of the theory of string. We start with fragments using only word equations, regular constraints, and length constraints, establishing these combinations as the baseline for defining new fragments by allowing additional operations. We query SMTQUERY to return the total number of instances in each fragment, providing insights into which fragments are relevant in practice. The results are presented in Table 1.

Word Equations, Regular, and Length Constraints. Following the approach of [12], we define the logical fragment containing only word equations as WE, and the fragment with only regular constraints (including string concatenations) as REG. Their combination is labeled WE+REG. Adding length constraints to any fragment appends +LEN to its name, resulting in six distinct fragments. Each instance is assigned to the minimal fragment (with respect to the set of constraints involved) that describes it. We use SMTQUERY to compute the number of benchmarks within each fragment. Notably, the majority of problems involve either exclusively word equations or regular constraints. Length constraints typically appear in combination with both word equations and regular constraints, a fragment whose decidability remains an important open question. Next, we explore additional fragments beyond these initial six categories, omitting those that do not contain instances for brevity.

§ *Substring and Indexing Operations.* The substring (`str.substr`) and indexing (`str.indexof`) operations extract a substring from a string and return the index at which a string occurs in another string, respectively. We denote the fragments by appending S and I, respectively. We view `str.at` as a special case of `str.substr`. Surprisingly, despite the frequent occurrence of `str.substr` and str.at operations, they rarely appear combined with word equations, regular, and length constraints. Notably, the largest fragment that includes these operations comprises only 2,776 instances.

String-Replacement Operations. We next examine the string-replacement operation str.replace, which replaces the first occurrence of a substring within a string. Notably, other replacement operations do not occur in the benchmarks. We denote the presence of string-replacement by appending an R to the fragment identifiers. Only 25 instances involve string replacement operations. Of the six resulting combinations with our baseline fragments, three are empty. Similar to substring operations, the operator plot reveals that string-replacement appears more frequently than reflected in our current fragments, suggesting a deeper analysis is needed to identify the fragments containing replacement operations.

String-Number Conversion. We investigate instances containing the string-number conversions str.to_int and str.from_int, which are relatively uncommon according to Fig. 5. We found 1818 instances that contain string-number conversion operations in combination with one of our baseline fragments.

The instances are nearly evenly distributed between the REG+LEN+SN and WE+REG+LEN+SN fragments, with only one instance in WE+LEN+SN. All these fragments are known to be undecidable, unlike fragments where word equations are absent, such as the decidable REG+LEN+SN fragment [15], in contrast to the undecidable WE+REG+LEN+SN fragment [7].

Categorisation by Decidability. We further categorize the benchmarks by the decidability of the fragments they fall into (see [2,7,23] and references therein). The classification along the number of instances falling into each respective category is shown in Table 2. Most instances (57,426) fall into a decidable fragments, whereas only 1,844 are in undecidable fragments. The second largest group contains the benchmarks for which satisfiability is unknown. All of them fall into WE+LEN or an extension of it. The decidability of this fragment is a major open question. The performance of the solvers seems to correlate with the decidability-status of the fragment a formula falls into, as shown in Fig. 6.

Table 2. Number of instances from decidable, undecidable, unknown fragments.

	Fragments	Number
Decidable	WE, REG, REG+LEN, REG+LEN+SN	57,426
Undecidable	WE+LEN+SN, WE+REG+LEN+SN, REG+LEN+SN, WE+R WE+LEN+R WE+REG+R, WE+LEN+I	1,844
Unknown	WE+LEN, WE+REG+LEN, WE+LEN+S	25,919

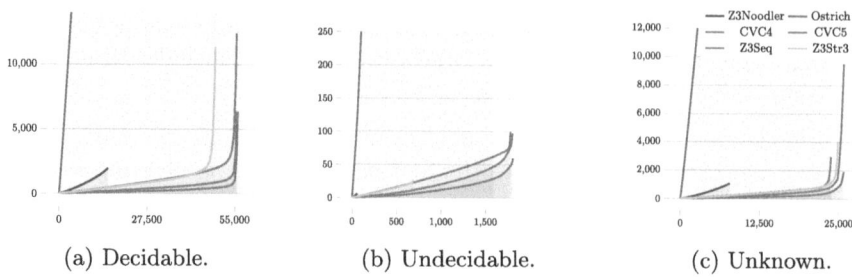

(a) Decidable. (b) Undecidable. (c) Unknown.

Fig. 6. Classification of benchmarks by decidability. The x-axis shows the total number of solved instances and the y-axis the accumulated runtime in seconds.

Extracting Information for Algorithm Selection Models. Utilizing SMTQUERY, we developed a machine-learning-based *algorithm selector* (e.g., [27]) that predicts the most reliable and efficient solver for an unseen problem based on its structural features. While similar approaches have been proposed for general SMT-solving (e.g., [29]), our focus is on applying this method specifically to the domain of string solving.

We used SMTQUERY to define a *feature* extractor, which compiles benchmarks into numerical features. For our experiment, we choose 21 features, which range from superficial ones (e.g., the number of regular or length constraints, the number of word equations), to deeper, string-solving specific properties like approximations of the number of states in finite automata accepting regular languages occurring in the formula. These features capture essential properties of the string constraint problems and appear to influence the solver performance. While computing these features can be time-consuming—especially for inherently difficult tasks such as determining the number of states in a minimal DFA from a given regular expression—SMTQUERY's internal AST and its INTELDICTIONARY allows reusing previously computed information. This optimisation helps speed up the process, making it feasible for practical applications.

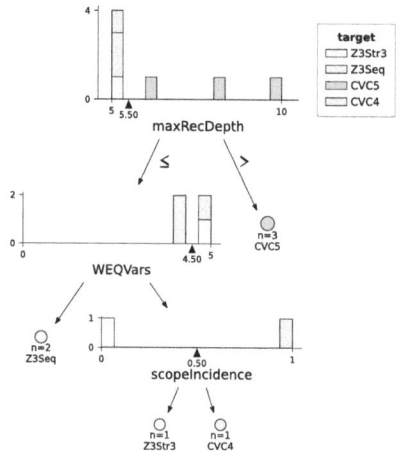

Fig. 7. Example decision tree resulting from training on a small subset of benchmarks stemming from [32]. Only the solvers that won (fastest and correct) at least one instance are displayed.

We used the extracted features to train a random forest model predicting the fastest solver for a new instance. We first trained the model on the collection of

Table 3. Accuracy of the random forest compared to the predictor always choosing CVC5 on the three tested benchmark sets.

	Instance Count	CVC5	Random Forest	Improvement
All Data	114,468	92.38%	93.79%	1.14
CVC5 > 85% omitted	9,067	66.98%	77.59%	10.61
CVC5 > 80% omitted	6,401	55.91%	74.01%	18.1

approximately 114,500 benchmarks introduced in Sect. 2. Due to CVC5's overall dominance on the complete benchmark set, and in order to understand the potential of this approach, we conducted two additional experiments, by excluding those subsets of the benchmark suite, where CVC5 was the fastest correct solver for more than 85% and, respectively, 80% of the instances. We chose this approach to have more diversity in our data while maintaining the superiority of CVC5. For each experiment, we randomly split the instances into a training set (75%) and a test set (25%), using one third of the training data for cross validation. Table 3 presents the accuracy of the predictor compared to a naive approach that always selects CVC5. The results demonstrate the effectiveness of our approach to predicting a reliable solver for new instances, based on the selected features.

Additionally, the random-forest-based algorithm facilitates direct visualization of the results, making it easy to trace the reasoning path from input to classification. For example, Fig. 7 visualized the decision tree resulting from training the model on the small `appscan` [32] subset of our benchmark suite. Following the branches of the decision reveals how specific properties influence solver selection. For example, the first node distinguishes CVC5 from other solvers by evaluating the maximal recursion depth, which reflects the complexity of nested constraints.

4 Conclusion

We introduced SMTQUERY, a framework for managing and analyzing SMT-LIB benchmarks alongside solver results, particularly focusing on string constraints. It leverages extensive caching to efficiently query information from diverse benchmark sets. Its modular architecture based on predicates, extractors, and mutators, together with the wide variety of out-of-the-box implementations, makes it adaptable to a broad range of use cases. Our toolbox offers a query language, allowing for a versatile interaction with the system. We demonstrated the utility of SMTQUERY through an extensive survey of publicly available benchmark sets, providing various insights. Additionally, we used SMTQUERY to train a proof-of-concept algorithm selection model, that predicts the most effective solver for specific instances. Continuing our efforts, we plan to expand SMTQUERY to support additional theories, such as integer arithmetic and bitvectors.

References

1. Abdulla, P.A., et al.: Norn: An SMT solver for string constraints. In: International conference on Computer Aided Verification, pp. 462–469. Springer (2015)
2. Amadini, R.: A survey on string constraint solving. ACM Comput. Surv. (CSUR) **55**(1), 1–38 (2021)
3. Aydin, A., Bang, L., Bultan, T.: Automata-based model counting for string constraints. In: Computer Aided Verification: 27th International Conference, CAV 2015, San Francisco, CA, USA, July 18-24, 2015, Proceedings, Part I, pp. 255–272. Springer (2015)
4. Backes, J., et al.: Semantic-based automated reasoning for AWS access policies using SMT. In: 2018 Formal Methods in Computer Aided Design (FMCAD), pp. 1–9 (2018)
5. Barbosa, H., et al.: cvc5: a versatile and industrial-strength SMT solver. In: International Conference on Tools and Algorithms for the Construction and Analysis of Systems, pp. 415–442. Springer (2022)
6. Berzish, M., et al.: String theories involving regular membership predicates: from practice to theory and back. In: Lecroq, T., Puzynina, S. (eds.) Combinatorics on Words, pp. 50–64. Springer International Publishing, Cham (2021)
7. Berzish, M., et al.: Towards more efficient methods for solving regular-expression heavy string constraints. Theor. Comput. Sci. **943**, 50–72 (2023)
8. Berzish, M., Ganesh, V., Zheng, Y.: Z3str3: a string solver with theory-aware heuristics. In: 2017 Formal Methods in Computer Aided Design (FMCAD), pp. 55–59. IEEE (2017)
9. Blahoudek, F., et al.: Word equations in synergy with regular constraints. In: Chechik, M., Katoen, J.P., Leucker, M. (eds.) Formal Methods, pp. 403–423. Springer International Publishing, Cham (2023)
10. Chen, T., Hague, M., Lin, A.W., Rümmer, P., Wu, Z.: Decision procedures for path feasibility of string-manipulating programs with complex operations. Proc. ACM Program. Lang. **3**(POPL), 49:1-49:30 (2019)
11. Day, J.D., Ehlers, T., Kulczynski, M., Manea, F., Nowotka, D., Poulsen, D.B.: On solving word equations using SAT. In: International Conference on Reachability Problems, pp. 93–106. Springer (2019)
12. Day, J.D., Ganesh, V., Grewal, N., Manea, F.: On the expressive power of string constraints. Proc. ACM Program. Lang. **7**(POPL), 278–308 (2023). https://doi.org/10.1145/3571203
13. Day, J.D., Kulczynski, M., Manea, F., Nowotka, D., Poulsen, D.B.: Rule-based word equation solving. In: Proceedings of the 8th International Conference on Formal Methods in Software Engineering, pp. 87–97 (2020)
14. De Moura, L., Bjørner, N.: Z3: An efficient SMT solver. In: TACAS 2008, pp. 337–340. Springer (2008)
15. Draghici, A., Haase, C., Manea, F.: Semënov arithmetic, affine VASS, and string constraints. In: 41st International Symposium on Theoretical Aspects of Computer Science, STACS 2024. LIPIcs, vol. 289, pp. 29:1–29:19. Schloss Dagstuhl - Leibniz-Zentrum für Informatik (2024). https://doi.org/10.4230/LIPIcs.STACS.2024.29
16. Hojjat, H., Rümmer, P., Shamakhi, A.: On strings in software model checking. In: Lin, A.W. (ed.) Programming Languages and Systems, pp. 19–30. Springer International Publishing, Cham (2019)

17. Jez, A.: Word Equations in Nondeterministic Linear Space. In: Chatzigiannakis, I., Indyk, P., Kuhn, F., Muscholl, A. (eds.) 44th International Colloquium on Automata, Languages, and Programming (ICALP 2017). Leibniz International Proceedings in Informatics (LIPIcs), vol. 80, pp. 95:1–95:13. Schloss Dagstuhl–Leibniz-Zentrum fuer Informatik, Dagstuhl, Germany (2017). http://drops.dagstuhl.de/opus/volltexte/2017/7408
18. Kan, S., Lin, A.W., Rümmer, P., Schrader, M.: Certistr: A certified string solver (technical report) (2021, to appear in CPP 2022). CoRR arxiv.org/abs/2208.08806
19. Kausler, S., Sherman, E.: Evaluation of string constraint solvers in the context of symbolic execution. In: Proceedings of the 29th ACM/IEEE International Conference on Automated Software Engineering. p. 259-270. ASE '14, Association for Computing Machinery, New York, NY, USA (2014). https://doi.org/10.1145/2642937.2643003
20. Kiezun, A., Ganesh, V., Artzi, S., Guo, P.J., Hooimeijer, P., Ernst, M.D.: Hampi: a solver for word equations over strings, regular expressions, and context-free grammars. ACM Trans. Softw. Eng. Methodol. **21**(4), 1 (2013). https://doi.org/10.1145/2377656.2377662
21. Kulczynski, M., Lotz, K., Nowotka, D., Poulsen, D.B.: Solving string theories involving regular membership predicates using sat. In: Legunsen, O., Rosu, G. (eds.) Model Checking Software, pp. 134–151. Springer International Publishing, Cham (2022)
22. Kulczynski, M., Manea, F., Nowotka, D., Poulsen, D.B.: ZaligVinder: a generic test framework for string solvers. J. Softw. Evol. Process, e2400 (2021)
23. Lin, A.W., Barceló, P.: String solving with word equations and transducers: towards a logic for analysing mutation xss. In: Proceedings of the 43rd Annual ACM SIGPLAN-SIGACT Symposium on Principles of Programming Languages, pp. 123–136 (2016)
24. Lotz, K., et al.: Solving string constraints using sat. In: Enea, C., Lal, A. (eds.) Computer Aided Verification, pp. 187–208. Springer Nature Switzerland, Cham (2023)
25. Mora, F., Berzish, M., Kulczynski, M., Nowotka, D., Ganesh, V.: Z3str4: a multi-armed string solver. In: FM 2021, pp. 389–406. Springer (2021)
26. Plandowski, W., Rytter, W.: Application of Lempel-Ziv Encodings to the Solution of Word Equations, pp. 731–742. Springer Berlin Heidelberg (1998). https://doi.org/10.1007/BFb0055097
27. Rice, J.R.: The algorithm selection problem. Adv. Comput. **15**, 65–118 (1976). https://doi.org/10.1016/S0065-2458(08)60520-3
28. Saxena, P., Akhawe, D., Hanna, S., Mao, F., McCamant, S., Song, D.: A symbolic execution framework for javascript. In: 2010 IEEE Symposium on Security and Privacy, pp. 513–528 (2010)
29. Scott, J., Niemetz, A., Preiner, M., Nejati, S., Ganesh, V.: Publisher correction: algorithm selection for SMT. Int. J. Softw. Tools Technol. Transf. **25**(5), 799–800 (2023). https://doi.org/10.1007/s10009-023-00714-1
30. Stanford, C., Veanes, M., Bjørner, N.: Symbolic boolean derivatives for efficiently solving extended regular expression constraints. In: Proceedings of the 42nd ACM SIGPLAN International Conference on Programming Language Design and Implementation. pp. 620–635. PLDI 2021, Association for Computing Machinery, New York, NY, USA (2021). https://doi.org/10.1145/3453483.3454066

31. Yu, F., Alkhalaf, M., Bultan, T.: STRANGER: an automata-based string analysis tool for PHP. In: Proceedings of the 16th International Conference on Tools and Algorithms for the Construction and Analysis of Systems, pp. 154–157. TACAS'10, Springer-Verlag, Berlin, Heidelberg (2010)
32. Zheng, Y., Zhang, X., Ganesh, V.: Z3-str: a z3-based string solver for web application analysis. In: ESEC/SIGSOFT FSE 2013, pp. 114–124 (2013)

Autonomous Vehicles Path Planning Under Temporal Logic Specifications

Akshay Dhonthi[1,2(✉)], Nicolas Schischka[1,3], Ernst Moritz Hahn[2], and Vahid Hashemi[1]

[1] AUDI AG, Auto-Union-Straße 1, 85057 Ingolstadt, Germany
[2] Formal Methods and Tools, University of Twente, Enschede, Netherlands
a.dhonthirameshbabu@utwente.nl
[3] Technical University of Munich, Munich, Germany

Abstract. Path planning is an essential component of autonomous driving. A global planner is responsible for the high-level planning. It basically performs a shortest-path search on a known map, thereby defining waypoints used to control the local (low-level) planner. Local planning is a runtime verification method which is repeatedly run on the vehicle itself in real-time, so as to find the optimal short-horizon path which leads to the desired waypoint in a way which is both efficient and safe. The challenge is that the local planner has to take into account repeatedly incoming updates about the information available of the environment. In addition, it performs a complex task, as it has to take into account a large variety of requirements, originating from the necessity of collision avoidance with obstacles, respecting traffic rules, sticking to regulatory requirements, and lastly to reach the next waypoint efficiently. In this paper, we describe a logic-based specification mechanism which fulfills all these requirements.

Keywords: path planning · signal temporal logics · trajectory optimization

1 Introduction

Autonomous driving has gained importance in the recent years. Path planning is one of the key aspects of automatically steering a driving vehicle. Here, a trajectory is generated between the current position and the goal position. A classical path planner consists of a global (high-level) planner and a local (low-level) planner. Before the start of a travel, the global planner must find a path to the final goal and generate a full route based on the environment map, thereby defining waypoints which it forwards to the local (low-level) planner. Global planning is typically defined as a reachability problem to find a path to the goal state. On the other hand, the local planner is a runtime validation entity which repeatedly and in real-time plans the next few seconds of a trajectory based on both static and dynamic obstacles. Learning from Demonstrations (LfD) is one of the path planning techniques, in which a demonstrator manually moves the vehicle from start to goal state. These demonstrations are then learned by the vehicle to reproduce a new path that is close to the demos. Most of the time, the reproduced trajectory fails to achieve the goal without violating road rules and hitting obstacles. For both planners, it is essential to verify during the runtime of the travel that a safe trajectory is generated.

The LfD method [12] that we use in this work encodes demonstrations using a discrete-state Hidden semi-Markov Model (HSMM) [10]. The states of this HSMM are then used as desired waypoints to generate the trajectories using Gaussian Mixture Models (GMM) [2] as depicted in Fig. 1(a). LfD for path planning, however, suffers from limitations to address safety concerns. Namely, reproduced paths must adhere to road-rules, for example to avoid crossing into the opposite lanes when not necessary. There can be other obstacles such as cars, bicycles, or pedestrians that might move into the planned trajectory. These obstacles can be static or dynamic. We depict these safety concerns as an example in Fig. 1(b) where we show how the reproduced trajectory fails to adhere to some of the safety concerns mentioned above.

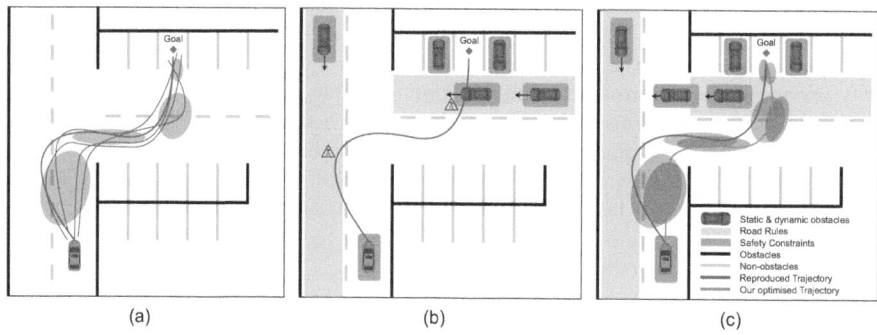

Fig. 1. Illustration of the approach. (a) Collection of human demos (in blue) and corresponding spatial GMM (red ellipses). Reproduced trajectory is in red. (b) Real-time scenario during runtime with three different constraint categories labelled in figure, the constraints breach is represented as yellow danger sign. (c) Optimized trajectory (in green) after running our algorithm (Color figure online).

To account for the latter and to address the aforementioned limitations, we propose a new method which will optimize the learned parameters of the LfD (also called model parameters) and generate optimal trajectories. We formalize safety properties using the logical specification called Signal Temporal Logics (STL) [9]. Safety properties could essentially also include requirements from relevant standards such as ISO 26262 [11] or SOTIF [13], and we use the logic to specify the requirements of these standards as STL formulas. Other potential safety properties are also driven by obstacles and road-rules. Synthesizing optimal model parameters needs a reward function which is a quantitative semantics calculated from the given STL property. We utilize the algorithm from our previous work [4] to achieve this. In Fig. 1(c), we illustrate the resultant optimal trajectory (in green) and optimized spatial GMMs (blue ellipses). As we can see, the new trajectory adheres to all the safety properties. In Fig. 1(c), we highlight the dynamicity of the obstacles by presenting them at a later time step. Our synthesized optimal trajectory can successfully avoid hitting those moving obstacles.

Similar to our work, there are few methods that define safety constraints via linear temporal logic (LTL) in the context of path planning [5,8,14]. Similar to our work, Barbosa et al. [1] use STL to incorporate different kinds of constraints and use them in a path planner algorithm called Rapid Exploring Random Tree* (RRT*) [6]. However, these methods do not use LfD for path planning and therefore cannot be scaled up for complex scenarios. GMR-RRT* [19] is one approach that is as well close to our work. This method also learns GMMs to fit human demonstrations but applies a Gaussian mixture regression on the demos unlike ours where we apply HSMM. The trajectory reproduction is based on a sampling process via the RRT* algorithm [6] and therefore does not output smooth trajectories. The core difference to this approach is that the reproduced paths of [6] do not account for safety constraints and dynamic obstacles.

Our approach, illustrated in Fig. 2, starts by collecting human demos from multiple start states and a single goal state. Using the trajectories from the demos, we fit an LfD model using the HSMM approach which learns model parameters that match the recorded demos best. Afterward, we define safety constraints based on real-world observations in the form of STL specifications. In the next step, we run a Bayesian optimizer to optimize the parameters of the LfD model so as to maximize the robustness degree computed using the defined STL specifications. Finally, we run the optimal trajectory obtained from the optimized LfD model parameters in a real-world environment.

Overall, our contributions in this paper are as follows:

- We evaluate the algorithm from our previous work [4] on a path planning use case.
- We propose a method for continuous path planning to use as a local planner.
- We define static and dynamic obstacles as temporal logic constraints and propose a new method to compute robustness for dynamic constraints.
- We evaluate the method on two scenarios of an automated valet parking use case.

2 Preliminaries

2.1 Learning from Demonstrations

In this section, we explain the HSMM-based LfD technique from [10] and how we utilize it in our approach. We first manually move the ego vehicle (the vehicle we are synthesizing the trajectory for) from the initial state to the goal state and record N demonstrations in the form of trajectories $\boldsymbol{\xi} = \{\boldsymbol{\xi}^i\}_{i=1}^N$, where $\boldsymbol{\xi}^i =$

$\{\boldsymbol{\xi}_t^i\}_{t=1}^T$ with $\boldsymbol{\xi}_t^i \in \mathcal{X} \subseteq \mathbb{R}^m$ is the state of the system in m dimensions. The m dimensions can be vehicle position, velocity, steering angle, etc. Each $\boldsymbol{\xi}^i$ records spatial co-ordinates and orientation angle (x, y, α) at each time step $t \in 1, \ldots, T$ as we utilize a non-holonomic kinematic model of a differential drive vehicle [7]. Note that the HSMM model we are using is not only restricted to the automotive area but can also easily be adapted to a different application.

Next, the recorded demonstrations $\boldsymbol{\xi}_t$ are associated with a discrete hidden state sequence $\{z_t\}_{t=1}^T$ with $z_t \in \{1, \ldots, K\}$, where K defines the number of components. Each component represents a specific segment of the trajectory (depicted as red ellipses in Fig. 1(a)). To move from one segment i to another j, a transition matrix $\boldsymbol{a} \in \mathbb{R}^{K \times K}$ is learned with $a_{i,j} = P(z_t = j | z_{t-1} = i)$. For the next state j, we fit multivariate Gaussian distributions written as $\{\boldsymbol{\mu}_j, \boldsymbol{\Sigma}_j\}$ that represent the demonstrations $\boldsymbol{\xi}_t$. The parameters $\{\mu_j^S, \Sigma_j^S\}$ denote the duration to stay in a state j for s consecutive steps; we learn their values by fitting a Gaussian $\mathcal{N}(s | \mu_j^S, \Sigma_j^S)$. We define the parameter space as $\boldsymbol{\theta} = \{\{a_{i,m}\}_{m=1}^K, \boldsymbol{\mu}_i, \boldsymbol{\Sigma}_i, \mu_i^S, \Sigma_i^S\}_{i=1}^K$. We refer the readers to [16] for more details about the approach. Since we are solving a non-linear system model, we replace the so-called linear quadratic tracker for the trajectory generation with an iterative linear quadratic regulator [17]. Using an expectation maximization algorithm, we then train these parameters using the likely state sequence $\boldsymbol{z}_t = \{z_1, \ldots, z_T\}$.

After learning $\boldsymbol{\theta}$ using the demonstrations, we can reproduce a deterministic trajectory $\boldsymbol{\xi}_t'$ (in red) as depicted in Fig. 1(a) (cf. [16]). We define $\boldsymbol{\delta} \subset \boldsymbol{\theta}$ to be the parameters to optimize, where $\boldsymbol{\delta} = \{\{a_{i,m}\}_{m=1}^K, \boldsymbol{\mu}_i, \mu_i^S\}_{i=1}^K$. The parameters $\{\boldsymbol{\mu}_i\}_{i=1}^K$ represent the spatial position of the Gaussian for HSMM state i; changing them will translate the Gaussian in (x, y) directions. These parameters are useful to correct the trajectory from going into the opposite lane, or to maintain a safe distance to obstacles. The parameters $\{\mu_i^S\}_{i=1}^K$ represent the temporal state for staying inside an HSMM state i and changing it will reduce or increase the time spent in a region. This parameter is useful to avoid hitting a moving obstacle by increasing the time spent in the previous state. Finally, the parameters $\{\{a_{i,m}\}_{m=1}^K\}_{i=1}^K$ represent the sequence in which each HSMM state has to be visited. It is useful to skip an HSMM state if it is not necessary anymore to satisfy the defined properties. In this work, we optimize parameters $\boldsymbol{\delta}$ to obtain $\hat{\boldsymbol{\theta}}$ which can in turn reproduce the trajectory $\hat{\boldsymbol{\xi}}_t$ (in green in Fig. 1(c)) that satisfies the set temporal logical constraints.

2.2 STL Specifications

We recursively define STL formulas according to the following grammar:

$$\varphi := \pi^\mu \mid \neg \varphi \mid \varphi_1 \wedge \varphi_2 \mid \mathbf{F}_{[a,b]} \varphi \mid \varphi_1 \mathbf{U}_{[a,b]} \varphi_2, \tag{1}$$

where φ_1, φ_2 are recursively defined STL formulas, $\pi^\mu \colon \mathcal{X} \to \mathbb{B}$ is an atomic predicate, the sign of a function $\mu \colon \mathcal{X} \to \mathbb{R}$ determines whether π^μ is true or false. By $\boldsymbol{\xi} \models \varphi$ we denote that the demonstration $\boldsymbol{\xi}$ satisfies the STL formula

φ. Therefore, $\boldsymbol{\xi} \models \mathbf{F}_{[a,b]}\varphi$ iff φ holds at some time step between $[a, b]$. Similarly, $\boldsymbol{\xi} \models \varphi_1 \mathbf{U}_{[a,b]}\varphi_2$, iff φ_1 holds until φ_2 eventually holds during a time step within $[a, b]$. We can then define the *globally* operator $\mathbf{G}_{[a,b]}\varphi = \neg \mathbf{F}_{[a,b]}(\neg\varphi)$, meaning, $\boldsymbol{\xi} \models \mathbf{G}_{[a,b]}\varphi$ holds within $[a, b]$.

The robustness degree or quantitative semantics for STL denoted as $r(\pi^\mu, \boldsymbol{\xi}, t)$ (or shortly as r^φ) is a real-valued function for signal $\boldsymbol{\xi}$ and time t, with the value being positive iff $\boldsymbol{\xi} \models \varphi$. We recursively define r for each operator as follows:

$$\begin{aligned}
r(\pi^\mu, \boldsymbol{\xi}, t) &= \mu(\boldsymbol{\xi}_t), \\
r(\neg\varphi, \boldsymbol{\xi}, t) &= -r(\pi^\mu, \boldsymbol{\xi}, t), \\
r(\varphi_1 \wedge \varphi_2, \boldsymbol{\xi}, t) &= \min(r(\varphi_1, \boldsymbol{\xi}, t), r(\varphi_2, \boldsymbol{\xi}, t)), \\
r(\mathbf{F}_{[a,b]}\varphi, \boldsymbol{\xi}, t) &= \max_{t_k \in [t+a, t+b]} (r(\varphi, \boldsymbol{\xi}, t_k)), \\
r(\varphi_1 \mathbf{U}_{[a,b]}\varphi_2, \boldsymbol{\xi}, t) &= \max_{t_{k1} \in [t+a, t+b]} \left(\min(r(\varphi_1, \boldsymbol{\xi}, t_{k1}), \min_{t_{k2} \in [t+a, t+t_{k1}]} r(\varphi_2, \boldsymbol{\xi}, t_{k2})) \right).
\end{aligned} \quad (2)$$

In this work, we utilize the modified robustness degree from [18] denoted as $\rho(\varphi_i, \boldsymbol{\xi}, t)$ (or shortly as ρ^φ) because its properties are optimal for faster convergence [3,4]. We define this robustness degree for the $\wedge$ operator as

$$(\varphi_1 \wedge \cdots \wedge \varphi_m) := \begin{cases} \dfrac{\sum_i r_{\min} e^{\rho_i} e^{\nu \rho_i}}{\sum_i e^{\nu \rho_i}} & s if \ r_{\min} < 0, \\ \dfrac{\sum_i r^{\varphi_i} e^{-\nu \rho_i}}{\sum_i e^{-\nu \rho_i}} & if \ r_{\min} > 0, \\ 0 & if \ r_{\min} = 0, \end{cases} \quad (3)$$

with

$$r_{\min} = \min(r^{\varphi_i} \cdots r^{\varphi_m}), \quad \rho_i = \frac{r^{\varphi_i} - r_{\min}}{r_{\min}}, \quad (4)$$

where $\nu > 0$ is a hyper-parameter and tends to traditional space robustness as $\nu \to \infty$.

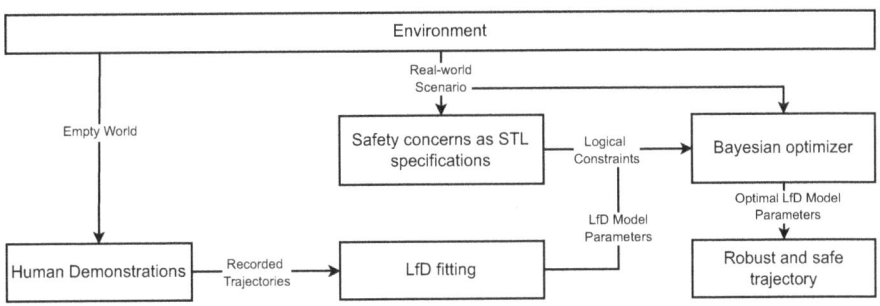

Fig. 2. Illustration of the approach.

3 Methodology

We now utilize all the concepts defined above and introduce our method for optimizing model parameters for safe path planning. After collecting the demonstrations and fitting an HSMM model, we obtain model parameters $\boldsymbol{\theta}$ which represent the task at hand. Now, based on the real-world scenarios we identify safety properties, such as static and dynamic obstacles, task-specific safety properties, or road-rules and convert them to STL semantics φ. We detail in Sect. 3.1, how our approach converts the safety properties to STL and computes the robustness degrees. We use these STL semantics and model parameters to optimize the parameters $\boldsymbol{\delta} \subset \boldsymbol{\theta}$. At any optimization step $n \in N$, we reproduce the trajectory $\boldsymbol{\xi}_n$ based on $\boldsymbol{\delta}_n$, compute the robustness degree $\rho_n(\varphi, \boldsymbol{\xi}_n, t)$ and, based on this, obtain new model parameters $\boldsymbol{\delta}_{n+1}$. Note that we initially modify the parameters $\boldsymbol{\delta}_1$ randomly. At the end of N steps, we obtain an optimal trajectory $\hat{\boldsymbol{\xi}}$ that follows all the safety properties, given $\hat{\boldsymbol{\xi}} \models \varphi$ and $\hat{\rho} > 0$.

The aforementioned method is suitable for a single instance of trajectory optimization. However, automotive applications in real-world scenarios have longer time steps, and path planning for the whole trajectory at once is not feasible. The reason is that the environment constantly changes, and the vehicle perception may be limited. Therefore, we propose an adapted version called *continuous multi-cycle path planning*. We break the demonstrations to M cycles, each cycle representing T_m time steps. This means that we divide the full task to M sets giving rise to M models, each represented as $\boldsymbol{\theta}_m$. At any cycle m, when the perception of the vehicle can cover the area of the next cycle $m+1$, we optimize $\boldsymbol{\delta}_{m+1}$ based on the current perception. Referring to the time taken to optimize the model parameters $\boldsymbol{\theta}$ as $t^{\boldsymbol{\theta}}$, our goal is to keep the time $t + t^{\boldsymbol{\theta}}_{m+1} < T_m$, so that the vehicle motion is continuous from the initial state until the goal state.

3.1 Safety Properties as STL Specifications

In this section, we introduce our approach to convert the safety properties to logical specifications. More specifically, the safety properties we define here are for avoiding static and dynamic obstacles, following traffic lights, and maintaining a safety distance to vehicles. We first define the logical specification for the obstacles as

$$\varphi_{obs} = \mathbf{G}_{[0,T]} \neg \varphi_{obs_1} \wedge \cdots \wedge \mathbf{G}_{[0,T]} \neg \varphi_{obs_O} \qquad (5)$$

with

$$\varphi_{obs_o} = (x_{o,lb} < x_o < x_{o,ub}) \wedge (y_{o,lb} < y_o < y_{o,ub}), \qquad (6)$$

where x_o, y_o are the co-ordinate position of an obstacle o coming from the observations, and we define the region of the obstacle with suffix lb, ub representing the lower and upper bounds of the obstacle in x and y axis, respectively. The robustness degree for this specification is defined as $\rho(\varphi_{obs}, \boldsymbol{\xi}, t)$.

Dynamic obstacles, however, change their position at every time step t and therefore, we define the obstacle positions as x^t_o, y^t_o and their bounds as

$x_{o,lb}^t, x_{o,lb}^t$. We get the obstacle positions from the real-world scenario by identifying the direction and velocity of each obstacle. From that, we extract the positions and bounds at each time step, assuming that the obstacle continues to move in the same direction. Our approach does not drastically affect the above-mentioned limitation because our total number of time-steps in one optimization cycle is small. We can expand the predicate φ_{obs_o} as

$$\varphi_{obs_o} = \varphi_{obs_o}^{t=1} \wedge \cdots \wedge \varphi_{obs_o}^{t=T} \tag{7}$$

with

$$\varphi_{obs_o}^t = (x_{o,lb}^t < x_o^t < x_{o,ub}^t) \wedge (y_{o,lb}^t < y_o^t < y_{o,ub}^t). \tag{8}$$

The computation of the robustness degree $\rho(\varphi_{obs}, \boldsymbol{\xi}, t)$ remains the same because we can directly use Eq. 3 due to the $\wedge$ operators between each predicate $\varphi_{obs_o}^t$. The only difference is that the inner predicates defined in Eq. 8 change at each time step t.

Similarly, we can define the STL specification for the road rules. The road rules can be of various kinds, for example, we can define the rule not to cross into the opposite lane by simply setting the opposite lane as a static obstacle. Some complex properties such as staying behind a traffic light until it is green can be formulated using the until operator as

$$\varphi_{safe} = \varphi_{avoid} \mathbf{U}_{[t_1, t_2]} \varphi_{stay}, \tag{9}$$

where the definition of φ_{avoid} is similar to the constraint for static obstacles, so that the region at the cross roads is avoided. t_1, t_2 define the time during which the traffic light stays red and φ_{stay} defines the event that the traffic light turns green.

4 Experiments

We utilize the *IR-SIM* simulation environment [15] to define two real-time automated valet parking scenarios. In these scenarios, the vehicle must plan a trajectory to reach a goal state which is a pre-defined parking place. We depict the two scenarios in Fig. 3 which consist of static and dynamic obstacles, some safety restrictions and a traffic light at the junction. For each scenario, we record 4 trajectories $\boldsymbol{\xi}_{i=1}^{N=4}$ with each $\boldsymbol{\xi}$ lasting for $T = 20$ s. The value of ν is set to 5.0 for optimal results based on multiple experimental evaluations. We use these scenarios to evaluate our single-cycle path planning and continuous multi-cycle path planning algorithms. The evaluation is based on the ability to address all the set constraints, and based on the time taken to obtain optimal trajectories.

The goal of Scenario (a) is to avoid the obstacles and to maintain a minimum safety distance to the vehicles adjacent to the parking place. We define the STL specification for the first scenario as

$$\varphi_1 = \mathbf{G}_{[0,20]} \neg \varphi_{obs_O} \wedge \mathbf{G}_{[0,20]} \varphi_{rules} \wedge \mathbf{F}_{[16,20]} \varphi_{safe}, \tag{10}$$

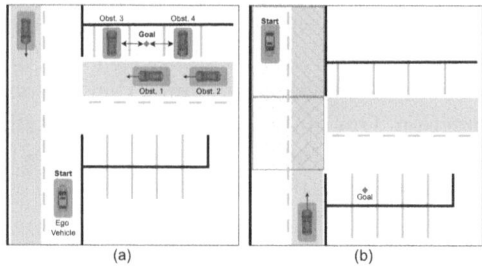

Fig. 3. Valet parking scenarios. The ego vehicle (in blue) must move from start to goal (depicted as diamond) while avoiding static (in red) and dynamic (in red with an arrow) obstacles. In (a), we depict the safety distance between the adjacent vehicles and the goal state. In (b), we depict the region to avoid (red cross-hatched) and region to stay (green hatched) when traffic light is red (Color figure online).

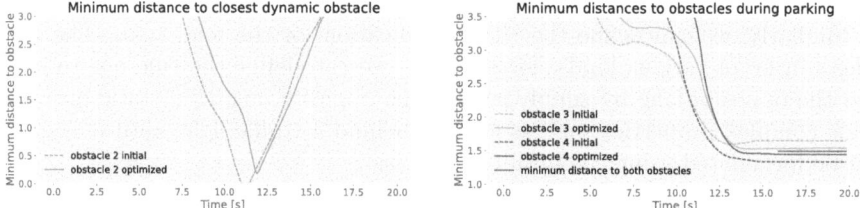

Fig. 4. We depict the distance to the obstacles over time before optimization (in dotted lines) and after optimization (in solid lines). A collision occurs when the distance is 0.0. The minimum distance constraint (on the left) during time 16 to 20 s is depicted as green line (Color figure online).

where φ_{obs_O} are the 5 obstacles as depicted in Fig. 3(a). The road rule to not cross to the opposite lane is defined as a region φ_{rules}. We define the safety distance between parked vehicles and ego vehicle as $\varphi_{safe} = x_o^t - x_{ego}^t < 1.5$, where x_{ego}^t is the position of the ego vehicle at time t in $x - axis$. Note that the time frame 16 to 20 s is identified from the simulation. In a continuous planner, we obtain the correct time intervals for the logic in real-time when the ego vehicle is close to the two vehicles and accordingly the trajectory in the next cycle is optimized. We can also relax the time interval restriction for φ_{rules} to a specific time if the car has to use other lanes, for instance when it has to cross the opposite lane for parking.

Figure 4 depicts the results of Scenario (a). As we can see, the collision into the dynamic obstacle φ_{obs_2} is avoided after the optimization. Also, the figure on the right shows that the minimum distance to the parked vehicles is also achieved as the distance to both obstacles coincides at 1.5 m. Overall, we achieved a positive reward, which means that the optimized trajectory addresses all the constraints set in φ_1.

Similarly, the goal of Scenario (b) is to avoid the obstacles and stay behind the junction in the first 4 s, when the traffic light is red. The STL specification for this scenario is

$$\varphi_2 = \mathbf{G}_{[0,20]} \neg \varphi_{obs_O} \wedge \mathbf{G}_{[0,20]} \varphi_{rules} \wedge \varphi_{avoid} \mathbf{U}_{[0,4]} \varphi_{stay}, \qquad (11)$$

where, as depicted in Fig. 3(b), φ_{avoid} is the red cross-hatched region and φ_{stay} is the green hatched region. Before optimization, Fig. 5 depicts the ego vehicle moving into the junction when the traffic light is red. This is avoided in the optimized trajectory because the ego vehicle waits behind the junction until the traffic light is green.

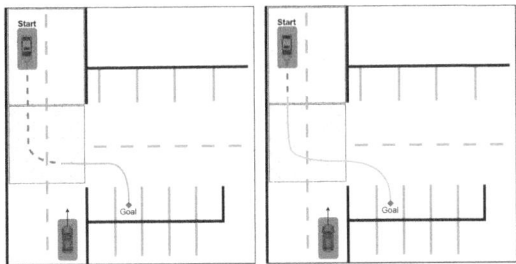

Fig. 5. We depict the ego vehicle trajectory when traffic light is red (as dotted red line) and when it is green (as solid green line) for both before optimization (left) and after optimization (right) (Color figure online).

Table 1. Runtime measurements for continuous multi-cycle path planning

Cycle	Initial robustness	Optimized robustness	Optimization time [s]	Simulation time [s]
1	–	–	6.73	–
2	1.432	1.619	7.118	7.65
3	1.199	1.278	6.636	8.172
4	−0.045	0.091	5.887	9.412
5	0.016	0.035	–	12.118

Table 1 depicts the optimization results of Scenario (a) for the continuous planner with minimal observation divided into 4 cycles. We partition the whole task into $M = 4$ cycles and at each cycle, we have the observation of obstacles in the next cycle. As we can see in Table 1, we obtain positive rewards in every cycle, which means all the constraints were satisfied. Additionally, as mentioned in Sect. 3, the time taken for optimization must be less than the total time of that cycle. We also achieved this, as depicted in the last two columns of the table. Therefore, we can say that our algorithm also works for continuous local planning when the observation is minimal.

The results above show that our method is powerful to incorporate various types of constraints and to address all of them at once to achieve safe trajectories. Using our reward function, we can verify that the generated trajectories are safe during the runtime. Our optimization algorithm can work for both minimal and full observation.

5 Conclusion

In this paper, we addressed the verification and optimization of path planning trajectories during runtime with both minimal and full observations. We defined static and dynamic obstacles, along with constraints from safety standards in the form of STL specifications, and used it to obtain optimal trajectories. Future work would include testing the approach on critical real-world scenarios and incorporating complex constraints using STL.

References

1. Barbosa, F.S., Karlsson, J., Tajvar, P., Tumova, J.: Formal methods for robot motion planning with time and space constraints. In: Formal Modeling and Analysis of Timed Systems: 19th International Conference, FORMATS 2021, Paris, France, August 24–26, 2021, Proceedings 19, vol. 12860, pp. 1–14. Springer (2021)
2. Calinon, S.: Stochastic learning and control in multiple coordinate systems. In: International Workshop on Human-Friendly Robotics, Italy, pp. 1–5 (2016)
3. Dhonthi, A., Schillinger, P., Rozo, L., Nardi, D.: Study of Signal Temporal Logic Robustness Metrics for Robotic Tasks Optimization. arXiv preprint arXiv:2110.00339 (2021)
4. Dhonthi, A., Schillinger, P., Rozo, L., Nardi, D.: Optimizing demonstrated robot manipulation skills for temporal logic constraints. In: 2022 IEEE/RSJ International Conference on Intelligent Robots and Systems (IROS), pp. 1255–1262. IEEE (2022)
5. Fainekos, G.E., Kress-Gazit, H., Pappas, G.J.: Temporal logic motion planning for mobile robots. In: Proceedings of the 2005 IEEE International Conference on Robotics and Automation, pp. 2020–2025. IEEE (2005)
6. Karaman, S., Frazzoli, E.: Sampling-based algorithms for optimal motion planning. Int. J. Robot. Res. **30**(7), 846–894 (2011)
7. Klancar, G., Zdesar, A., Blazic, S., Skrjanc, I.: Wheeled Mobile Robotics: from Fundamentals Towards Autonomous Systems. Butterworth-Heinemann (2017)
8. Lacerda, B., Faruq, F., Parker, D., Hawes, N.: Probabilistic planning with formal performance guarantees for mobile service robots. Int. J. Robot. Res. **38**(9), 1098–1123 (2019)
9. Mehdipour, N., Vasile, C.I., Belta, C.: Arithmetic-geometric mean robustness for control from signal temporal logic specifications. In: 2019 American Control Conference (ACC), pp. 1690–1695. IEEE (2019)
10. Murphy, K.P.: Hidden Semi-Markov Models (HSMMs) (2002)
11. Palin, R., Ward, D., Habli, I., Rivett, R.: ISO 26262 safety Cases: Compliance and Assurance (2011)
12. Pignat, E., Calinon, S.: Learning adaptive dressing assistance from human demonstration. Robot. Auton. Syst. **93**, 61–75 (2017)

13. Pimentel, J.: Safety of the Intended Functionality, vol. 3. SAE International (2019)
14. Rizaldi, A., Immler, F., Schürmann, B., Althoff, M.: A formally verified motion planner for autonomous vehicles. In: International Symposium on Automated Technology for Verification and Analysis, vol. 11138, pp. 75–90. Springer (2018)
15. Ruihua, H.: Intelligent Robot Simulator (IR-SIM) (2024). https://github.com/hanruihua/ir_sim/releases/tag/v2.1.0
16. Tanwani, A.K., et al.: Generalizing robot imitation learning with invariant hidden semi-Markov models. In: Algorithmic Foundations of Robotics XIII: Proceedings of the 13th Workshop on the Algorithmic Foundations of Robotics 13, pp. 196–211. Springer (2020)
17. Tassa, Y., Erez, T., Todorov, E.: Synthesis and stabilization of complex behaviors through online trajectory optimization. In: 2012 IEEE/RSJ International Conference on Intelligent Robots and Systems, pp. 4906–4913. IEEE (2012)
18. Varnai, P., Dimarogonas, D.V.: On robustness metrics for learning STL tasks. In: 2020 American Control Conference (ACC), pp. 5394–5399. IEEE (2020)
19. Wang, J., Li, T., Li, B., Meng, M.Q.H.: GMR-RRT*: sampling-based path planning using gaussian mixture regression. IEEE Trans. Intell. Veh. **7**(3), 690–700 (2022)

Formal Semantics and Verification of UML Models

A CSP Semantics for UML State Machines Aiming at Hidden Formal Methods Verification

Diego Ferreira[✉] and Lucas Lima

Departamento de Computação, Universidade Federal Rural de Pernambuco,
Recife-PE, Brazil
{diego.pires,lucas.albertins}@ufrpe.br

Abstract. The increasing complexity of software systems, especially in safety-critical domains, requires rigorous verification methodologies to ensure reliability and correctness. This paper presents a semantics for UML state machines using the formal language CSP to support automatic property verification. Our approach integrates the intuitive modeling capabilities of UML with the precise verification tooling available for CSP, thus facilitating the detection and correction of design errors at the early stages of system development. We implemented a framework as a plugin for the Astah modeling tool, which translates UML diagrams into CSP specifications and utilizes the FDR model checker for verification. The results are traced back to the diagram level, thus hiding the complexity of formal notations and tools. A case study of a flashlight system demonstrates the practical applicability and benefits of our approach, highlighting its ability to identify and solve design issues early in the development process.

Keywords: state machine · semantic · deadlock · nondeterminism · CSP

1 Introduction

We have recently noticed a paradigm shift from traditional system engineering towards a model-based approach, known as Model-based system engineering (MBSE). Some of the reasons for this include better support for digitalization processes and tackling the growing complexity of systems. In this context, the Unified Modeling Language (UML) [15] is widely adopted for its intuitive modeling capabilities for system and software projects. Within UML, state machines are frequently used to describe system behavior [16]. As systems become more complex, there is a growing need for robust and secure methods to represent and analyze behaviors, emphasizing the importance of verification during the modeling phase to avoid costly and time-consuming rework due to unnoticed defects [7].

In industry, project development typically moves from abstract to concrete models, where the choice between formal and informal semantics greatly affects project quality. Informal models are user-friendly but susceptible to subjective interpretation errors [10], while formal models provide exact semantics and tool support, improving reliability but needing mathematical handling. UML, widely recognized for software and system modeling, includes structural and behavioral aspects, with state machine diagrams commonly used for event-oriented objects in reactive systems [16]. In particular, the verification of these models is crucial in safety-critical industries, such as automotive, aerospace, and healthcare, where errors in system behavior can lead to catastrophic failures or significant financial loss.

This paper bridges the gap between these paradigms by presenting a framework for the automated verification of UML state machine diagrams using CSP (Communicating Sequential Processes) [8] as the underlying semantic domain. Our approach combines UML's intuitive modeling capabilities with CSP's precise verification tools, enabling early detection and correction of design errors. By translating UML state machine diagrams into CSP specifications, our solution leverages model-checking tools like FDR [5] to verify properties such as deadlock freedom and determinism. This approach ensures that critical system behaviors are rigorously validated before implementation, reducing the risk of costly post-deployment fixes. Our framework improves traceability by generating diagrammatic counterexamples when verification fails. This allows designers to trace errors back to specific UML model elements without requiring knowledge of the underlying formalism, streamlining debugging, and correction. This approach of hiding from the user the complexity of formal notations and formal tools is commonly known as hidden formal methods [9,11,20].

The structure of this paper is as follows: Sect. 2 discusses the fundamental concepts of our research, including UML state machines and the formal language CSP. In Sect. 3, we describe our semantics for UML state machines using CSP. Section 4 provides an overview of the tool support developed for verification. Section 5 situates our contributions within the broader context of existing research. Finally, Sect. 6 presents the conclusion and outlines directions for future work.

2 Background

In this section, we present UML and state machine diagrams, and we describe CSP, which is used as the semantic domain for our UML state machine semantics.

2.1 Unified Modeling Language (UML)

Unified Modeling Language (UML) [15] is a standardized modeling language used to specify, visualize, construct, and document the artifacts of software systems. UML provides a variety of diagrams to represent different aspects of a system, including structural diagrams (such as class diagrams and object diagrams) and behavioral diagrams (such as use case diagrams and state machine diagrams). Among these, state machine diagrams are one of the most used to model the event-driven behavior of reactive systems [16]. They capture the states of an object and the transitions triggered by events, thus describing how the system reacts to internal and external stimuli.

2.2 State Machine Diagrams

A state machine diagram is a powerful modeling tool used to represent the dynamic behavior of a system by depicting its states and the transitions between those states triggered by events. These diagrams are essential for modeling event-driven systems, where the behavior of the system depends on both internal and external stimuli. A state machine diagram consists of states, pseudostates, transitions, events, and actions.

States represent the various conditions during the life of an object. Each state can be a simple state or a composite state. Simple states are indivisible, representing a single condition or activity. For example, in the Flashlight state machine diagram (Fig. 1), the Off state is a simple state. Composite states, on the other hand, can contain nested states, providing a hierarchical structure. In the same diagram, the state On includes substates NormalMode and SOSMode, making it a composite state. Transitions connect states and are triggered by events. A transition typically includes a trigger (the event that causes the transition), a guard (a condition that must be true for the transition to occur), and an action (an operation executed during the transition). For instance, in the Flashlight state machine diagram (Fig. 1), the transition from Recharging to On is triggered by the event turnOn, a guard [battery > 0] and action battery = max(0, battery - 1).

Events are occurrences that can trigger transitions. These events can be generated by user interactions, system signals, or other sources. For example, in the Flashlight state machine diagram, the event batteryDepleted might trigger a transition from the On state to the Off state. Actions are activities that are executed in response to a transition or while in a state. Actions include entry actions (executed upon entering a state), do actions (performed while in the state), and exit actions (executed upon exiting a state). In the Flashlight diagram, the Recharging state has the entry, do, and exit actions, indicating activities to be performed upon entering, while in, and upon exiting the state.

Pseudostates are special states used to control the flow within the state machine. Common pseudostates include initial, final, junctions, and choices. Junctions are used to merge or split transitions, while choices allow branching based on conditions. In the Flashlight diagram, a choice pseudostate might decide between transitioning to On or Recharging, based on the battery level. We give more details about the meaning of each element within state machine diagrams in Sect. 3.2 using the Flashlight model in Fig. 1 as our running example.

2.3 CSP

The CSP language (Communicating Sequential Processes) [8], proposed by Hoare in 1985, provides a formal approach for specifying concurrent systems with formally unambiguous semantics and automated refinement calculation mechanisms, such as those offered by the FDR tool (Failures-Divergences Refinement) [5]. FDR allows checking the absence of deadlocks, livelocks, and nondeterminism of CSP specifications.

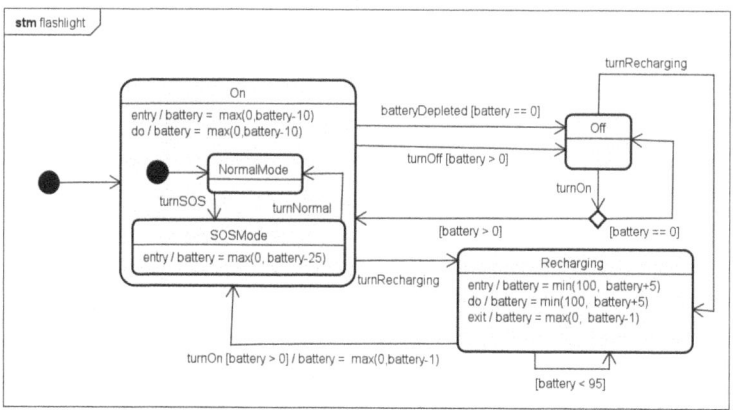

Fig. 1. Flashlight State Machine Diagram.

The behavior model in CSP is described through processes, the fundamental units of description. These processes, defined in terms of events or other processes, can be composed in parallel in a synchronized or interleaved manner, providing flexibility in modeling concurrent behaviors. The function $\alpha(P)$ represents the set of events that a process P can communicate. The basic process, $SKIP$, represents successful termination. A process of the form $a \to P$ presents the event a to the environment and then behaves as the process P. CSP channels are used to abstract sets of events that share a common prefix. The syntax $c?x$ denotes a channel c receiving a value x, where x is a value of a type that also types channel c. The value for x is determined by the environment. The syntax $c.e$ ($c!e$) represents an expression e communicated through channel c.

Sequential composition in CSP notation, denoted by $P1 ; P2$, works in a way that when $P1$ is completed, control is then passed on to $P2$. Although CSP lacks a specific operator for recursion, a process name can be used within its definition. For instance, if we define the process P as $a \to P$, it will first communicate the event a and then behave as P. In parallel composition, the operator $P1 \underset{cs}{\parallel} P2$ synchronizes the events between $P1$ and $P2$ based on the set of events cs, while any events not present in cs occur independently. Additionally, the external choice operator $\Box$ in CSP represents a decision point where a process can choose between multiple possible events, with the environment determining which event occurs. This allows for modeling nondeterministic behavior, where the exact sequence of events is not predetermined, adding another layer of flexibility in describing concurrent systems. The interruption operator ($\triangle$) allows a process to be interrupted by another. The process $P \triangle Q$ behaves as P until Q communicates an event. When this happens, we say that P has been interrupted by Q. The renaming operator $P[\![R]\!]$ takes a process P and a renaming relation R that contains a list of pairs $a \leftarrow b$. The process $P[\![a \leftarrow b]\!]$ behaves like the process P, but occurrences of the event a are replaced by occurrences of the event b.

The CSP process algebra is a very versatile way to specify systems that consist of interactive components. Each component functions independently and has its interface designed for interaction with the environment. This formalism provides us with tools to define and analyze the interactions among the different components. In our case, these components are the nodes of the diagrams.

3 A Formal Semantics for State Machines in CSP

This section presents an overview of the CSP semantics for state machines and demonstrates the application of translation rules that result in the CSP specifications corresponding to the elements of UML state machines.

3.1 Overview

The formal semantics for state machine diagrams consider various elements present in the diagrams, such as states, transitions, pseudostates, and events. The formalization of these elements in terms of the CSP language aims to unambiguously represent the dynamic behavior of the system.

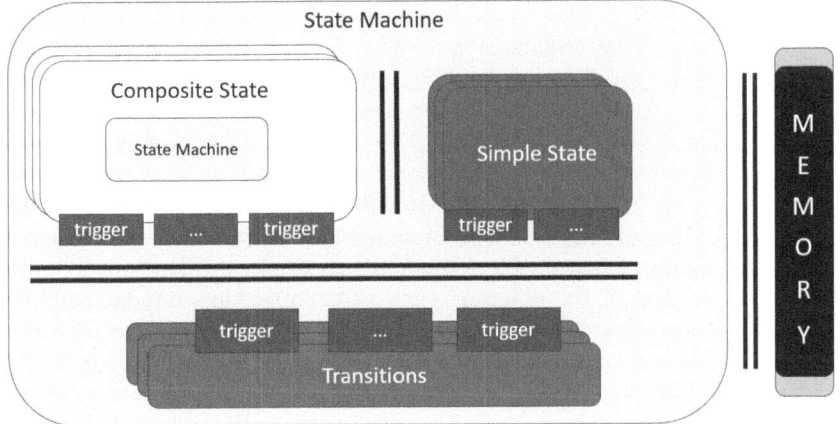

Fig. 2. State machine diagram semantics in CSP.

Figure 2 illustrates our CSP semantics for state machines using roundtangles to represent CSP processes and parallel bars to indicate synchronization between them. This semantics considers the reactive and event-driven nature of the model. Events trigger state transitions, with each state linked to specific actions. Although inspired by RoboChart's semantics [12,13], which is a framework for modeling and verifying robotic controllers using state machines using an underlying formal semantics based on CSP, our implementation is independent with unique design choices. Simple states form the foundation of this diagram type, residing within the state machine or nested in composite states. These simple states, composite states, transitions, and memory are each modeled as separate CSP processes operating concurrently.

Moreover, states or pseudostates within a state machine are linked to transition processes. These transitions are activated by trigger events, specified as CSP channels, forming a crucial synchronization mechanism. This concurrency allows parallel state flows, enabling system progression. Synchronization via key events in CSP channels ensures coherence in state transitions. The entire state machine is also placed in parallel composition with the Memory, which controls the access to the variables used inside the state machine. In essence, the generated semantics use CSP processes composed in parallel. The synchronization of key events accurately emulates the modeled behavior of a state machine, ensuring that interactions and state transitions reflect the intended design.

3.2 Semantics

This subsection delves into the formalization of UML state machine elements into CSP specifications. We cover the semantics of events (triggers), memory, transitions, internal actions, states, pseudostates (choice), composite states, and the controller. Due to size restrictions, instead of showing the translation rules, we illustrate their application to our flashlight running example.

Starting with events, in UML state machines, they represent specific occurrences that can trigger transitions between states. These events can originate from user interactions, system signals, or other sources within the system. In the context of CSP, these triggers are modeled as channels that enable the communication and synchronization between concurrent processes. Each event in the UML model corresponds to a distinct channel in CSP.

In Fig. 3, the `datatype STATES_ID_Flashlight` defines unique IDs for all states and pseudostates in the diagram, each identified by its own name, such as `SOSMode`. Channels for triggers, like `internal` and `turnOn`, are also defined. The `internal` channel triggers transitions without a specific event trigger, for example, using only a guard. The remaining channels are determined by the names of the triggers in the diagram, such as `turnOn`, `turnOff`, `turnSOS`, etc. These channels are critical in CSP for modeling the system, as they are used to synchronize the states and transitions.

Memory in UML state machines is crucial for maintaining the state information and variables across transitions. This allows the state machine to remember past interactions and make decisions based on this history. In CSP, memory is

```
datatype STATES_ID_Flashlight = Off | On | Recharging | SOSMode |
  NormalMode | Choice
channel internal, turnOn, turnOff, turnRecharging, batteryDepleted,
  turnSOS, turnNormal
```

Fig. 3. Triggers and datatypes.

```
MEMORY(battery) = (end → SKIP) □ get_battery!battery → MEMORY(battery)
 □ set_battery?y → MEMORY(y)
 □ (battery>0) & turnOff → MEMORY(battery)
 □ (battery==0) & batteryDepleted → MEMORY(battery)
 ...
 □ (battery>0) & turnOn → MEMORY(battery)
```

Fig. 4. Memory process.

handled by maintaining state variables within processes. These variables can influence transitions and actions, ensuring the correct context and behavior of the state machine are preserved and updated as transitions occur.

The semantics of the memory process is illustrated in Fig. 4. It is composed of an external choice between terminating the process, accessing the value of the variable (get_battery channel), setting the value of the variable(set_battery channel), or verifying if the variable's value satisfies a guard condition. These guards are associated with transitions that use the variable for validation, and if the guard condition is true, the trigger can be executed. This mechanism is inspired by RoboChart [12]. For example, the state On has two transitions to Off, triggered by turnOff and batteryDepleted, each with a different guard. For this transition to be active, the guard in memory must be true. This synchronization ensures that memory is consistent with both states and transitions. When the state machine process terminates, we also need to terminate its inner processes. This is performed by synchronizing them on the end event. This applies not only to the memory process in Fig. 4 but also to other processes that are described further.

Transitions in UML state machines represent movements between states triggered by events. They may include guards (conditions that must be met for the transition) and actions (activities performed during the transition). In CSP, a transition is modeled as a process that changes from an outgoing state to an incoming state when a triggering event occurs. The triggering event acts as the first event of the process. Through parallelism between states and transitions, the transition process waits for the triggering event before it begins. Guard conditions are handled in the memory process. Actions associated with transitions are converted into CSP events, which are executed during the transition process after performing the exited event of the outgoing state and before executing the enter event of the incoming state. The transition process synchronizes with the memory process to store any variable updates.

In Fig. 5, the transition from the Recharging state to the On state starts with a turnOn trigger, synchronizing with the state through parallel composition. Although we omit here due to simplification, the unique IDs of the transitions are defined by the UML model, which generates unique identifiers for each transition. Once triggered, the transition activates. The source state performs its exit actions (exit and exited events), followed by the enter event in the target state. If there is an action, it occurs between the exited and enter events. In this case, the action reduces the battery value: max(0, battery - 1).

```
Tr_id_3 = ((turnOn → exit.Recharging → exited.Recharging →
    get_battery_flashlight?battery →
    set_battery_flashlight!(max(0,battery-1)) → enter.On → SKIP))
```

Fig. 5. Transition semantic—CSP Semantics

In UML state machines, the entry action happens when the state is entered, enabling initialization or setup. The do action occurs while the state is active, representing ongoing or periodic behaviors. The exit action occurs when the state is exited, allowing for cleanup or finalization before transitioning to another state. In CSP, these actions are modeled as sequential processes within the state process, representing entry, do, and exit actions.

```
EntryProc(Recharging) = entry.Recharging → ActionBehaviourEntry;
    State_Recharging_Do
DoProc(Recharging) = do.Recharging → ActionBehaviourDo △
    interrupt.Recharging → SKIP
ExitProc(Recharging) = exit.Recharging → ActionBehaviourExit;
    exited.Recharging → State_Recharging
```

Fig. 6. Internal Actions Process — CSP Semantics

In Fig. 6, the internal actions are for the Recharging state. The EntryProc process corresponds to the entry action for the state Recharging. It performs the entry event, followed by an action process, which in this case involves memory operations (we omit the action processes for simplification). Upon completion, it transitions to State_Recharging_Do to continue with the state's process. The DoProc(Recharging) process handles the do action, which involves ongoing activities while the state is active. This process might be interrupted by an interrupt.Recharging event. The interrupt serves to halt the ongoing action if a transition leaving the state is triggered. This synchronization is achieved by renaming all transition trigger events to the corresponding interrupt events in CSP, as will be detailed later in this section. Finally, the ExitProc(Recharging) process handles the exit action occurring between the exit and exited events. It performs a specified action and then returns to the initial state process State_Recharging, waiting for the next activation by a transition.

In UML, states define specific conditions or situations in an object's lifecycle where it performs activities or waits for events. States can be simple or composite. Simple states are atomic and indivisible, while composite states can include nested state machines. In CSP, simple states are modeled as individual processes waiting for events to trigger transitions, incorporating entry, do, and exit actions. Composite states, on the other hand, are modeled as CSP processes that encompass the behavior of their nested states. This encapsulation allows the nested state machine to operate independently while still being part of the larger state machine structure.

```
State_Recharging = ((enter.Recharging
  → State_Recharging_Entry) □ (end → SKIP)
State_Recharging_Entry = EntryProc(Recharging)
State_Recharging_Do = (DoProc(Recharging)); ExitProc(Recharging)
```

Fig. 7. Simple State with internal actions — CSP Semantics

For a simple state as in Fig. 7, like Recharging, the semantics is composed of three sequential processes: State_Recharging, State_Recharging_Entry, and State_Recharging_Do. The first process, State_Recharging, represents entering a state through the enter event, synchronizing with a transition process, meaning that a state is being entered. After this, State_Recharging_Entry is invoked, executing the previously explained EntryProc(Recharging) process. Upon completion, the State_Recharging_Do process sequentially executes the processes for the do and exit actions, also previously explained in Fig. 6.

In Fig. 7, the state has internal actions. However, if a state does not have a particular internal action, it is not necessary to include its corresponding process. Only the synchronization events are required. For instance, if the Recharging state does not have internal actions, the State_Recharging_Entry and State_Recharging_Do process can be omitted, and State_Recharging will be responsible for all events. Only the enter, interrupt, exit, and exited events are needed. The same logic holds for pseudostates, as they do not have internal actions, as illustrated in Fig. 8.

Pseudostates, such as choices and joins, play a crucial role in state machine diagrams by facilitating complex state transitions and control flows. Choice pseudostates, for instance, allow for branching based on guard conditions, enabling the state machine to select different transition paths depending on the evaluation of these guards. In CSP, pseudostates are modeled as simple state processes without internal actions that implement these decision points using conditional expressions in the memory process synchronizing on their corresponding events.

```
State_Choice = (enter.Choice → interrupt.Choice →   SKIP; exit.Choice
  → exited.Choice → State_Choice)
  ☐ (end → SKIP)
```

Fig. 8. Choice process—CSP Semantics

This can be exemplified by the pseudostate choice, which occurs after the transition from the state Off and is represented by a diamond shape, in the Flashlight example from Fig. 1. In Fig. 8, first, the enter event occurs, followed immediately by the interrupt event, and finally, the exit and exited events. The interrupt event is renamed in the States_id process (shown in Fig. 9) to two internal events related to the outgoing transitions without triggers that synchronize with the memory process. Hence, this pseudostate can lead to any of these two transitions when their guards are true.

```
States_id = On   ‖   Off   ‖   Recharging   ‖   Choice
                 end      end             end
Transitions_id = Tr_id_1;Transitions_id ☐ ... ☐ Tr_id_n;Transitions_id
  ☐ end → SKIP
StartSync_id = States_id [[interrupt.On <- batteryDepleted,
  interrupt.On <- turnOff, ..., interrupt.Off <- turnRecharging]]
        ‖              Transitions_id        ‖           MEMORY(30)
  triggers,events,end           triggers,actions,end
```

Fig. 9. Sync Controller — CSP Semantics

In this framework, the synchronization controller orchestrates the coordination of processes within the state machine translation to CSP. The StartSync process serves as the central component, responsible for managing the overall behavior of the state machine, ensuring that all parallel regions and initial states are properly coordinated, and setting up the initial context for execution. The States_id process uses renaming to handle interrupts. This means it renames all interrupts associated with states to the corresponding trigger events that could cause those interrupts, that is, transition triggers outgoing states. This renaming ensures that interrupts are correctly synchronized with their triggering events, allowing the state machine to respond appropriately to state changes. The States_id and Transitions_id processes only contain information relevant to their respective layers. For example, in Fig. 9, States_id only includes information about On, Off, Recharging, and Choice. This happens because composite states have their own StartSync synchronization processes with states and transitions that occur within them. However, the MEMORY process is composed in parallel only with the top-level StartSync process (related to the state machine), but as the other composite processes are part of the top-level StartSync process, they can also synchronize with the MEMORY process.

StartSync itself operates through parallel composition, combining processes encompassing States_id (all states in a parallel composition, synchronizing on the end event), Transitions_id (all transitions in external choice), and the MEMORY process with the initial value for the battery variable (30 in this case). This orchestration synchronizes trigger events and standard events. Standard events are those typically used within state machines to manage the lifecycle of a state, ensuring that transitions between states occur in a well-defined and coordinated manner, such as enter, do, exit, end, and interrupt. The synchronization controller depicted in Fig. 9 shows how the processes are composed to emulate the flow of execution, ensuring synchronized and coordinated state changes throughout the state machine model.

Finally, the composite states in UML provide a structured approach for modeling hierarchical state behaviors, allowing states to encapsulate nested state machines. This hierarchical modeling is essential for managing complex system behaviors through state decomposition. In CSP, composite states are translated by combining the behaviors of their substates using both parallel and sequential compositions. This ensures that the composite state accurately reflects its internal state transitions and concurrent activities.

Furthermore, in this semantic model, a composite state functions similarly to a standalone state machine. It operates within the context of its parent state, and when invoked, its State_st_id_Do process calls the composite state StartSync process. One notable distinction is that a composite state can be interrupted at any point by its parent state, allowing for dynamic control over its execution. This interruption capability facilitates flexible state management and supports responsive state transitions within the overall state machine structure. To handle

```
CtrlAux(s) = #s>0 & head(s) → CtrlAux(tail(s)) □ #s==0 & SKIP
Control_On_CompositeState(s) = #s==0 & enter.On →
   Control_On_CompositeState(<exit.On, exited.On>^s)
□ #s<n & enter?state:{NormalMode, SOSMode} →
   Control_On_CompositeState(<exit.state, exited.state>^s)
□ #s>0 & head(s) → Control_On_CompositeState(tail(s))
□ #s<n & interrupt.On → ControlAux(s);
   Control_On_CompositeState(<>)) □ (end → SKIP)
```

Fig. 10. Control Process for Composite States — CSP Semantics

the complexities of composite states, particularly the nested transitions, we have introduced two helper processes called Ctrl_On_CompositeState and CtrlAux, as presented in Fig. 10, related to the On composite state.

The Ctrl_On_CompositeState process, which handles the control flow within the On composite state, ensures the correct order of exiting actions by guaranteeing that most internal states are exited first. It keeps a list containing pairs of exit events, and it is composed in parallel with the Start_Sync composite state process synchronizing on their enter, exit, and exited events to ensure their correct order of execution. This process has five external choices. The first choice occurs when first entering the composite state and the list s is empty, allowing the process to perform enter.On to enter the composite state. The second choice allows entering a substate (?state is a set of possible substates, including nested ones, within the composite state). In both cases, the corresponding exit actions <exit.state, exited.state> are appended to the list s, preserving the trace of active states-those that have been entered but not yet exited. The n value in the condition #s<n corresponds to the maximum number of exit events that can be added to the list. This is related to the depth of composite states. For example, a composite state that has another composite state can have three active states, one in the first level (the root composite state), another in the second level, and the last in the innermost level. Then, the list s can have at most 6 exit events, and n would be 7 (assuming they do not have more than one region). In the Flashlight example, n has a value of 5 because it just has one sublevel (two events from the On state plus two from one of its substates). These conditions on the n value restrict how the sequence parameter (s) grows, which makes the analysis feasible, avoiding state space explosion.

The third external choice synchronizes the exiting of a substate, assuring their related events are removed from the list in the correct order. This ensures that the first state to enter is the first to exit. The fourth external choice represents exiting the composite state (interrupt.On) due to the triggering of one of its outgoing transitions. In this particular case, the most internal substates should be exited first. This is achieved by using the CtrlAux process, which sequentially clears the list by removing the exit events from the list in the correct order. This synchronous process ensures that active states perform their exit and exited actions in order, from the innermost to the outermost, maintaining the integrity of state transitions, especially when dealing with nested composite states. After CtrlAux completes, Ctrl_On_CompositeState(<>) is executed to ensure the list is empty and the process is ready to be executed again.

Finally, the fifth external choice is the end event, which, when triggered, terminates the Ctrl_On_CompositeState process, indicating the end of the state machine diagram. The detailed explanation of the Ctrl_On_CompositeState process and its external choices highlights the robustness of our approach to managing the complexities of composite states in UML state machines. This method ensures that transitions and actions are performed correctly and in the proper sequence, facilitating accurate modeling and verification of complex hierarchical behaviors in CSP. This approach supports the development of reliable and consistent systems by providing a robust framework for analyzing state transitions and interactions within composite states.

4 Tool Support

The proposed framework is implemented as a plugin for the Astah modeling tool [19], providing an integrated environment for modeling and verifying UML state machines. The plugin automates the translation of UML diagrams to CSP specifications and interfaces with the FDR model checker to perform verification.

Our framework has been implemented as a plug-in, BPV (Behaviour Property Verifier), for the Astah modeling environment[1]. This plug-in can verify state machine diagrams. Figure 11 illustrates how the plug-in and its dependencies are organized. Our framework is built upon the UML version of Astah, which allows the use of plug-ins to introduce new features and runs on the JVM (Java Virtual Machine). Thus, we used the Astah API to create a new plug-in and to programmatically read, verify, and analyze the state machine.

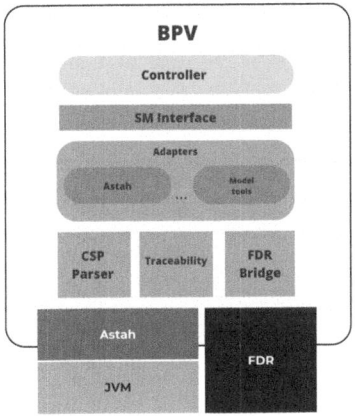

Fig. 11. Plug-in Architecture.

The developed plug-in is divided into five modules. The `Controller` module is responsible for managing, receiving, and returning information between our tool and the modeling environment. The `Adapters` module transforms the tool representation of these diagrams to our internal representation available in the `SM Interface`. The `CSP Parser` module is responsible for translating these representations to CSP_m according to the semantics in Sect. 3. The parser ensures that all necessary CSP constructs are correctly generated and that the resulting specification is both syntactically and semantically valid. The `FDR Bridge` module, in turn, is responsible for sending the information translated into CSP

[1] https://github.com/Open-MBEE/apv/tree/statemachine

to the FDR tool. This process occurs in the background, eliminating the need for the user to interact directly with CSP or FDR. Finally, the Traceability module is responsible for receiving a trace that identifies a CSP counterexample (if any) from the verified diagram and building a state machine counterexample that can be navigated to illustrate the sequence of events that led to the issue.

To illustrate its usage, we intentionally modified the Flashlight state machine diagram to introduce both a deadlock and nondeterminism within the state Choice in Fig. 12. To introduce a deadlock, the trigger and guard conditions for the transition from Off to Recharging were changed. The original guard [battery >= 0] was changed to [battery > 0]. This leads to a deadlock because the two transitions from the Choice state are now [battery > 0]. Consequently, when the battery level is 0, there is no valid transition out of the Choice state, causing the system to be deadlocked. We want to clarify that a deadlock happens in CSP when reaching a dead-end state in the specification. At the diagrammatic level, this can happen not only due to the lack of covered conditions, as in the shown example, but also due to the lack of communication between elements, isolated states, or other ill-designed models.

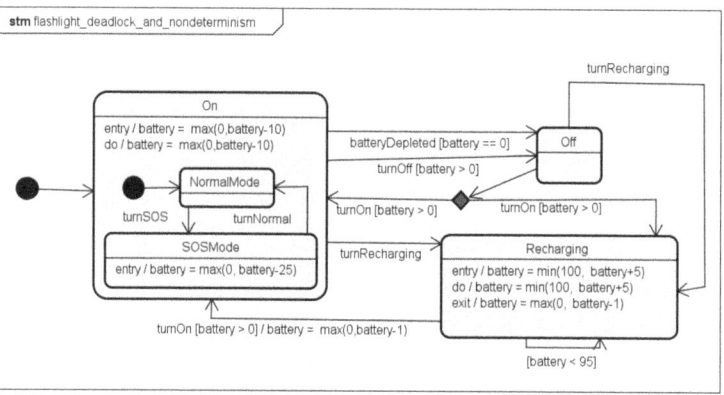

Fig. 12. Deadlock and nondeterminism on flashlight.

Additionally, nondeterminism was introduced by adding the trigger turnOn. Both transitions originating from the Choice state now share the same trigger, turnOn, and identical guards. This results in non-deterministic behavior because when the turnOn trigger is activated, the system has to make a non-deterministic choice between the two transitions, both of which are enabled simultaneously.

These modifications are depicted in Fig. 12. The Choice state, highlighted in purple, is where both the deadlock and nondeterminism occur. The tool effectively identifies and reports these issues, pinpointing the exact location of deadlock or nondeterminism within the state machine diagram. Also, the tool allows users to navigate through the counterexample trace using forward and backward buttons. As users step through the trace, the current state/transition is highlighted in red, providing a clear visual indication of the progression. When the final element causing the deadlock or nondeterminism is reached, it is marked in purple.

By detecting these issues and allowing interactive navigation through the counterexample trace, the tool aids designers in identifying potential problems early in the design phase, enabling corrections during the design phase. The ability to visualize counterexamples and highlight the exact state or transition causing the issue significantly enhances understanding of the root causes, thereby facilitating a more robust and accurate design process.

5 Related Work

The work by Miyazawa et al. [12,13] laid the foundation for formalizing UML state machine diagrams using CSP, demonstrating the feasibility and benefits of this approach. Their study focused on defining formal semantics for UML diagrams and verifying properties using CSP-based tools. The semantics provided by Miyazawa et al. provide support as the formal representation of the RoboChart language in CSP. It served as an inspiration and basis for our project. However, our approach includes modifications and additions to the original semantics, such as introducing the `ControlAux` process to manage composite states effectively. Our tool extends RoboChart's capabilities by integrating with the Astah modeling tool and the FDR model checker, offering a user-friendly environment for designers. It also enhances the understanding of counterexamples by providing detailed navigation through the trace, highlighting states and transitions. This interactive navigation aids designers in comprehending the root causes of issues, thus facilitating a more robust and accurate design process. The user does not have direct access to the formal semantics or the current state of the memory. The user interface only provides access to the interactive counterexample, as described in Sect. 4, which is generated after a verification process.

Model checking of state machines is fully automated and supported in the Gamma Framework [6]. Traceability is provided through back annotations of the resulting trace in sequence diagrams, hiding the formal aspects from the users. While this work focuses on reachability properties, our work emphasizes verifying properties such as deadlock freedom and nondeterminism, crucial for ensuring the robustness and correctness of system designs.

Ng et al. [14] are among the first to propose a formalization of UML state diagrams using CSP. Their work tackled the lack of rigorous behavioral semantics for UML state machines, offering solutions for transitions and handling entry and exit actions, and do-activities. However, their approach was based on an older version of UML, meaning several newer constructs introduced in more recent UML versions were not available at the time. Despite the solid foundation they laid, their formalization does not address some of the complexities found in modern UML state machines, limiting its applicability to newer models. Additionally, they developed a prototype tool to translate UML state diagrams into

CSP specifications, which could then be verified using the FDR model checker. Our approach, while building on the same principle of translating UML diagrams into CSP for formal verification, extends the scope by supporting the latest UML constructs and integrating the verification process directly into the Astah modeling tool, offering a more comprehensive and user-friendly experience.

Zhang and Liu [21] propose an approach for translating UML state machines into CSP#, an extension of CSP, specifically designed for use with the PAT model checker [17]. Their method covers a broad subset of UML state machine features, including fork, join, history, and submachine states. However, despite its extensive feature support, there is uncertainty regarding the correct encoding of the run-to-completion step within their framework. Additionally, their approach lacks detailed traceability, which could make it difficult for users to pinpoint the source of errors in the original model. Our approach improves on this by ensuring better traceability through diagrammatic counterexamples and maintaining a clear focus on deadlock freedom and nondeterminism while fully integrating the formal verification process into the Astah modeling tool.

Djaaboub et al. [4] present an approach for translating UML state machines into flat state machines and subsequently into LOTOS (Language of Temporal Ordering Specification) [1]. Their method employs a graph grammar for the translation and leverages the AToM [18] meta-modeling tool to support the process. However, the approach addresses only the translation process. While this work offers a practical solution for transforming UML state machines into LOTOS, it requires knowledge of the LOTOS toolchain to perform property verification. Also, no form of traceability is discussed.

Börger et al. [2] pioneered the formalization of UML state machines using Abstract State Machines (ASMs) [3]. Their work addresses a wide range of features, including orthogonal composite states, event deferral, and run-to-completion, providing a structured framework for formalizing UML behavior. However, despite the clarity and flexibility of their approach, no automated

Table 1. Related work.

Work	Semantics			Automation			Formalism	Purpose
	IA	CS	MM	AT	HV	TC		
[2]	✓*	X	X	X	X	X	ASM	Semantic definition
[4]	✓*	✓	X	✓	X	X	LOTOS	Automated translation
[6]	X	✓	✓	✓	✓	✓	Gamma	Reachability properties
[12]	✓	✓	✓	✓	X	X	CSP	Classical and User-defined properties
[14]	✓	✓	X	✓	X	X	CSP	Classical and User-defined properties
[21]	✓	✓	X	✓	X	X	CSP#	Safety and liveness properties
Our Work	✓	✓	✓	✓	✓	✓	CSP	Deadlock and nondeterminism

translation tool based on this formalization was developed, limiting its practical applicability for automated verification. Our approach contrasts with theirs by focusing on automating the entire verification process, including translation, and providing traceability, with an emphasis on deadlock freedom and nondeterminism.

Table 1 provides a comparative overview of various works related to the formalization and verification of UML state machines. We use ✓, ✓*, and X to indicate coverage, partial coverage, and not covered, respectively. We split the comparison into two groups. The first group relates to the coverage of semantic concepts. The columns `IA`, `CS`, and `MM` refer to internal actions, composite states, and memory management, respectively. These elements are crucial for understanding the behavior and structure of state machines within the formal semantics. The second group focuses on automation, where `AT` indicates if the translation to the formal notation is automated, `HV` stands for hidden verification, i.e., the user does not need to manipulate formal methods tooling to perform analysis and traceability features, and `TC` details if there is a traceability mechanism to return results back to the user. These dimensions are essential for assessing the usability and effectiveness of the proposed methodologies in practical applications. Furthermore, we describe the formalism employed in each work, and the last column outlines the purpose of the respective approaches.

In contrast to previous works, our approach provides a more comprehensive integration of CSP-based formal verification with UML, focusing specifically on deadlock freedom and nondeterminism in state machine diagrams. Our modifications to the original RoboChart semantics, such as the `ControlAux` process, ensure better handling of composite states, which is an improvement not addressed by earlier approaches. Furthermore, the integration of FDR within the Astah modeling tool provides a more seamless and user-friendly environment compared to previous methods. These aspects distinguish our work from other existing formal verification frameworks and tools, making it uniquely suited for ensuring both accessibility and rigor in system verification.

6 Conclusion

This paper presented a framework for the automatic verification of UML state machine diagrams using CSP. By integrating UML's intuitive modeling capabilities with CSP's rigorous verification tools, our approach facilitates early detection and correction of design errors in software systems. The implementation as an Astah plugin demonstrates the practical applicability of our method, providing a seamless and user-friendly environment for formal verification.

The developed semantics, inspired by the RoboChart [12] framework, is tailored to suit our specific needs, including the introduction of the `CtrlAux` process to manage composite states effectively. This enhancement ensures accurate synchronization of state transitions, especially within nested composite states, thereby improving the robustness of the verification process. The case study of the `Flashlight` system illustrates the effectiveness of the framework, highlighting its ability to identify and resolve issues such as deadlock and nondeterminism in complex models. Additionally, the tool's interactive counterexample navigation aids users in understanding and addressing the root causes of these issues. The integration of formal methods into commonly used modeling tools not only bridges the gap between practical design and theoretical rigor, but also promotes broader adoption of formal verification techniques in industry.

Future work will focus on extending the framework to support additional UML diagram types and enhancing the scalability of the verification process. In particular, exploring verification across larger, more complex systems will be crucial to expanding the framework's applicability. This will further solidify the utility of our approach in various modeling and verification scenarios, contributing to the development of reliable and correct software systems.

References

1. Bolognesi, T., Brinksma, E.: Introduction to the ISO specification language LOTOS. Comput. Netw. ISDN Syst. **14**(1), 25–59 (1987)
2. Börger, E., Cavarra, A., Riccobene, E.: Modeling the meaning of transitions from and to concurrent states in uml state machines. In: Proceedings of the 2003 ACM Symposium on Applied Computing, pp. 1086–1091. SAC '03, Association for Computing Machinery, New York, NY, USA (2003). https://doi.org/10.1145/952532.952745
3. Börger, E., Stärk, R.F.: Abstract State Machines: A Method for High-level System Design and Analysis; with 19 Tables. Springer (2003)
4. Djaaboub, S., Kerkouche, E., Chaoui, A.: From UML statecharts to LOTOS expressions using graph transformation. In: Dregvaite, G., Damasevicius, R. (eds.) Information and Software Technologies, pp. 548–559. Springer International Publishing, Cham (2015)
5. Gibson-Robinson, T., Armstrong, P., Boulgakov, A., Roscoe, A.: Fdr3 -a modern refinement checker for csp. In: Àbrahàm, E., Havelund, K. (eds.) Tools and Algorithms for the Construction and Analysis of Systems. Lecture Notes in Computer Science, vol. 8413, pp. 187–201. Springer Berlin Heidelberg (2014). https://doi.org/10.1007/978-3-642-54862-8_13
6. Graics, B., Molnár, V., Vörös, A., Majzik, I., Varro, D.: Mixed-semantics composition of statecharts for the component-based design of reactive systems. Soft. Syst. Model. **19**, (2020). https://doi.org/10.1007/s10270-020-00806-5
7. Haskins, B., Stecklein, J., Dick, B., Moroney, G., Lovell, R., Dabney, J.: 8.4.2 error cost escalation through the project life cycle. INCOSE Int. Symp. **14**, 1723–1737 (2004). https://doi.org/10.1002/j.2334-5837.2004.tb00608.x
8. Hoare, C.A.R.: Communicating and Sequential Processes. Prentice Hall (1985)
9. Horváth, B., et al.: Model checking as a service: towards pragmatic hidden formal methods. In: Proceedings of the 23rd ACM/IEEE International Conference on Model Driven Engineering Languages and Systems: Companion Proceedings. MODELS '20, Association for Computing Machinery, New York, NY, USA (2020). https://doi.org/10.1145/3417990.3421407
10. Khendek, F., Bourduas, S., Vincent, D.: Stepwise design with message sequence charts. In: Kim, M., Chin, B., Kang, S., Lee, D. (eds.) Formal Techniques for Networked and Distributed Systems, pp. 19–34. Springer, Boston (2001)

11. Kiniry, J.R., Zimmerman, D.M.: Secret ninja formal methods. In: Cuéllar, J., Maibaum, T.S.E., Sere, K. (eds.) FM 2008: Formal Methods, 15th International Symposium on Formal Methods, Turku, Finland, May 26-30, 2008, Proceedings. Lecture Notes in Computer Science, vol. 5014, pp. 214–228. Springer (2008). https://doi.org/10.1007/978-3-540-68237-0_16
12. Miyazawa, A., Ribeiro, P., Li, W., Cavalcanti, A., Timmis, J., Woodcock, J.: Robochart: modelling and verification of the functional behaviour of robotic applications. Softw. Syst. Model. **18**(5), 3097–3149 (2019). https://doi.org/10.1007/s10270-018-00710-z
13. Miyazawa, A., Ribeiro, P., Ye, K., Cavalcanti, A., Li, W., Woodcock, J., Timmis, J.: Robochart reference manual. Tech. rep. University of York (2017). https://robostar.cs.york.ac.uk/publications/techreports/reports/robochart-reference.pdf
14. Ng, M.Y., Butler, M.: Towards formalizing UML state diagrams in CSP. In: First International Conference onSoftware Engineering and Formal Methods, 2003, Proceedings, pp. 138–147 (2003). https://doi.org/10.1109/SEFM.2003.1236215
15. Object Management Group: OMG Unified Modeling Language (OMG UML), version 2.5.1. Tech. rep. OMG (2017)
16. Reggio, G., Leotta, M., Ricca, F., Clerissi, D.: What are the used UML diagrams? A preliminary survey. In: EESSMOD@MoDELS, vol. 1078, pp. 3–12 (2013)
17. Sun, J., Liu, Y., Dong, J.S., Pang, J.: Pat: towards flexible verification under fairness. In: Bouajjani, A., Maler, O. (eds.) Computer Aided Verification, pp. 709–714. Springer Berlin Heidelberg, Berlin, Heidelberg (2009)
18. Syriani, E., Vangheluwe, H., Mannadiar, R., Hansen, C., Van Mierlo, S., Ergin, H.: Atompm: a web-based modeling environment. In: Joint proceedings of MODELS'13 Invited Talks, Demonstration Session, Poster Session, and ACM Student Research Competition co-located with the 16th International Conference on Model Driven Engineering Languages and Systems (MODELS 2013): September 29-October 4, 2013, Miami, USA, pp. 21–25 (2013)
19. Vision, C.: Astah (2019). http://astah.net/
20. Visser, W., Dwyer, M., Whalen, M.: The hidden models of model checking. Softw. Syst. Model. **11**(4), 541–555 (2012)
21. Zhang, S., Liu, Y.: An automatic approach to model checking UML state machines. In: IEEE International Conference on Secure Software Integration and Reliability Improvement Companion, pp. 1–6 (06 2010). https://doi.org/10.1109/SSIRI-C.2010.11

Verifying Integrated Designs of UML State Machines and Activities Using CSP

Diego Ferreira[✉] and Lucas Lima

Departamento de Computação, Universidade Federal Rural de Pernambuco, Recife-PE, Brazil
{diego.pires,lucas.albertins}@ufrpe.br

Abstract. This paper presents a framework for verifying deadlock and nondeterminism in UML state machines integrated with activities, addressing the critical need for automated checks in UML projects. The framework aims to support architects and system designers in modeling and verifying properties of state machine diagrams integrated with activity diagrams, emphasizing the absence of deadlock and nondeterminism, crucial aspects of critical systems. We implemented this tool as a plug-in for the Astah modeling environment, utilizing the Astah API to read the components used in state machine and activity diagrams. We consider the formal language CSP as the underlying semantic domain, and we verify the translated models using the FDR tool. In the case of an issue is found, an interactive counterexample is generated in the modeling platform, facilitating the identification of the reasons for the failure and to hide the complexity of the rigorous notation and manipulation of formal method tooling. The paper also discusses the developed semantics, a case study, and the functionalities of the framework. Additionally, it compares this work with related approaches and discusses its limitations and future directions.

Keywords: UML state machines · UML activities · deadlock · nondeterminism · CSP

1 Introduction

The increasing complexity of systems and software projects has prompted the intensive use of models for representing and refining ideas. In this context, the Unified Modeling Language (UML) [19] stands out as a widely adopted modeling language. Within the realm of UML, state machine and activity diagrams are frequently employed for describing system behavior [23].

As modern systems become increasingly complex, there is a growing demand for a more robust and secure approach to representing and analyzing system behaviors. Many studies emphasize the importance of conducting verifications to identify flaws during the system modeling phase, as unnoticed defects can lead to detrimental consequences for the project, such as high costs associated with bug correction and significant time loss due to necessary rework [8]. However, when using informal models, such as those expressed in UML, there is a significant risk of ambiguities in understanding the system's behavior, leading to imprecise decisions prone to errors due to subjective interpretation.

In industry, project development typically evolves from an abstract model to a concrete model. The choice between formal or informal semantics for these models can significantly impact project quality. Informal models are more accessible. Their interpretation is subjective and depends on the designer's experience, presenting significant risks [11]. On the other hand, formal models offer precise semantics and tool support to increase reliability, but understanding these models is more challenging due to the manipulation of mathematical concepts.

The UML language, recognized as an essential standard for software and system modeling, encompasses both structural and behavioral aspects. When considering behavioral diagrams, the state machine diagram stands out as a widely used notation in the industry to describe event-oriented objects in reactive systems [23]. This diagram, composed of vertices connected by transitions, is activated by events, outlining the possible state flows in a system. The visual representation of this model incorporates simple and composite states, pseudo-states, and various notations, enriching the understanding of the dynamic behavior of the system. The activity diagram, also part of UML, provides a comprehensive view of the system's dynamics, illustrating how different actions are interconnected and the possible complex flows of execution. Both diagrams play crucial roles in behavioral modeling, providing a holistic understanding of the system at different levels of abstraction.

It is essential to note that state machine and activity diagrams already have initiatives for hidden formal methods [10,16,17], which is a field that aims to support the usage of formal methods in the background avoiding end users to manipulate complex notations or formal methods tools [12,26]. Hidden verification involves checking an abstract model of the system through a semantic translation into a logical formula and tracing back the results to the user level. Subsequently, the formula is verified using formal methods. For example, [16] proposes a tool for the verification of an activity diagram by transforming it into a formal notation, performing the necessary checks, and returning a counterexample in the diagrammatic notation if needed. There are also works that perform a similar process using state machines instead [7,17]. However, it is quite common for system engineers to model system behavior using both state machines and activities. More precisely, state machines whose actions can invoke activities. As an example, we can observe these dynamics in the open SysML model of the Thirty-Meter Telescope [22], which has been developed in the context of the OpenMBEE community [21] as an industrial-scale application. This cohesion between the two diagrams offers a more complete and detailed view of the system, enabling the modeling of complex behaviors. However, there is still a lack of specific automated verification tools for these integrated diagrams.

Our work aims to fill this gap, contributing to the advancement of critical systems modeling and verification. We propose an innovative approach for the automatic verification of these diagrams, combining the advantages of UML modeling with the robustness provided by formal semantics, specifically using the CSP (Communicating Sequential Processes) process algebra [9]. It is noteworthy to mention that while our discussions primarily focus on UML, the techniques and methodologies introduced herein are equally applicable to the equivalent diagrams in SysML [25]. We concretize our approach as an implementation of a plug-in for the Astah modeling environment. We hope this tool will provide architects and system designers with an automated way to model and verify properties in state machines combined with activities.

The remainder of this paper is organized as follows. In Sect. 2, we present the fundamental concepts used in our work, encompassing UML concepts for state machines and activity diagrams and the formal language CSP. Section 3 introduces the semantics of activities and state machines in terms of CSP. Section 4 outlines the tooling support we provide to enable verification. Section 5 illustrates our approach using a case study. Section 6 discusses related works, placing our contributions within the context of existing research. The conclusion and discussion of initiatives for future work are presented in Sect. 7.

2 Background

In this section, we present the baseline concepts that are used in our approach. Section 2.1 details the behavioral elements of UML/SysML that we support, in this case, state machines and activities. Section 2.2 describes the semantic domain we use to represent the behavior semantics of state machines and activities, which is the process algebra CSP.

2.1 UML/SysML models

Activity Diagram is a type of UML diagram consisting of activity nodes connected by edges. Activity nodes come in three types: action, control, or object nodes. Action nodes perform a behavior determined to be executed upon passing through that node. There are various types of action nodes, such as basic action, accept event, send signal, and call behavior. Control nodes, on the other hand, organize the flows of the activity diagram. Control nodes play a crucial role in sequencing flows, acting as traffic controllers on the edges of the diagram. The types of control nodes include initial, flow final, activity final, merge, decision, fork, and join. Finally, object nodes hold data arriving at their incoming edges and offer them to the outgoing edges. Object nodes have some variations, like basic objects, pins, and activity parameters.

It is important to emphasize that the execution semantics of an activity diagram involve the flow of tokens through directed edges and nodes. Tokens move from the origin activity node to the destination activity node, but this flow is contingent upon the readiness of the destination to accept the token. Certain nodes generate tokens, such as an initial node at the start of an activity, while others, like flow final and activity final nodes, only consume tokens. Object nodes have the capacity to hold multiple tokens before passing them on to subsequent nodes. For an action node to execute, all incoming edges must offer tokens, and upon completion, the node must provide tokens on its outgoing edges. The detailed semantics of each constructor and its specific execution can be found in the UML specification [19].

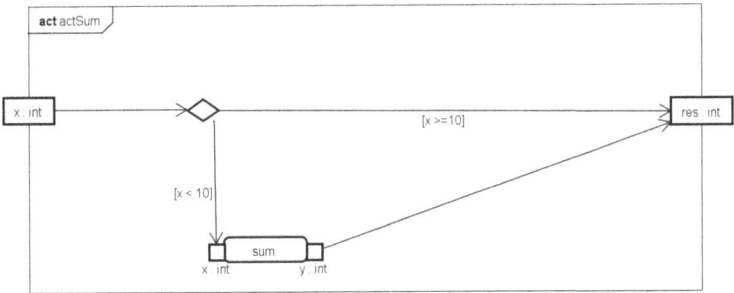

Fig. 1. A simple activity diagram that increments a received input when less than 10.

In Fig. 1, a simple activity diagram named actSum is depicted featuring an action named sum with an input pin and an output pin, a decision node, two activity parameters, and four edges, two of which include guards. It is not explicit here, but assume that the sum action increments the input received in x and outputs the result in y. This diagram functions as follows: a value is passed as an attribute to the input parameter of the diagram. If it is greater than or equal to 10, it will be returned through the output parameter of the diagram. If the value is less than 10, the designated action in sum occurs, defined in this example as the addition of one unit, and is then returned by the output parameter.

State Machine Diagram is comprised of various vertices connected by transitions, activated by a series of events, determining possible activity flows. Vertices can be categorized into states and pseudostates, with states further divided into simple and composite states. Simple states are those without substates, and they can have internal actions: entry, do, exit. Entry performs a behavior upon entering a state; Do may execute a behavior during the state passage; Exit performs a behavior upon exiting the state. These behaviors can be treated as actions, allowing, for instance, the invocation of activity diagrams. Thus, there is an integration between state machine diagrams and activity diagrams, which can occur both within entry, do, and exit actions, as well as within actions performed by transitions. Composite states, in contrast to simple states, have substates. Pseudostates, in turn, serve specific functions depending on their type. Among them are the following types: initial, final, choice, junction, fork, join, entry, exit, deep history, and shallow history.

Finally, concerning transitions, they can include triggers, actions, and guards in their notation. Basically, a trigger enables a transition to be executed from a source state to the target state. After the trigger is fired, if the guard evaluates to true, then the action is performed before activating the target state. The detailed semantics of each constructor can be found in the UML specification [19].

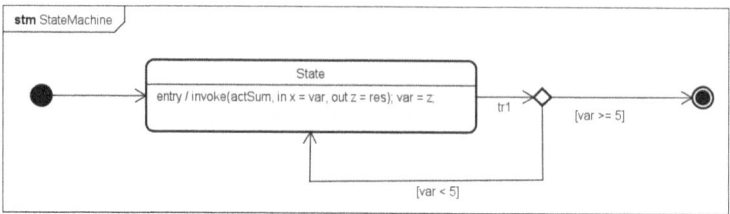

Fig. 2. A state machine diagram with an entry action that invokes an activity diagram

In Fig. 2, we show a state machine diagram featuring a simple state, initial, choice and final pseudostates, and four transitions, two of which include guards. After the initialization of this diagram, in the first state, it is possible to notice an entry action performing an activity call. After concluding the state behavior, the exit transition can be triggered, leading to the choice pseudostate. If the variable var currently has a value less than 5, it will return to State. However, if the value of var is greater than or equal to 5, the process will proceed to the final pseudostate, and consequently, the diagram will terminate.

This example has no issues. However, if we simply change the logical operator in the guard condition from $[var \geq 5]$ to $[var < 5]$, there will be no outgoing path for the case where var is equal to 5, thereby preventing this behavior from advancing. In our proposed approach, such a situation can be detected by performing a deadlock check, which will be detailed further in Sect. 4.

2.2 CSP

The CSP language (Communicating Sequential Processes) [9], proposed by Hoare in 1985, provides a formal approach for specifying concurrent systems. With formally unambiguous semantics and automated refinement calculation mechanisms, such as those offered by the FDR tool (Failures-Divergences Refinement) [6]. FDR allows checking the absence of deadlocks, livelocks, and nondeterminism of CSP specifications. When an issue is found, FDR returns a counterexample describing the list of events that led to the property violation.

The behavior model in CSP is described through processes, the fundamental units of description. These processes, defined in terms of events or other processes, can be composed in parallel in a synchronized or interleaved manner, providing flexibility in modeling concurrent behaviors. The function $\alpha(P)$ represents the set of events that a process P can communicate. The basic process, $SKIP$, represents successful termination. A process of the form $a \rightarrow P$ presents the event a to the environment and then behaves as the process P. CSP channels are used to abstract sets of events that share a common prefix. The syntax $c?x$ denotes a channel c receiving a value x, where x is a value of a type that also types channel c. The value for x is determined by the environment. The syntax $c.e$ ($c!e$) represents an expression e communicated through channel c. Sequential composition in CSP notation, denoted by $P1; P2$, works in a way that is similar to the process $P1$. When $P1$ is successfully completed, control is then passed on to $P2$. Although CSP lacks a specific operator for recursion, a process name can be used within its definition. For instance, if we define the process P as $a \to P$, it will first communicate the event a and then behave as P. In parallel composition, the operator $P1 \parallel_{cs} P2$ synchronizes the events between $P1$ and $P2$ based on the set of events cs, while any events not present in cs occur independently.

The choice of CSP as the formal language in our framework stems from its established use in prior work [5,14,16], where semantic translations of UML state machines and activities were already defined. CSP is highly expressive, offering a wide range of constructs that facilitates the definition of our formal semantics in a compositional manner. Furthermore, CSP has mature tooling supported by FDR, providing automated checks for deadlock and nondeterminism, which is crucial for ensuring system reliability.

3 Formal Semantics of State Machine and Activity Diagrams

In this section, we will discuss the formal semantics of state machine diagrams and activity diagrams. The semantics defined here are based on related works [14, 16–18] that established the semantics for these diagrams. These semantics have been studied and outlined to achieve efficient and accurate translations from UML diagrams to CSP_m code, which is a machine-readable version of CSP that is accepted by the FDR tool.

Furthermore, in this section, we will explain how this work has developed the integration semantics between state machine diagrams and activity diagrams, which is the main contribution of our paper. Although there are tools that verify diagrams independently, the verification of these diagrams, when integrated, still lacks specific tools.

3.1 Overview on the Individual Semantics of Activities and State Machines

The formal semantics for activity diagrams are constructed on the foundations proposed by previous works [14,16] . Key elements, such as action nodes, control nodes, and objects, are addressed in terms of their interactions and sequential or concurrent executions. The formal representation of these elements in the CSP language aims to ensure fidelity in the transition from the activity model to the formal description of the system's behavior. Figure 3 illustrates the semantics of an activity diagram in CSP graphically. The roundtangles represent CSP processes, and the arrows represent CSP events. The activity is encapsulated within the MainProcess process. This process is exclusively triggered by the startActivity event and is designed to conclude upon the occurrence of the endActivity event. It assumes a central role, comprehensively encompassing the entire activity.

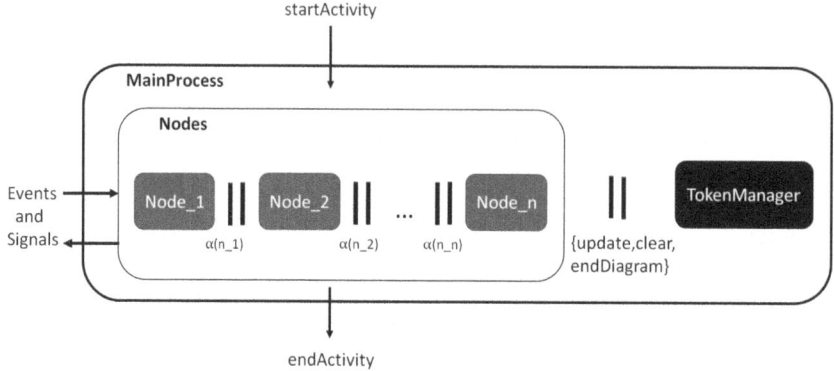

Fig. 3. Activity diagram semantics in CSP [16].

Within MainProcess, a process referred to as Nodes represents the fundamental units of the activity. Each Node_x corresponds to a specific CSP process related to an activity node, executed in parallel synchronizing on the edges as CSP events (denoted as α(n_x)). This parallelization is crucial for mirroring the concurrent nature of activities and actions transpiring simultaneously and ensuring a coherent and synchronized execution of the nodes according to their interconnected edges.

In addition to the Node processes, there is another process that controls and supervises them (known as TokenManager), acting as a coordinator, ensuring that Nodes are executed as expected and that the memory associated with tokens is managed appropriately. It also controls the termination of the whole activity. To ensure a cohesive and controlled flow of activities throughout the entire process, Nodes synchronizes with the TokenManager process on specific events such as update for changing the current number of active tokens, clear to erase all active tokens (e.g., when reaching an activity final node), and endDiagram to synchronize the termination of the diagram with all internal processes.

On the other hand, the formal semantics for state machine diagrams covers several elements, such as states, transitions, pseudostates, and events. It takes into account the reactive and event-driven nature of the model. Events trigger state transitions, and each state and transition may be associated with specific actions, which represent the execution of some behavior, for example, an assignment to a variable. Our semantic implementation was inspired by the RoboChart semantics for state machines in terms of CSP [17,18]. In Fig. 4, we observe an overview of this semantics [5]. Simple states constitute the foundation of this diagram type, residing within the state machine or even nested within composite states.

States or pseudostates within a state machine are intricately linked to transition processes. These transitions are activated through trigger events occurring in CSP channels . Simple states, composite states, transitions, and memory, all represented as distinct CSP processes, work concurrently. This synchronized concurrency emulates the flow of states, enabling the progression of the system. The synchronization occurs through key events in CSP channels, ensuring coherence in the simulated state transitions. Moreover, states and transitions operate in parallel concerning the state machine's memory, which functions as a shared resource among the processes. The memory, managed by a controller, facilitates the sending or modification of predefined variables as specified in the diagram.

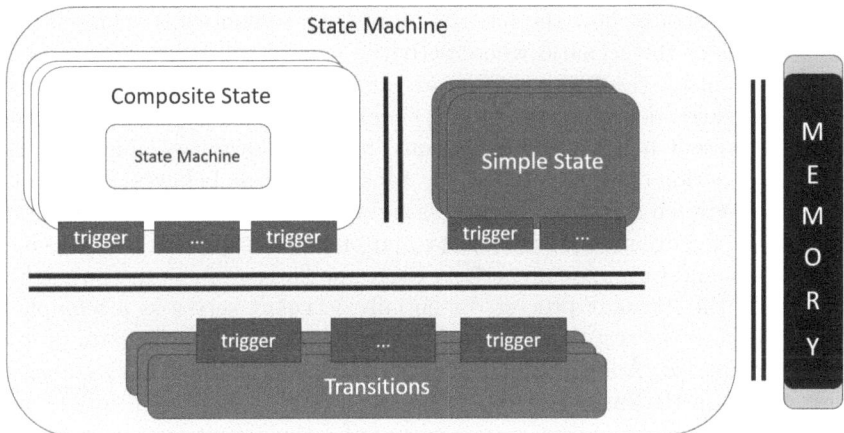

Fig. 4. State machine diagram semantics in CSP.

In essence, the generated semantics employ CSP processes to function either sequentially or in parallel composition. The parallel synchronization of key events is instrumental in achieving an accurate execution of the modeled behavior of both state machine and activity.

3.2 Integrated Semantics of State Machines and Activities

Our contribution is to provide a notion for a common usage of state machine and activity diagrams. While individual semantics were established considering the peculiarities of each diagram, integration requires an approach that encompasses communication between both. There are tools that verify diagrams independently, but the lack of support addressing the verification of these diagrams when integrated is a gap that this work seeks to fill.

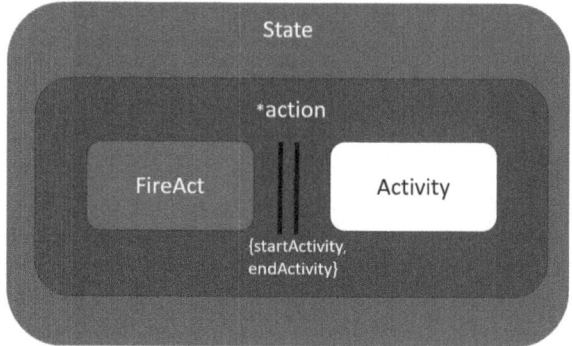

Fig. 5. Semantic integration of state machine and activity

Figure 5 illustrates how the integration of both semantics is achieved. Our work only tackles the scenario where activities can be called by state machine actions. Then, inside the State process, we can have other processes related to its actions (e.g., entry, do, exit actions). For simplification, here we call it *action. We do not present a figure for transitions, but it follows the same principle. Whenever an action calls an activity, the *action process behaves as a parallel composition between the FireAct process and the activity diagram process, synchronizing on the events startActivity and endActivity, which act as channels to initiate and terminate an activity diagram. These events are also the first two events of the FireAct process. Essentially, FireAct serves as a semaphore that only releases the state machine behavior after the activity diagram process has been completed. Additionally, startActivity and endActivity transport tokens, where, in the case of startActivity, the tokens represent inputs, and endActivity is a channel that carries outputs for the activity parameters.

In this way, it is possible to visualize the state machine diagram presented in Fig. 2 and how the integration between the two different types of UML diagrams would work. The integration can be observed through the function present in the Entry action of the State. This function aims to invoke an activity diagram, passing the necessary inputs for its execution and receiving the outputs upon completion. This function has the following structure:

```
invoke(actName, in i1 = q, ..., out j = o1, ...)
```

It necessarily has the name of the activity being invoked as its first parameter. The subsequent parameters pertain to the structure of inputs and outputs of the selected activity. For each input, the in term should be added to indicate that it is an input, followed by the respective activity input parameter name, then = and the value to be sent. For each output, the out term should be added to indicate that it is an output, followed by the variable that will receive the value, then = and the name of the activity output parameter. For instance, in i1 = q represents an input for activity parameter i1 receiving the state machine variable q, while `out j = o1` assigns to variable j the activity output parameter o1.

Thus, the function `invoke(actSum, in x=var, out z=res)` in Fig. 2 details the entry action will invoke the activity diagram `actSum`, represented in Fig. 1, passing the variable `var` to the input `x`, and receiving `res` in `z` as the output. Afterwards, `z` is assigned to `var` in `var = z`.

Therefore, it can be verified that the diagrams represented in Figs. 1 and 2, respectively, can be integrated simply through a function that allows efficient translation to the formal CSP model and consequently allows the verification of properties on models that use both diagrams.

Next, we show the CSP representation for this scenario. It is described in terms of the `EntryProc` process, where the `entry` event initiates the entry action procedure. Subsequently, the activity diagram is invoked in parallel with `FireAct` process, synchronizing on the `startActivity` event to pass the inputs and `endActivity` event to receive the outputs. During the execution of the `FireAct`, the value of the variable `var` is collected from the memory through the `get_var` event. At the conclusion of the `FireAct` process, the value of the variable `var` is updated by the output through the `set_var` event.

After the completion of the `actSum` and `FireAct` processes, the next process is initiated through sequential composition. In this case, the next process corresponds to the do action specified in the `State_st_State_Do_StateMachine` process.

$$EntryProc(st) = entry.st \rightarrow get\_var?var \rightarrow (actSum(id)$$
$$\underset{startActivity\_actSum, endActivity\_actSum}{\parallel}$$
$$FireAct(id))\,;\,State\_st\_State\_Do\_StateMachine$$
$$FireAct(i) = startActivity.i!var \rightarrow endActivity.i?z \rightarrow set\_var!(z) \rightarrow SKIP$$

It's important to note that we illustrate the scenario for the `Entry` process, but this pattern can be used for any type of action within the state machine. The generic structure allows for the seamless integration of different actions, ensuring a cohesive and adaptable design within the state machine.

4 Tool Support

This section addresses the tooling support for applying the semantics defined in Sect. 3. Our framework has been implemented as a plug-in for the Astah modeling environment. This plug-in can verify activity and state machine diagrams in isolation, and now, their integration as well. Our framework is built upon the UML version of Astah, which allows the use of plug-ins to introduce new features and runs on the JVM (Java Virtual Machine). Thus, we used the Astah API to programmatically read, verify, and analyze state machine and activity diagrams.

The automatic translation of diagrams is performed with translation rules directly embedded in the Java program that has been developed. This translation process is based on the semantics of Lima et al. [16] for activity diagrams and

Miyazawa et al. [17] for state machine diagrams. In addition to adapting these two works for the tool, it was necessary to create a bridge that connects the two and can thus perform an integrated verification of the diagrams. While this automated process may introduce inconsistencies due to coding errors, we have taken measures to mitigate this by adopting a Test-Driven Development (TDD) approach [2]. In this approach, we initially define test cases outlining the expected translation behavior before proceeding to implement the parser code.

Users can check if a state machine diagram or an activity diagram is deadlock-free or deterministic by clicking on the option in the user interface. Once the plug-in is installed, the menu shown in Fig. 6 is available, allowing users to select the type of verification for the current diagram. For deadlock-freedom verification, in the case of a state machine diagram integrated with an activity diagram, users should select the root diagram, which is the state machine.

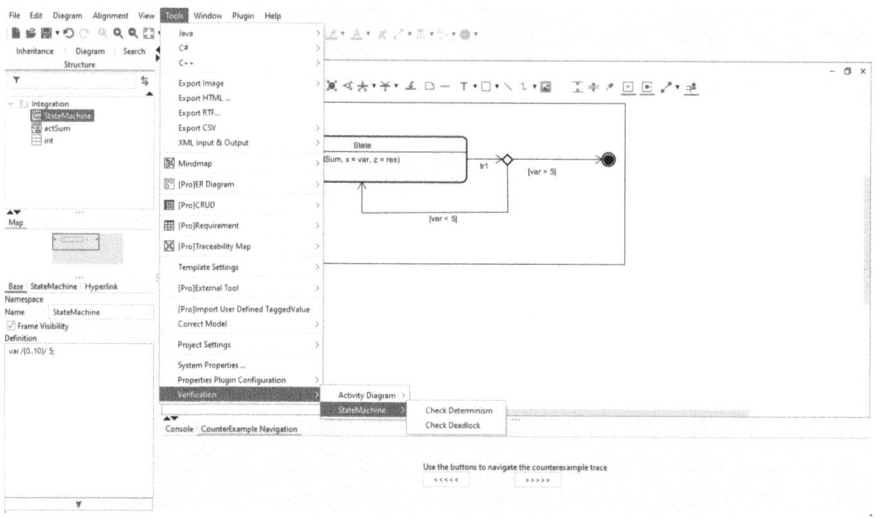

Fig. 6. Steps to use the plug-in in Astah and the interactive navigation buttons

In this example, the tool performs the following tasks: it generates the corresponding CSP specification for all related diagrams, loads it into FDR, and invokes the deadlock-freedom assertion. If FDR detects a deadlock, it provides a counterexample trace that shows the sequence of events that led to the deadlock. This trace is an ordered list of events that shows the path leading up to the point where the flaw occurred. Our tool creates an interactive and diagrammatic counterexample using this returned list. In this counterexample, you can navigate forward or backward the elements of the diagram that belong to this trace. The current element is highlighted in red, and when the user reaches the last element, it is highlighted in purple. This interactive counterexample helps the user to understand how the issue occurred.

At this point, it is important to note that the current version of the framework is limited to verifying deadlock and nondeterminism properties only. Other analysis features available in the FDR tool, such as checking livelock or refinement properties, are not accessible through this framework. This limitation could be addressed in future work if needed, but as of now, the scope of the tool focuses exclusively on these two properties.

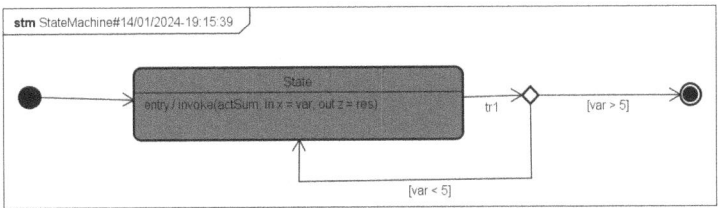

Fig. 7. First step from deadlock counterexample navigation in Astah.

The diagram presented in Fig. 7 is the same as the one shown in Fig. 2, except the condition `var ≥ 5` has been replaced with `var < 5`. This change causes a deadlock in the translated CSP specification. We want to clarify that in CSP, a deadlock happens when there is a state in the specification where we cannot advance further. At the diagrammatic level, this can happen not only due to the lack of covered conditions, as in the shown example, but also due to the lack of communication between elements, isolated states/nodes, or other ill-designed models. When we check this property, the counterexample diagram can be navigated using the forward and backward buttons, as illustrated at the bottom of Fig. 6. Each step forward in the trace reveals the next node or transition. In this example, the first event in the trace is the state `State`, which is highlighted in red to make it easier to follow, as can be seen in Fig. 7. Following this node, the next event in the trace is the transition `tr1`, followed by the choice pseudostate. The deadlock occurs at the choice pseudostate because there is a path for `var > 5` and `var < 5`, but there is no path for when `var` is equal to 5. Therefore, in Fig. 8, the choice pseudostate is painted in purple to indicate the end of the counterexample trace.

There were no major obstacles when using the Astah plug-in environment to build the tool. The most challenging aspect was generating the navigable counterexamples, which required careful handling of event traces and their mapping to diagrammatic elements. However, this was successfully implemented, allowing users to trace back the issues in an intuitive manner.

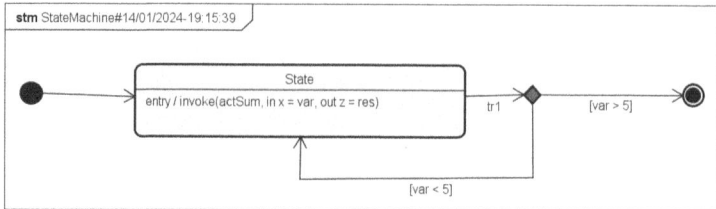

Fig. 8. Last step from deadlock counterexample navigation in Astah.

5 Case Study

The diagram model, represented in Fig. 9, is designed to represent a common flashlight characterized by a battery that runs out with use. Additionally, the flashlight features a charger for replenishing the battery. The main purpose is to simulate the dynamic behavior of the flashlight in different states, such as on, off, in the recharging process, and in SOS mode.

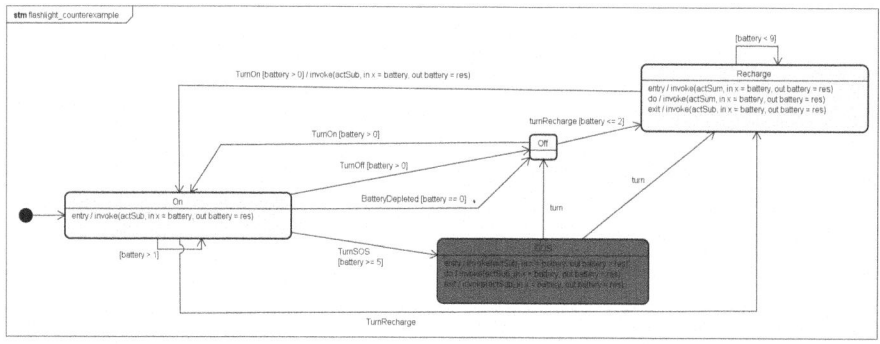

Fig. 9. Flashlight State Machine counterexample for nondeterminism

The structure of the model comprises a state machine diagram representing the flashlight and two activity diagrams depicting operations of addition (actSum) and subtraction (actSub), respectively. The activity diagram actSum can be found in Fig. 1, while the diagram actSub is omitted due to space limitation. However, it follows the same principles as actSum but performs the subtraction operation instead. The state machine diagram consists of four simple states (On, Off, Recharge, SOS), an initial pseudostate, and 12 transitions, with eight of them having guards.

The states On, SOS, and Recharge contain associated actions. For instance, the Recharge state has entry, do, and exit actions. It also has two outgoing transitions, one with a loop in Recharge, allowing the recharge process to repeat. The entry action executes the actSum activity, using the battery as input and receiving an incremented value, simulating the recharging process. The do action performs the same operation, interruptible at any moment, and the exit action executes the `actSub` activity, representing a slight battery consumption.

While verifying the model, the tool detects nondeterminism and generates a counterexample diagram. The navigation using interactive buttons led to the `SOS` state, indicated by the highlighted (purple) color. This nondeterminism happens because of the two outgoing transitions with the same trigger `turn`, resulting in distinct situations depending on the path taken. The proposed solution involves changing the trigger's name, replacing `turn` with `TurnOff` and `TurnRecharge`, differentiating the transitions, and eliminating the nondeterminism.

The analysis of the model in FDR took 0.03 seconds to compile the CSP file, which generates a Labeled Transition System with 2880 states and 3905 transitions, and 0.7 seconds to perform the verification process to check nondeterminism. This scenario shows that our framework can possibly tackle simple to medium complexity models. Nevertheless, further investigation needs to be performed to evaluate how our approach scales and identify possible bottlenecks.

6 Related Work

In this section, we refer to works related to the verification of activity diagrams and state machine diagrams, aiming to analyze properties as well as examine the existence of counterexamples.

The work by Miyazawa et al. [17] focuses on the modeling and verification of the functional behavior of robotic applications. They propose an approach to model robotic applications and provide support for the verification of such modeling through model checking. For this purpose, RoboChart employs a translation process from state machines to CSP, utilizing the FDR tool to verify if the model is deadlock-free. In case a deadlock is detected, a counterexample in the form of a CSP trace is provided to the user. This work does not cover activity diagrams and, consequently, their integration with state machine diagrams. However, our semantic approach draws inspiration from Miyazawa et al.'s work, incorporating certain aspects into our methodology. Unlike Miyazawa's work, our methodology provides traceability of counterexamples to the diagram, enhancing user understanding by linking errors back to the visual representation. This is a distinct feature as Miyazawa's work lacks traceability of counterexamples to the diagram, requiring users to possess a deep understanding of CSP and FDR to check and comprehend errors. Lima et al. [16] focus on the UML activity diagram and offer a framework for automatically verifying deadlocks and nondeterminism in it. Our work considerably augmented [16]'s work not only by supporting state machines and the integration with activities but also by new tool features like the navigable counterexamples.

Horváth et. al [10] propose a cloud-based, end-to-end verification workflow for SysML State Machines and reachability properties using sequence diagrams. Model checking is fully automated and supported via the Gamma Framework [7]. Traceability is provided through back annotations of the resulting trace provided in sequence diagrams. In this way, formal aspects are hidden from the users, as in our case. However, they do not support the combination of state machines and activities to describe behavior.

Kohlmeyer et al. [13] have presented an innovative approach for characterizing software models using UML 2 state machines, activities, and interactions. This methodology utilizes Abstract State Machines (ASMs) [3] as formal semantics for facilitating communication between these diagrams. They cover communication between sequence diagrams to activities, and activities calling state machines. The latter is the opposite of our approach, so in this sense, our work is complimentary to them. Tooling support is provided by the tool ActiveCharts. However, no further details are provided regarding the verification process or traceability mechanisms. Nevertheless, we plan to investigate the discussed connecting scenarios for incorporation into our framework in the future.

Abdelhalim et al.'s [1] approach involves translating a subset of fUML [20] to CSP to leverage the FDR tool as a template checker. Their work primarily focuses on deadlock checks. Additionally, users are required to manually manipulate the formal result and the tool to conduct the verification process.

Elmansouri et al. [4] introduced a method for verifying UML 2.0 activity diagrams by automatically transforming them into CSP models. However, users must specify the properties for verification, utilizing the GROOVE [24] model checker. This approach can detect deadlock and livelock scenarios but lacks traceability for errors and counterexamples.

Table 1. Related work.

Work	Verif. AD	Verif. SMD	Integ.	Trac.	Form.	Purpose
[1]	✓*	X	X	X	CSP	Deadlock
[4]	✓*	X	X	X	CSP	Property Verification
[10]	X	✓*	X	✓*	Gamma	Reachability Properties
[13]	✓*	✓*	✓	X	ASM	Property Verification
[16]	✓	X	X	✓	CSP	Deadlock and Nondeterminism
[17]	X	✓	X	X	CSP	Deadlock
Our Work	✓	✓	✓	✓	CSP	Deadlock and Nondeterminism

We summarize the comparison between our work and others in Table 1. The characteristics considered in this comparison include automated verification of activity diagrams, automated verification of state machine diagrams, integration between these two types of verification, traceability, formalism, and purpose. We use the symbol ✓ to indicate that the feature is addressed, ✓* means that it is partially addressed, while X indicates that it is not addressed.

7 Conclusion

In the conclusion of this work, we present a comprehensive summary of the contributions and results achieved. Our approach focused on defining formal semantics for the integration of state machine and activity diagrams, exploring the efficient translation of these models into the CSP language. In addition to the proposed semantics, we implemented a tool that verifies behaviours described by the combination of state machines that call activities and traces back the results to the UML level, this way truly supporting hidden formal methods.

We acknowledge some limitations of our work. We have not fully analyzed the scalability of the framework, as only a limited number of case studies were conducted. Also, we only explored communication from state machines to activities, which we believe is the most commonly used. But we are aware that the opposite direction is also possible. Finally, the framework does not yet allow navigable counterexamples for activity diagrams, only a static one.

For future work, we plan to expand the coverage of the current plug-in with more model elements and more features. Further research should also focus on scalability and conducting more extensive case studies, including the TMT [22] case study from OpenMBEE [21]. Finally, we plan to investigate and expand the framework to support communication in the opposite direction, from activities to state machines. For that, the work from [13] can inspire some paths to be followed. However, as we use different semantic domains, a proper semantics in CSP may be defined for this purpose. Moreover, integration with sequence diagrams should also be possible. We plan to support this using the semantics presented in [15].

References

1. Abdelhalim, I., et al.: Formal verification of Tokeneer behaviours modelled in fUML using CSP—. In: Proceedings of the 12th International Conference on Formal Engineering Methods and Software Engineering, pp. 371–387. ICFEM'10, Springer-Verlag, Berlin, Heidelberg (2010). http://dl.acm.org/citation.cfm?id=1939864.1939895
2. Beck: Test Driven Development: By Example. Addison-Wesley Longman Publishing Co., Inc., Boston, MA, USA (2002)
3. Börger, E., Stärk, R.: Abstract State Machines. A Method for High-Level System Design and Analysis (2003). https://doi.org/10.1007/978-3-642-18216-7
4. Elmansouri, R., Meghzili, S., Chaoui, A.: A UML 2.0 activity diagrams/CSP integrated approach for modeling and verification of software systems. Comput. Sci. **22**, (2021). https://doi.org/10.7494/csci.2021.22.2.3478

5. Ferreira, D., Lima, L.: A CSP semantics for UML state machines aiming at hidden formal methods verification. In: Formal Methods: Foundations and Applications - 27th Brazilian Symposium, SBMF 2024, Vitória, Brazil, December 04–06, 2024, Proceedings. Lecture Notes in Computer Science (2024)
6. Gibson-Robinson, T., Armstrong, P., Boulgakov, A., Roscoe, A.: Fdr3—a modern refinement checker for csp. In: Ábrahám, E., Havelund, K. (eds.) Tools and Algorithms for the Construction and Analysis of Systems. Lecture Notes in Computer Science, vol. 8413, pp. 187–201. Springer Berlin Heidelberg (2014). https://doi.org/10.1007/978-3-642-54862-8_13
7. Graics, B., Molnár, V., Vörös, A., Majzik, I., Varro, D.: Mixed-semantics composition of statecharts for the component-based design of reactive systems. Softw. Syst. Model. **19**, (2020). https://doi.org/10.1007/s10270-020-00806-5
8. Haskins, B., Stecklein, J., Dick, B., Moroney, G., Lovell, R., Dabney, J.: 8.4.2 error cost escalation through the project life cycle. INCOSE Int. Symp. **14**, 1723–1737 (2004). https://doi.org/10.1002/j.2334-5837.2004.tb00608.x
9. Hoare, C.A.R.: Communicating and Sequential Processes. Prentice Hall (1985)
10. Horváth, B., et al.: Model checking as a service: towards pragmatic hidden formal methods. In: Proceedings of the 23rd ACM/IEEE International Conference on Model Driven Engineering Languages and Systems: Companion Proceedings. MODELS '20, Association for Computing Machinery, New York, NY, USA (2020). https://doi.org/10.1145/3417990.3421407
11. Khendek, F., Bourduas, S., Vincent, D.: Stepwise design with message sequence charts. In: Kim, M., Chin, B., Kang, S., Lee, D. (eds.) Formal Techniques for Networked and Distributed Systems, pp. 19–34. Springer, Boston (2001)
12. Kiniry, J.R., Zimmerman, D.M.: Secret ninja formal methods. In: Cuéllar, J., Maibaum, T.S.E., Sere, K. (eds.) FM 2008: Formal Methods, 15th International Symposium on Formal Methods, Turku, Finland, May 26–30, 2008, Proceedings. Lecture Notes in Computer Science, vol. 5014, pp. 214–228. Springer (2008). https://doi.org/10.1007/978-3-540-68237-0_16
13. Kohlmeyer, J., Guttmann, W.: Unifying the semantics of UML 2 state, activity and interaction diagrams. In: Pnueli, A., Virbitskaite, I., Voronkov, A. (eds.) Perspect. Syst. Inform., pp. 206–217. Springer Berlin Heidelberg, Berlin, Heidelberg (2010)
14. Lima, L., Didier, A., Cornélio, M.: A formal semantics for SYSML activity diagrams. In: Iyoda, J., de Moura, L. (eds.) Formal Methods: Foundations and Applications, pp. 179–194. Springer Berlin Heidelberg, Berlin, Heidelberg (2013)
15. Lima, L., Iyoda, J., Sampaio, A.: Refinement verification of sequence diagrams using CSP. In: Ribeiro, L., Lecomte, T. (eds.) Formal Methods: Foundations and Applications - 19th Brazilian Symposium, SBMF 2016, Natal, Brazil, November 23–25, 2016, Proceedings. Lecture Notes in Computer Science, vol. 10090, pp. 235–252 (2016). https://doi.org/10.1007/978-3-319-49815-7_14
16. Lima, L., Tavares, A., Nogueira, S.C.: A framework for verifying deadlock and nondeterminism in UML activity diagrams based on CSP. Sci. Comput. Program. **197**, 102497 (2020). https://doi.org/10.1016/j.scico.2020.102497
17. Miyazawa, A., Ribeiro, P., Li, W., Cavalcanti, A., Timmis, J., Woodcock, J.: Robochart: modelling and verification of the functional behaviour of robotic applications. Softw. Syst. Model. **18**(5), 3097–3149 (2019). https://doi.org/10.1007/s10270-018-00710-z
18. Miyazawa, A., Ribeiro, P., Ye, K., Cavalcanti, A., Li, W., Woodcock, J., Timmis, J.: Robochart reference manual. Tech. rep. University of York (2017). https://robostar.cs.york.ac.uk/publications/techreports/reports/robochart-reference.pdf

19. Object Management Group: OMG Unified Modeling Language (OMG UML), superstructure, version 2.4.1. Tech. rep. OMG (2011)
20. Object Management Group: Semantics of a Foundational Subset for Executable UML Models (FUML). Tech. rep., Object Management Group (2013). OMG Document Number: formal/2013-08-06
21. OpenMBEE: Open Model Based Engineering Environment. https://www.openmbee.org/. Accessed on 2023 Dec 10
22. OpenMBEE: TMT-SysML-Model. https://github.com/Open-MBEE/TMT-SysML-Model. Accessed on 2023 Jan 16
23. Reggio, G., Leotta, M., Ricca, F., Clerissi, D.: What are the used UML diagrams? A preliminary survey. In: EESSMOD@MoDELS, vol. 1078, pp. 3–12 (2013)
24. Rensink, A.: The groove simulator: a tool for state space generation. In: Pfaltz, J.L., Nagl, M., Böhlen, B. (eds.) Applications of Graph Transformations with Industrial Relevance, pp. 479–485. Springer Berlin Heidelberg, Berlin, Heidelberg (2004)
25. The Object Management Group: OMG Systems Modeling Language. Standard 1.7 beta, Object Management Group, Milford, MA, USA (2022). https://www.omg.org/spec/SysML/1.7/Beta1
26. Visser, W., Dwyer, M., Whalen, M.: The hidden models of model checking. Softw. Syst. Model. **11**(4), 541–555 (2012)

An Integrated Framework for Analysing, Simulating and Testing UML Models

Gustavo Carvalho[1]( ), José Dihego[2], and Augusto Sampaio[1]

[1] Centro de Informática, Universidade Federal de Pernambuco,
Recife 50.740-560, Brazil
`{ghpc,acas}@cin.ufpe.br`
[2] Departamento de Computação, Instituto Federal de Educação, Ciência e Tecnologia da Bahia, Salvador, Brazil
`jose.dihego@ifba.edu.br`

Abstract. UML is widely adopted for modelling object-oriented software systems, including diagrams that cover the several facets of the entire development life cycle. Approaches to formal semantics of UML tend to concentrate on individual diagrams and, so far, no complete, standard, semantics is available. Here, we explore a different path and define a natural-language semantics for a component UML model that embodies state machines and composite structure diagrams. We then integrate with the NAT2TEST strategy to provide means for analysis (via model checking and theorem proving), simulation and testing. The integration is based on a systematic process (mapping rules), and its soundness has been validated considering an independent reference formal semantics. The developed tool support automates the translation from UML models to natural-language requirements directly based on the proposed mapping rules. We illustrate our contributions and tool support with respect to two case studies: the classical Dijkstra's dining philosophers problem, and a distributed ring-buffer model.

Keywords: UML · Controlled Natural Language · NAT2TEST · CSP · model checking

1 Introduction

UML is widely accepted as the de facto standard graphical notation for modelling object-oriented software systems [24,31]. It provides structural and behavioural diagrams to capture the various views of the development life cycle, from requirements to deployment. Unfortunately, UML does not yet have a complete and standard semantics. There are some relevant contributions in this direction, including: the semantics of a foundational subset for executable UML models (fUML) [27], Precise Semantics of UML State Machines (PSSM) [29], and Precise Semantics of UML Composite Structures (PSCS) [28]. Nevertheless, these do not cover the full notation, and are not integrated into a unified formalism.

There have been several attempts to formalise UML for specific reasoning purposes, typically by mapping a subset of UML diagrams into a formal notation like Alloy, B, CSP, Petri nets, and Z, among others. Many of these approaches are limited in that they address either a structural or a behavioural view in isolation. Moreover, most of the works related to reasoning about UML models involves either mapping into a formalism for the purpose of analysis (model-checking or theorem proving) or for test case generation, but typically not both.

Differently, we target the integration of two behavioural and structural diagrams (state machines and composite structures). Furthermore, we aim at a broad application of techniques and tools, enabling simulation, testing, and formal verification by means of model checking and (interactive) proof development.

We are also concerned with natural-language descriptions generated from UML models: our target is a controlled natural language (CNL) with a well-defined syntax and semantics that can then be automatically processed. A benefit of the generated CNL description is that it can be useful as a textual documentation of the model. It can also be useful as an implementation reference. Our main focus here, however, is to carry out formal analysis, simulation and testing from CNL descriptions. This is achieved via integration with the NAT2TEST tool [5] that provides all these facilities by taking as input CNL requirements.

Soundness of such translations is always an important concern. A standard characterisation is to show that the semantics of the obtained CNL descriptions preserve the behaviour of the respective UML models. We take advantage of the fact that NAT2TEST automatically generates a reactive semantics (interaction with the environment by responding to external stimuli) of CNL descriptions in the CSP [9] process algebra, and show trace conformance with respect to the CSP semantics mechanically given in [17] to the same UML diagrams. A complete proof is left as a topic for future work.

In summary, the main contributions of this work are as follows. (1) we propose a systematic and compositional process (mapping rules) for translating from state machine and composite structure diagrams to CNL requirements; (2) we validate the translation by establishing a correspondence between the CSP traces semantics obtained from the NAT2TEST strategy and the one described in [17]; (3) we provide tool support for the devised integration; and, (4) we explore the benefits of our approach by presenting some case studies. As yet another, by-product, contribution of integrating with the NAT2TEST framework, (5) we have devised some guidelines to express state machines and composite structured diagrams in CNL. Therefore, this can also be used as a direct input, and not constrained to the translation process presented here.

In Sect. 2, we comment on background information. In Sect. 3, we delve into the details of our translation to CNL descriptions. In Sect. 4, we present the developed tool support. In Sect. 5, we address related and future work.

2 Background

In Sect. 2.1, we cover UML. In Sect. 2.2, we show how CSP can be used to give formal semantics to UML diagrams. In Sect. 2.3, we present the NAT2TEST strategy (used here to analyse, simulate, and test UML models).

2.1 UML

UML is the industry standard for specifying and visualizing software systems [26]. UML diagrams [3] are the primary input for our strategy, specially those that define how components connect with each other and how they behave.

State machines provide a notation for representing the states of an object (or component), the transitions between these states, and the events triggering such transitions. Consider the classical Dijkstra's dining philosophers problem [15]. Figure 1 shows a state machine that models the behaviour of a fork. It has tree states: available, Busy1 and Busy2. Initially, the fork is available and can be picked up by a philosopher on its right or left. If it is picked up by a philosopher on its right, signalled by the event fork_right.picksup, the machine transitions to Busy1, indicating that the fork is in use by the philosopher on its right-hand side. When the philosopher releases the fork, triggered by the event fork_right.putsdown, and the machine returns to the available state. The behaviour for picking up and putting down the fork by a philosopher on its left is symmetric.

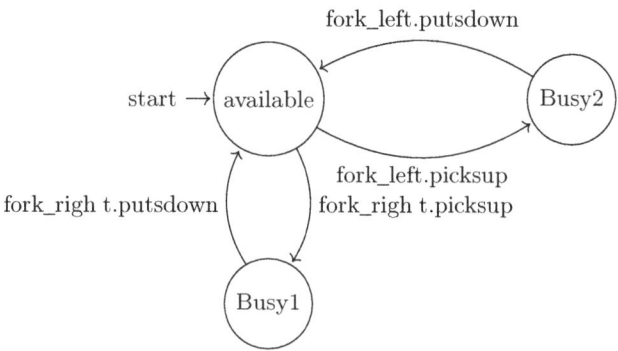

Fig. 1. Fork's state machine

State machines address behavioural aspects, while structural diagrams model the configurations of system components. Figure 2 illustrates a fragment of the structure diagram of the dining philosophers including three components: fork1, phil1 and phil2 connected through communication ports. These connections allow interactions based on the behaviours defined by their state machines.

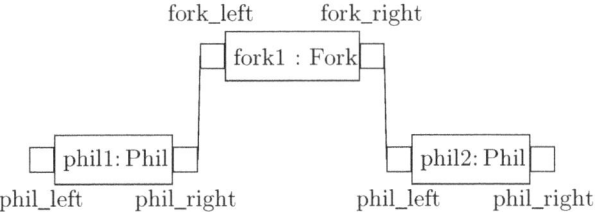

Fig. 2. Composite structure diagram connecting fork and philosopher instances

2.2 CSP

Communicating Sequential Processes (CSP) [20] is a formal language for specifying concurrent systems. The Failures-Divergence Refinement (FDR) tool [30] supports the verification of CSP specifications, enabling the analysis of classical behavioural properties such as deadlock and livelock freedom, and determinism. The state machine in Fig. 1 can be represented in CSP as follows:

```
Fork = Available
Available = fork_right.picksup -> Busy1
            [] fork_left.picksup -> Busy2
Busy1 = fork_right.putsdown -> Available
Busy2 = fork_left.putsdown -> Available
```

The Fork process behaves as the Available process that provides an external choice ([]) between the events fork_right.picksup and fork_left.picksup. Depending on which philosopher picks up the fork, it behaves as Busy1 if picked up by the right philosopher, or as Busy2 if picked up by the left philosopher. Both processes behave like Available when the fork is put down.

Processes can be parameterised to create additional instances. In our example, we can instantiate forks as follows:

```
N=3
Fork(i) = Available(i)
Available(i) = fork_right.picksup!i!i  -> Busy1(i)
               [] fork_left.picksup!((i-1)%N)!i -> Busy2(i)
Busy1(i) = fork_right.putsdown!i!i -> Available(i)
Busy2(i) = fork_left.putsdown!((i-1)%N)!i -> Available(i)
```

For i=1, Fork(1) can be picked up by philosopher Phil(1) on its right or by Phil(0) on its left. Busy1(1) and Busy2(1) behave accordingly. The expression ((i-1)%N) stands for modular arithmetic subtraction. For instance, Fork(0) can be picked up by Phil(0) or by Phil(2). CSP provides operators to combine processes in parallel. Bellow, FORKS combines N forks in parallel. In this case, the processes execute independently (interleaving, |||), without communication among them.

```
FORKS = ||| i:{0..N} @ FORK(i)
```

Philosophers can operate in parallel using PHILS. By synchronizing them on picks and putsdown events, we model the dining philosophers' example in CSP:

```
PHILS  = ||| i:{0..N} @ PHIL(i)
FORKS  = ||| i:{0..N} @ FORK(i)
SYSTEM = PHILS [|{|picksup, putsdown|}|] FORKS
```

Note that, by parameterising the specification with the number of forks and philosophers (N), one can instantiate it to obtain different configurations, capturing the behaviour of a UML composite structure diagram.

2.3 The NAT2TEST Strategy

The NAT2TEST strategy [8] provides means for testing systems whose inputs and outputs can be seen as signals. The system behaviour needs to be described using a Controlled Natural Language (CNL) called SysReq-CNL. Generally speaking, this CNL allows for writing system requirements in the form of guarded actions; when the conditions are met, the associated actions shall be performed by the system.

Although not devised initially to describe transitions of a state machine, we realised that this is entirely feasible. For instance, considering the dining philosophers example, one can use SysReq-CNL to represent the transition from *available* to *Busy1* (see Fig. 1) as follows.

```
When the fork state is available,
and the event fork_right_picksup becomes true,
the fork component shall assign Busy1 to the fork state.
```

Note that, since this CNL was proposed to a context of input and output as signals, we describe the occurrence of the event *fork_right.picksup* as the corresponding signal becoming true.

We emphasise that these guidelines are themselves a relevant contribution, since they allow to express UML diagrams in a textual way, and can be used in contexts other then the translation presented here. An alternative would be mapping UML diagrams directly to DFRSs or other notations (e.g., CSP) adopted by the NAT2TEST strategy, but this would not be straightforward, and could also limit the use of a broader range of techniques and tools.

In Fig. 3, we have an overview of the NAT2TEST, emphasising its use of different notations, techniques and tools for generating test cases, but also enabling simulation and verification (the latter via both model checking and proof development). After syntactic and semantic analyses, the system description is formalised as a Data-Flow Reactive System (DFRS), which plays a central role in this strategy; DFRSs are the source for the translation to different formalisms, such as CSP_M (the machine-readable version of CSP).

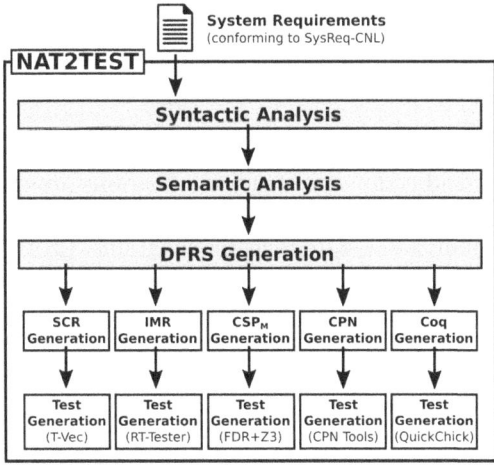

Fig. 3. The NAT2TEST strategy

There are two types of DFRSs: a symbolic (s-DFRS) and an expanded (e-DFRS) one. An s-DFRS is a 6-tuple $(I, O, T, gcvar, s0, F)$, where I, O, and T comprises input and output signals, and timers, respectively. The variable $gcvar$ represents the system global clock, and s_0 denotes the initial state. The system behaviour is captured by F, which is a set of functions. Each function encodes symbolically how the system reacts when certain conditions are met. Therefore, a function is a set of pairs relating conditions with actions. There is a direct correspondence between systems requirements and pairs of a given function.

Differently, an e-DFRS encodes the system behaviour as a state-based machine. Formally, it is a 7-tuple $(I, O, T, gcvar, s_0, S, TR)$, where TR is a transition relation associating states in S by means of delay and function transitions. The former models time passing, when new input signals are perceived, whereas the latter models instantaneous system reactions. We refer the reader to [6] for a more comprehensive explanation of DFRSs. Information about the associated tool support is available in [5].

3 From UML Diagrams to Natural-Language Requirements

In order to employ the NAT2TEST strategy to analyse, simulate and test UML models, we translate UML diagrams to natural-language requirements adhering to the grammar of SysReq-CNL. This is performed automatically and totally transparent to the user. In Sect. 3.1, we discuss an overview of our translation process. Afterwards, in Sects. 3.2 and 3.3, we systematise this process by defining mapping rules.

Finally, in Sect. 3.4, we validate the mapping rules. Regarding the dining philosophers example, we prove a correspondence between the CSP semantics associated with the derived DFRS and the one obtained mechanically and directly from UML diagrams, as proposed in [17].

3.1 Overview of Translation

UML state machines and composite structure diagrams are mapped to SysReq-CNL requirements according to three major phases: (1) mapping rules are applied to translate individual state machine diagrams, (2) the output of Phase 1 is replicated based on the number of instances in the composite structure diagram, and (3) additional mapping rules are applied to the output of Phase 2 to take into account the connections described in the composite structure diagram. In what follows, we provide an intuition for these phases. Afterwards, they are properly addressed and systematised.

Phase 1. Initially, a sentence (requirement) is generated for each transition of the given state machine (see the example). The indentation is solely for explanation purpose. Remember that sentences in SysReq-CNL can be seen as guarded actions. The conditions associated with transitions are translated to guards, whereas their effects (i.e., the state change and others) are translated to actions.

```
When the STM_Fork_state is available,
 and the STM_Fork timer is greater than 0,
the STM_Fork_component shall:
 assign true to the fork_right_picksup,
 assign Busy1 to the STM_Fork_state,
 reset the STM_Fork timer.
```

An output signal (variable) is created to represent the current system state (e.g., `STM_Fork_state`). The transition's source state is added as a condition (e.g., `the STM_Fork_state is available`); the change to the target state is represented as an action (e.g., `assign Busy1 to the STM_Fork_state`).

At this moment, the occurrence of an event is represented as an action (e.g., `assign true to the fork_right_picksup`). Later, in the third phase, based on the information about input/output ports provided in the composite structure diagrams, we adjust this accordingly: the output represents an action, whereas the input represents a condition. This is necessary since the communication model of DFRSs is based on shared memory, instead of message passing (as in CSP). Therefore, considering the above example, there will be a sentence with something like `When ... the fork_right_picksup becomes true`.

Although the dining philosophers model is an untimed system, there is an implied order for the occurrence of events. According to the e-DFRS semantics, successive function transitions happen instantaneously. Therefore, it is necessary to enforce time elapsing between events. This is the rationale for `STM_Fork timer` in the above sentence. When the actions described by a sentence occur, a timer is reset, and other actions can only occur after some delay transition that evolves the system global clock and all timers as well. Synchronous events do not follow this rationale. This is addressed just in Phase 3, when dealing with the composition of instances of state machines.

Recall that an s-DFRS comprises a set of functions F (see Sect. 2.3). The sentences derived from a given state machine are grouped into one of these functions. In the above example, this is denoted by the STM_Fork_component.

Phase 2. In the second phase, the sentences are replicated considering the number of instances of a given state machine. Elements of different instances are differentiated by appending the instance name to the corresponding identifiers. For example, regarding the dining philosophers, our rules create names such as STM_Fork_state_fork1 and STM_Fork_component_fork1, where fork1 is the name of an instance of the Fork state machine.

Phase 3. In the last phase, we address the connections between instances of state machines, which are provided in the composite structure diagram (see Fig. 2). Besides the connections, connected ports are classified as input or output. Based on this information, we update the result of the second phase.

To give a concrete example, consider the following two sentences. The first one describes the situation where the second philosopher (phil2) wants to pick up the first fork (fork1). Since the communication over picksup is synchronised, we define phil_left_picksup_phil2__fork_right_picksup_fork1 as the variable used to handle such a synchronous communication. Moreover, as the philosopher-side port is defined as an output, the philosopher is the one who assigns true to this channel to indicate the desire to pick up the fork. However, this can only be done if the corresponding fork is on the available state.

```
When the STM_Phil_state_phil2 is HoldForkL,
 and the STM_Phil timer is greater than 0,
 and the STM_Fork_state_fork1 is available,
the STM_Phil_component_phil2 shall:
 assign true to the
   phil_left_picksup_phil2__fork_right_picksup_fork1,
 assign PutsDownR to the STM_Phil_statephil2,
 reset the STM_Phil timer.

When the STM_Fork_state_fork1 is available,
 and the STM_Fork timer is greater than 0,
 and the
   phil_left_picksup_phil2__fork_right_picksup_fork1 becomes true,
the STM_Fork_component_fork1 shall:
 assign false to the
   phil_left_picksup_phil2__fork_right_picksup_fork1,
 assign Busy1 to the STM_Fork_state_fork1,
 reset the STM_Fork timer.
```

The second sentence has a symmetric behaviour. As the fork-side port is an input one, the fork monitors the variable aforementioned to detect when it becomes `true`. When this happens, the shared variable is reset to `false`. These two sentences also update the states of the philosopher and the fork accordingly. In what follows, we formalise this translation process in terms of mapping rules.

3.2 Phase 1: Mapping Rules for State Machine Diagrams

The process of mapping state machines into phrases involves several steps. Initially, we generate a textual representation of the state machine. This representation is then mapped to corresponding objects. Finally, these objects are used to populate a template with the relevant values. Considering the first step, the following represents the state machine in Fig. 1.

```
machine STM_Fork
state Available
state Busy1
state Busy2
transition Available fork_right.picksup Busy1
transition Available fork_left.picksup Busy2
transition Busy1 fork_right.putsdown Available
transition Busy2 fork_left.putsdown Available
```

Afterwards, we use a textual representation of a state machine, such as the one above, to instantiate a collection of objects corresponding to the classes illustrated in Fig. 4. For our example, this process yields a `StateMachine` object, which encapsulates three `State` objects and four `Transition` objects.

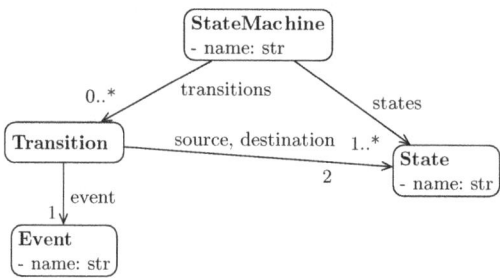

Fig. 4. Metamodel fragment for state machines

The final step in translating UML state machine diagrams to DFRS involves applying a set of compositional translation rules, as outlined below. The mapping rule *generate_phrases* creates a list of phrases, one for each transition in S. This is done by applying the mapping rule *generate_phrase* to each transition. The latter rule employs a template, encoded as a string, to format a phrase from the data encoded in a `Transition` object.

Templates are just string (str) constant values and are presented in detail in Sect. 4. The function *format* processes a template—a pre-formatted string with placeholders—and sequentially populates it with data extracted from various objects, such as state machines and transitions.

Mapping Rule 1 (generate_phrases) : StateMachine ⟶ list[str]

$generate\_phrases(S) = [generate\_phrase(t, S.name) \mid t \in S.transitions]$

Mapping Rule 2 (generate_phrase) : Transition × str ⟶ str

$generate\_phrase(T, stm\_name) = format((T, stm\_name), temp)$

3.3 Phases 2 and 3: Mapping Rules for Composite Structure Diagrams

The mapping rules for compositions must deal with component instances connected through channels. As before, we generate a textual representation of the composition diagram. This representation is then mapped to corresponding objects. Finally, these objects are used to populate a template with the relevant values. The following represents one of the compositions in Fig. 2.

```
instance phil1 type STM_Phil in phil_right
instance fork1 type STM_Fork out fork_left
```

This composition is mapped into objects according to the classes depicted in Fig. 5. In our example, this mapping results in the creation of an instance of the Connection class, which links a ComponentInstance for phil1 and another for fork1. Additionally, two instances of the Channel class are created: one representing phil_right and another representing fork_left.

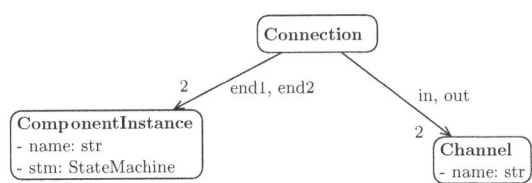

Fig. 5. Metamodel fragment for composite structure diagram

The final step in translating composition diagrams into phrases involves applying a set of mapping rules, illustrated by the two following rules. For a set of connections, Mapping Rule 3 generates a list of phrases in terms of Mapping Rule 4. The latter, outputs two phrases for each connection, one for the input and one for the output event, using a template for each case. In Sect. 4.1 we explain how these rules have been implemented, and we provide further examples. The implementation of all rules can be found in the provided artefact [7].

Mapping Rule 3 (generate_composition_phrases)
: set[Connection] ⟶ list[str]

$$generate\_composition\_phrases(C_L) = \\ [generate\_composition\_phrase(c) \mid c \in C_L]$$

Mapping Rule 4 (generate_composition_phrase)
: Connection ⟶ str × str

$$generate\_composition\_phrase(C) = format(C, t_{in}), \ format(C, t_{out})$$

3.4 Validation of the Mapping Rules

When translating between notations, a typical and important concern is the soundness of such translations. Here, we provide a validation notion supported by classical examples. We take advantage of the fact that NAT2TEST automatically generates a reactive semantics of DFRSs in the CSP process algebra, and show trace conformance of this semantics with respect to the CSP semantics independently and mechanically given in [17] for the same UML diagrams. To address the bias of different approaches targeting the same input notation (UML diagrams), we go further, and prove that the obtained CSP semantics of DFRSs is trace-equivalent to an abstract and classical CSP specification reported in the literature. A complete proof of soundness is left as a topic for future work.

Our example proof has been verified using FDR. Let S_NAT2TEST be the CSP semantics of the DFRS derived from the CNL requirements, which were automatically generated from the UML diagrams. It is important to say that we employ a number of (semantics preserving) compression functions[1] provided by FDR to reduce the size of this model. In general terms, reduction is achieved by eliminating internal transitions and states using strong bisimulation. Let S_UML be the CSP semantics given in [17] for UML diagrams. Let S_Classical be a classical CSP specification given in the literature, such as the one provided by Roscoe to the dining philosophers problem[2]. S_NAT2TEST' is defined by hiding all events (\ { ... }), apart from the ones related to the communication between instances of state machines. Concerning S_UML' and S_Classical', we also hide all events, except from the ones related to the communication between components of the model. Additionally, we rename ([[... <- ...]]) the visible events to match the names of those from S_NAT2TEST'.

---

[1] Link: https://cocotec.io/fdr/manual/cspm/prelude.html#compressions.
[2] Link: https://cocotec.io/fdr/manual/examples/index.html#dining-philosophers.

```
S_NAT2TEST' = S_NAT2TEST \ { ... }
S_UML' = S_UML [[ ... <- ... ]] \ { ... }
S_Classical' = S_Classical [[ ... <- ...]] \ { ... }
```

FDR is used to check a number of assertions. Each one (L [T= R) verifies whether the right model (R) is a trace-refinement of the left one (L). This implies that the traces of R is a subset of the traces of L. By verifying this in both directions, we ensure that both models have precisely the same trace semantics. A complete account of the semantics used in this verification can be found in the associated artefact [7].

```
assert S_NAT2TEST' [T= S_UML'
assert S_UML' [T= S_NAT2TEST'

assert S_NAT2TEST' [T= S_Classical'
assert S_Classical' [T= S_NAT2TEST'
```

4 Tool Support

In this section, we detail the developed tool support. In Sect. 4.1, we describe how the mapping rules previously defined are realised as a number of scripts. Then, in Sect. 4.2, we present how this integrates into the NAT2TEST tool.

4.1 Translator to Natural-Language Requirements

UML benefits from extensive tool support and interoperability, making the choice of a specific tool often hinge on particular features and requirements. We chose Astah UML [10] for two primary reasons: it allows for customisation through our own plugins and enables data extraction from models using a well-documented API. These features significantly enhance our ability to tailor the tool to our specific needs and integrate it seamlessly into our development workflow.

To create sentences from state machines we first create a JavaScript code to extract the relevant data for our strategy. The choice of JavaScript is driven by its widespread support across various tools and its integral role as the primary language for interacting with models in AstahUML. The code outputs textual representations of UML diagrams as the one shown in the beginning of Sect. 3.2. These then serve as the input for other scripts written in Python that implement the mapping rules previously defined, in a very direct way. For example, the transition

```
transition Available fork_right.picksup Busy1
```

is mapped to

When the STM_Fork_state is available, and the STM_Fork timer is greater than 0, the STM_Fork_component shall: assign true to the fork_right_pickup, assign Busy1 to the STM_Fork_state, reset the STM_Fork timer.

To implement the generation in Python we use text templates. For state machines the following template is employed to generate the previous phrase.

When the {1}_state is {2}, and the {3} timer is greater than 0, the {4}_component shall: assign true to the {5}, assign {6} to the {7}_state, reset the {8} timer.

In this context, the placeholders are mapped as follows: {1} ↦ STM_Fork (as well as {3}, {4}, {7} and {8}), {2} ↦ available, {5} ↦ fork_right_pickup and {6} ↦ Busy1.

The Python script systematically implements our approach by reading a state machine textual representation and extracting its transitions. For each transition, the script applies a corresponding template file. Finally, it outputs the resulting data. These functions follow directly from our mapping rules.

```
# inside StateMachine class
def generate_phrases(self) ->list:
    return [ t.generate_phrase(self.name)
            for t in self.transitions]
# inside Transition class
def generate_phrase(self, data)->str:
    template = open('stm.template').read()
    return template.format(data)
```

The `generate_phrases` function calls `generate_phrase` for every transition in `self.transitions` of the state machine (`self`). The `generate_phrase` function reads and applies the `stm.template` for each transition encoded in `data`.

In the next phase of the translation, we focus on instances and their actions; see Fig. 2. Each instance operates its own state machine, with events communicated via channels. These channels establish connections between components, requiring synchronisation for event communication. Additionally, each synchronised event is an output from one state machine and an input to another. For instance, the connection between `phil1` and `fork1` is extracted as:

```
instance phil1 type STM_Phil in  phil_right.picksup
instance fork1 type STM_Fork out fork_left.picksup
instance phil1 type STM_Phil in  phil_right.putsdown
instance fork1 type STM_Fork out fork_left.putsdown
```

For each event in a channel, a corresponding textual representation is generated. Considering the `phil_right` channel, there are two events: `picksup` and `putsdown`. These events act as inputs for `phil1` and outputs for `fork1`. Each event in a channel connection results in two phrases: one for the component where the event is an input and another for the component where it is an output. For concrete examples, see Sect. 3. Similarly to state machines we also use templates. In this case we have two templates, one for the event as an input and another for the event as an output. We omit these templates here.

The following Python script consolidates the translation process. It reads the textual representation of a component diagram, loads the input and output templates, and for each synchronised event, it generates two phrases: one for the event as an input and another for the event as an output. As before, the functions follow directly from our mapping rules.

```
def generate_composition_phrases(connections):
  phrases = []
  for c in connections:
      in_p, out_p = generate_composition_phrase(c)
      phrases.extend([in_p, out_p])
  return phrases

def generate_composition_phrase(connection):
  t_in, t_out = load_templates('in.template','out.template')
  phrase_in = t_in.format(connection)
  phrase_out = t_out.format(connection)
  return phrase_in, phrase_out
```

Model-to-text transformation frameworks, such as ATL, could be employed for translating UML to CNL. However, given the structure of the models involved, we opted for a more straightforward and targeted approach.

4.2 Integration with NAT2TEST

After deriving CNL requirements from UML diagrams, we provide these sentences as input to the NAT2TEST framework. In Fig. 6, one can see a screenshot of this tool. The derived requirements can be seen on the right panel.

Exploring the tool capabilities, we generate the corresponding s-DFRS, whose e-DFRS can be simulated by the custom embedded animator (see a screenshot in Fig. 6). Initially, the second philosopher picks its left fork. Then, we have two possible scenarios. In the left branch, this philosopher picks its right fork, and now the forks can be returned to the table. In the right branch, the first philosopher picks its left fork, reaching a deadlock. Although our illustration uses 2 forks and 2 philosophers, for simplicity, any configuration is possible.

In addition to simulation, our integration with NAT2TEST enables other analysis possibilities. For instance, one can use Coq [2] to define and prove custom properties of interest. FDR can also be used to check classical concurrency properties. Moreover, one can generate test cases by two different approaches: a combination of Coq and property-based testing [22], or via FDR and Z3 [14]. Due to space restrictions, we do not address these possibilities in details here.

4.3 Case Study: Ring Buffer

Besides the dining philosophers, we considered other more challenging case studies; particularly, a ring-buffer algorithm [17], which is found in many embedded systems. In this example, a bounded buffer comprises a ring of storage cells with a controller. This structure resembles a circular queue with FIFO data characteristics. It can be used to control requests to a single shared resource.

In the cell component, the data is restricted to binary values, and we have read and write operations described by means of a state machine diagram. An n-ring buffer (Fig. 7) comprises a control unit connected to n cells.

Fig. 6. The integration with the NAT2TEST tool

We have successfully applied our proposal to process these diagrams, and provided the obtained sentences to the NAT2TEST strategy. The files associated with this case study are also included in the provided artefact [7].

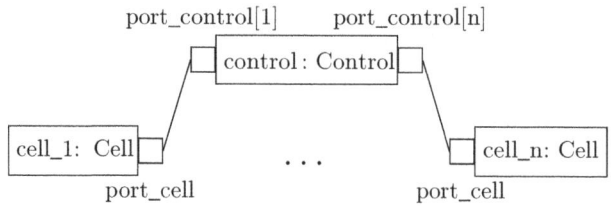

Fig. 7. Composite structure diagram connecting cells and control instances

5 Conclusion

In this paper, we conceived a strategy to provide means for the analysis, simulation, and testing of UML models specified using a combination of behavioural and structural models, namely, composite structure diagrams and state machines, respectively. To accomplish this, we propose a systematic and compositional process supported by mapping rules for translating such diagrams to CNL requirements. As a by-product, we create a textual representation of these diagrams, which may be relevant in a wider context than that explored here. This allowed the integration of a component model formed of UML diagrams with the NAT2TEST framework. Moreover, the conceived textual convention can also be used as a direct input to NAT2TEST, and not confined to our translation. The soundness of the translation is addressed by providing a formal argument, where we mechanise and prove for some examples that the obtained CSP semantics is trace-equivalent to the semantics obtained from other independent means. We also provide tool support for the devised integration with the NAT2TEST tool.

5.1 Related Work

In addition to aid problem understanding and to serve as documentation, creating executable UML models provides valuable benefits, but also challenges [13]. The absence of a complete and standard semantics for UML models stimulates the development of partial and inconsistent solutions. In many situations, the approaches address either a structural or a behavioural view in isolation. For example, in [1], it is presented a comprehensive survey on the formalisation of UML state machines for automated verification.

A possible alternative is to focus on a subset or tailored versions of UML. For instance, the CHESS modelling language (CHESS-ML) [12] (defined as a UML profile, including tailored subsets of SysML and MARTE profiles) allows for the integration of different views (requirements, components, deployment, analysis), and supports simulation, formal analysis, and code generation.

Similarly, the Gamma Statechart Composition Framework [18,25] offers elements similar to that of UML and SysML aiming at simulation, testing, formal analysis, and code generation as well. Within this framework, model-based testing is enabled by using model checkers [19].

Another general approach is proposed in [11], where rCOS (a method of Refinement of Component and Object Systems) is used to provide formal definitions of models in a UML-based development process. Refinement is performed by means of model transformation.

In what follows, we focus on related work addressing directly UML and SysML models. Table 1 summarises our analyses; ○, ◐, and ● denote no, partial and total fulfilment, respectively. In [4], it is proposed a model checker that is capable of analysing properties via direct interpretation of SysML models, that is, it is not required to translate the models to internal formal representations. The model checker is integrated into TTool[3], also supporting simulation. Also

---

[3] Link: https://ttool.telecom-paris.fr/.

targeting SysML models, in [23], the authors propose an integrated semantics for formal analysis (consistency checking and refinement) of different diagrams.

A pragmatic verification and validation process is devised in [21] to a subset of SysML behavioral and structural modelling elements. The process is significantly comprehensive, since it takes into account simulation, test generation (via model checkers) and execution, formal analysis, and also code generation.

In [16], the authors report on inconsistencies and missing clarifications associated with the semantics of doActivity behaviours in UML state machine diagrams. Besides state machines, the work considers activity diagrams to detail complex behaviours. Sequence diagrams are used for simulation. Test generation is not a concern here, but running previously defined test cases is used to collect evidence about the semantics of doActivity behaviours.

In [17], formal semantics is given to state machine and composite structure diagrams, aiming at compositional verification. Simulation is also supported.

Table 1. Related work, where Ac = activity, BD = block definition, IB = internal block, CS = composite structure, SM = state machine, and Sq = sequence diagrams.

	Behavioural diagrams	Structural diagrams	Simulation	Testing	Formal analysis	Code generation
[4]	SM	BD, IB	●	○	●	○
[23]	Ac, SM, Sq	BD, IB	○	○	●	○
[21]	Ac, SM, Sq	BD, IB	●	●	●	●
[16]	Ac, SM, Sq	–	●	◐	○	○
[17]	SM	CS	●	○	●	○
This work	SM	CS	●	●	●	○

In summary, the most comprehensive approach is reported in [21]. Whereas simulation is addressed by all the approaches, except for [23], testing is only fully supported by our approach and the one discussed in [21]. All the approaches, except for [16], offer formal methods related facilities. Code generation features are provided only by [21]; this is not in our scope. In terms of diagrams, these works consider both structural and behavioural views (except for [16]), but only our approach and [17] handles composite structure diagrams.

5.2 Future Work

As future work, we plan to extend our approach to take into account more complex constructs (e.g., entry-exit actions, parallel regions, etc.) and other UML diagrams. Consider other case studies and further explore the capabilities of the NAT2TEST in terms of verification and testing are also in our agenda.

Acknowledgments. This work is partially supported by CNPq grant 432198/2018-0 and also by INES (www.ines.org.br), CNPq grant 465614/2014-0, CAPES grant 88887.136410/2017-00, and FACEPE grants APQ-0399-1.03/17.

Disclosure of Interests. The authors have no competing interests to declare that are relevant to the content of this article.

References

1. André, E., Liu, S., Liu, Y., Choppy, C., Sun, J., Dong, J.S.: Formalizing UML state machines for automated verification - a survey. ACM Comput. Surv. **55**(13s) (2023). https://doi.org/10.1145/3579821
2. Bertot, Y., Casteran, P.: Interactive Theorem Proving and Program Development. Springer, Heidelberg (2004). https://doi.org/10.1007/978-3-662-07964-5
3. Booch, G., Rumbaugh, J., Jacobson, I.: The Unified Modeling Language User Guide. Addison-Wesley, Reading (1999)
4. Calvino., A., Apvrille., L.: Direct model-checking of SysML models. In: Proceedings of the 9th International Conference on Model-Driven Engineering and Software Development - MODELSWARD, pp. 216–223. INSTICC, SciTePress (2021). https://doi.org/10.5220/0010256302160223
5. Carvalho, G., Barros, F., Carvalho, A., Cavalcanti, A., Mota, A., Sampaio, A.: NAT2TEST tool: from natural language requirements to test cases based on CSP. In: Calinescu, R., Rumpe, B. (eds.) SEFM 2015. LNCS, vol. 9276, pp. 283–290. Springer, Cham (2015). https://doi.org/10.1007/978-3-319-22969-0_20
6. Carvalho, G., Cavalcanti, A., Sampaio, A.: Modelling timed reactive systems from natural-language requirements. Form. Asp. Comput. **28**(5), 725–765 (2016). https://doi.org/10.1007/s00165-016-0387-x
7. Carvalho, G., Dihego, J., Sampaio, A.: Artefact associated with this paper: "an integrated framework for analysing, simulating and testing UML models" (2024). https://zenodo.org/doi/10.5281/zenodo.13323735
8. Carvalho, G., Meira, I.: Validating, verifying and testing timed data-flow reactive systems in Coq from controlled natural-language requirements. Sci. Comput. Program. **201**, 102537 (2021). https://doi.org/10.1016/j.scico.2020.102537, https://www.sciencedirect.com/science/article/pii/S0167642320301453
9. Carvalho, G., Sampaio, A., Mota, A.: A CSP timed input-output relation and a strategy for mechanised conformance verification. In: Groves, L., Sun, J. (eds.) ICFEM 2013. LNCS, vol. 8144, pp. 148–164. Springer, Heidelberg (2013). https://doi.org/10.1007/978-3-642-41202-8_11
10. Change Vision, Inc.: Astah UML User's Guide (nd). https://astah.net/support/astah-uml/. Accessed 25 June 2024
11. Chen, Z., Liu, Z., Ravn, A.P., Stolz, V., Zhan, N.: Refinement and verification in component-based model-driven design. Sci. Comput. Program. **74**(4), 168–196 (2009). https://doi.org/10.1016/j.scico.2008.08.003, https://www.sciencedirect.com/science/article/pii/S0167642308000890. Special Issue on the Grand Challenge
12. Cicchetti, A., et sl.: CHESS: a model-driven engineering tool environment for aiding the development of complex industrial systems. In: 2012 Proceedings of the 27th IEEE/ACM International Conference on Automated Software Engineering, pp. 362–365 (2012). https://doi.org/10.1145/2351676.2351748
13. Ciccozzi, F., Malavolta, I., Selic, B.: Execution of UML models: a systematic review of research and practice. Softw. Syst. Model. **18**(3), 2313–2360 (2019). https://doi.org/10.1007/s10270-018-0675-4
14. de Moura, L., Bjørner, N.: Z3: an efficient SMT solver. In: Ramakrishnan, C.R., Rehof, J. (eds.) TACAS 2008. LNCS, vol. 4963, pp. 337–340. Springer, Heidelberg (2008). https://doi.org/10.1007/978-3-540-78800-3_24
15. Dijkstra, E.W.: Solution of a problem in concurrent programming control. Commun. ACM **8**, 569 (1965). https://doi.org/10.1145/365559.365617

16. Elekes, M., Molnár, V., Micskei, Z.: To do or not to do: semantics and patterns for do activities in UML PSSM state machines. IEEE Trans. Softw. Eng. **50**(8), 2124–2141 (2024). https://doi.org/10.1109/TSE.2024.3422845
17. Falcão, F., Lima, L., Sampaio, A., Antonino, P.: A formal component model for UML based on CSP aiming at compositional verification. Softw. Syst. Model. **23**(3), 765–798 (2024). https://doi.org/10.1007/S10270-023-01127-Z
18. Graics, B., Molnár, V., Vörös, A., Majzik, I., Varró, D.: Mixed-semantics composition of statecharts for the component-based design of reactive systems. Softw. Syst. Model. **19**(6), 1483–1517 (2020). https://doi.org/10.1007/s10270-020-00806-5
19. Graics, B., Mondok, M., Molnár, V., Majzik, I.: Model-based testing of asynchronously communicating distributed controllers. In: Cámara, J., Jongmans, S.S. (eds.) FACS 2023. LNCS, vol. 14485, pp. 23–44. Springer, Heidelberg (2024). https://doi.org/10.1007/978-3-031-52183-6_2
20. Hoare, C.: Communicating Sequential Processes. Prentice-Hall International (1985)
21. Horváth, B., et al.: Pragmatic verification and validation of industrial executable SysML models. Syst. Eng. **26**(6), 693–714 (2023). https://doi.org/10.1002/sys.21679, https://incose.onlinelibrary.wiley.com/doi/abs/10.1002/sys.21679
22. Lampropoulos, L., Pierce, B.C.: QuickChick: Property-Based Testing in Coq, Software Foundations, vol. 4. Electronic textbook (2023). http://softwarefoundations.cis.upenn.edu. Version 1.3.2
23. Lima, L., et al.: An integrated semantics for reasoning about SysML design models using refinement. Softw. Syst. Model. **16**(3), 875–902 (2017). https://doi.org/10.1007/s10270-015-0492-y
24. Malavolta, I., Lago, P., Muccini, H., Pelliccione, P., Tang, A.: What industry needs from architectural languages: a survey. IEEE Trans. Softw. Eng. **39**(6), 869–891 (2013)
25. Molnár, V., Graics, B., Vörös, A., Majzik, I., Varró, D.: The gamma statechart composition framework: Design, verification and code generation for component-based reactive systems. In: Proceedings of the 40th International Conference on Software Engineering: Companion Proceeedings, ICSE 2018, pp. 113–116. Association for Computing Machinery, New York (2018). https://doi.org/10.1145/3183440.3183489
26. Object Management Group (OMG): UML Resource Page. https://www.omg.org/spec/UML/. Accessed 12 June 2024
27. Object Management Group (OMG): Semantics of a Foundational Subset for Executable UML Models, Version 1.3. OMG Document Number formal/17-07-02 (2017). https://www.omg.org/spec/FUML/1.3/
28. Object Management Group (OMG): Precise Semantics of UML Composite Structures, Specification v1.2. OMG Document Number: formal/19-05-01 (2019). https://www.omg.org/spec/PSCS/1.2/
29. Object Management Group (OMG): Precise Semantics of UML State Machines, Specification v1.0. OMG Document Number: formal/19-05-01 (2019). https://www.omg.org/spec/PSSM/1.0/
30. Roscoe, A.: The Theory and Practice of Concurrency. Prentice Hall (1997)
31. Rumbaugh, J., Jacobson, I., Booch, G.: The Unified Modeling Language Reference Manual. Pearson Higher Education (2004)

Formal Verification and Proof Techniques in Algorithms and Logics

Brzozowski's Algorithm for Automata Minimization Verified in Coq

Filipe Ramos[1], Karina Girardi Roggia[1]($\boxtimes$), and Rafael Castro G. Silva[2]

[1] State University of Santa Catarina, Joinville, Brazil
karina.roggia@udesc.br
[2] University of Copenhagen, Copenhagen, Denmark
rasi@di.ku.dk

Abstract. Deterministic finite automata are abstract machines that play a vital role in computer science and control engineering, aiding in the development of compilers, search algorithms, modeling of discrete event systems and more. With the aim of optimizing computational resources, minimization algorithms have been developed to eliminate unreachable and indistinguishable states in these automata. Brzozowski's algorithm is one such method which involves reversing and determinizing the automaton twice. Despite its apparent simplicity, proving the correctness of this minimization method requires various inductive strategies. For this purpose, the Coq proof assistant was employed to streamline the proof and provide a means of verification for the algorithm. In addition to the related demonstrations, this paper contributes with a straightforward representation of automata in functional programming languages. This approach uses only lists and types with decidable equality, so that common data structures can be utilized to represent finite automata. It also offers an accessible explanation for the reasoning process.

Keywords: Brzozowski's algorithm · finite automata · Coq

1 Introduction

Finite automata are a fundamental concept that represents abstract machines with a finite number of states that process strings of symbols. These automata transition from one state to another based on the input symbols, enabling them to recognize specific patterns within the strings they process. A non-deterministic finite automaton (NFA) allows state transitions to be non-deterministic, meaning one state can transition to multiple other states with a same input symbol. On the other hand, a deterministic finite automaton (DFA) is a specific type of NFA where each state has at most one transition for every possible input symbol. This determinism ensures that the automaton's behavior is entirely predictable and repeatable, making DFAs a powerful tool for various applications in theoretical computer science and practical programming tasks.

As the set of strings recognized by finite automata, regular languages play a crucial role in computer science and control engineering. They provide a foundation for designing compilers, constructing search algorithms, modeling discrete event systems, diagnosing unobservable events of the latter systems, among other applications [5,7]. The efficiency of these applications often depends on the simplicity of the finite automata that recognize the targeted regular languages.

Minimizing a DFA involves reducing the number of states to the smallest possible while preserving the language it recognizes. This process has the advantages of optimizing computational resources—namely space reduction for representation within data structures—and simplifying the state arrangement to make the automaton easier to understand, while keeping the language semantics.

Many courses in Automata Theory follow Hopcroft's text book [7] which includes an automaton minimization procedure using a table-filling algorithm to compute equivalent states. In contrast, Brzozowski's algorithm works by reversing the automaton's transitions, swapping the start states with the final (accepting) ones, converting the resultant automaton back into a DFA, and then repeating these steps once. For a beginner student, Brzozowski's algorithm is probably easier to execute as it does not involve computing equivalent states. However, the lack of intuition behind Brzozowski's algorithm makes its correctness less obvious. This motivated the undergraduate final project of Ramos [11], and later the development of this work.

Proofs of theorems about finite automata, including the correctness of minimization algorithms like Brzozowski's, may be challenging. The abstract nature of these models often necessitates deep intuition and rigorous formalization, making manual methods for verification difficult to employ effectively. In fact, notwithstanding its plainness, the correctness of Brzozowski's algorithm is not immediately apparent, which makes it an ideal candidate for further exploration through formal verification techniques.

This is where Coq, a proof assistant, becomes invaluable. Proof assistants are software tools that streamline the creation and validation of mathematical proofs by automating tedious verification tasks and offering intuitive interfaces to accelerate the writing process. Coq is a popular option of proof assistant, having its foundations in the calculus of (co)inductive constructions [2], a higher order lambda calculus with (co)inductive definitions, such as (co)recursive functions and relations. Coq's advantages include a broad user community, the ability to automate simpler proofs or parts of more complex proofs and a set of tactics that break down the proof process into more manageable steps.

The use of Coq not only ensures the rigor and accuracy of our demonstrations but also validates the practical benefits of computer-assisted theorem proving in handling complex theoretical challenges. We utilized its version 8.18.0 and all code can be found at https://github.com/fil1pe/brzozowski-algorithm. Our key contribution is the Coq proof of the correctness of Brzozowski's algorithm, which includes the following lemmas:

- reversal produces an automaton that accepts the strings reversed from the source language;

- after reversal and determinization, the paths of the new automaton connect set states that have original states connected by reverse paths;
- the minimized automaton is deterministic;
- the language of the minimized DFA is the same as that of the input automaton;
- all constructed states are reachable and distinguishable.

The structure of this work is the following: the next section is a non-exhaustive collection of related work, focusing on the mechanical formalization of finite automata minimization algorithms; Sect. 3 introduces basic automata definitions in Coq used in this work; Sect. 4 explains Brzozowski's minimization algorithm and formalizes it in Coq; Sect. 5 proves the correctness of the algorithm; the last section overviews this work and suggests future steps.

2 Related Work

Several significant contributions have been made in the area of formal verification of automata and regular languages. However, as far as we know this is the first Coq verification of Brzozowski's algorithm.

In the work by Doczkal et al. [6], the authors present a constructive theory of regular languages in Coq, where they prove some theorems and lemmas about finite automata. These include the pumping lemma and the correctness of DFA minimization through table-filling algorithm. Deterministic and non-deterministic finite automata are defined using two different datatypes, the former has a function to represent state transitions, and the latter uses a relation. In contrast, our development uses a single datatype to represent non-deterministic finite automata, and a predicate that specifies when an automaton is deterministic. The use of a single datatype showed to be an advantage in our development because we avoided type conversions in our proofs. The authors relied on the Mathematical Components' libraries, which supply finite type construction.

The work done by Athalye [1] focuses on input-output automata (IO automata). These automata, whose transitions are associated with actions, are used to model components of distributed systems, serving as mathematical formalisms to ensure the correctness of distributed algorithms and protocols. The work implements a framework for verification of properties about the design of distributed systems. As highlighted by the author, combinatorial explosion results from model checking, making this technique impractical for verifying real systems, which is why deduction verification in Coq is an efficient alternative.

Braibant et al. [4] proposes a Coq tactic for solving equations of regular expressions in Kleene algebras. The algorithm developed for the reflexive tactic decides if two given regular expressions are equal by applying consecutive transformations over them. First, they are normalized in order to build, for each, a non-deterministic finite automaton with epsilon transitions that recognizes its language. Then, the epsilon transitions are removed, and each automaton is determinized with the aim of checking the equivalence by coinduction. The states and symbols in this implementation are assumed to be numbers, and the transition function is represented by a matrix. The implemented determinization uses a depth-first enumeration algorithm optimized for large automata.

The pen-and-paper proof of the correctness of Brzozowski's algorithm [3] uses universal algebra and coalgebra to model reachability and observability respectively. A deterministic finite automaton is reachable if all states are reachable from the start state and is observable if the states recognize different languages. The authors apply category theory to prove that these concepts are dual and to derive the correctness of Brzozowski's algorithm as a corollary from this duality. They extend the applicability of the algorithm to deterministic Moore machines and generalize it to automata with infinitely many states. Although this work is related, the proof techniques they employed differ significantly from those in the present study, which seeks methods more familiar to computer science students. Nonetheless, we benefit from their observation that a DFA is minimal if it is observable—in other words, if all states are distinguishable.

Paulson [9] formalizes hereditarily finite sets in Isabelle/HOL, and defines finite automata as a case study of it. These sets are shown as a way to work around HOL's limited type system that does not allow machines to polymorphic on the type of states. In our development in Coq, to quantify over types of states is not a challenge. His work includes proofs of the Myhill-Nerode theorem and the correctness of Brzozowski's minimization algorithm. Paulson implements a method to reverse a DFA and another to determinize the resulting automaton through the powerset construction. Brzozowski's algorithm is built over these two constructions and proved correct by the demonstration that it yields a DFA with only reachable states and no pair of indistinguishable states.

Although the above contributions have inspired various aspects of this work, our approach differs in the representation of finite automata. Unlike other representations, we define finite automata as lists, which allows for a more straightforward induction over the automaton term. This choice simplifies the inductive hypotheses, making them more manageable. It also leads to predicates that are easier to understand and reason about. By leveraging this list-based structure, our formalization enhances the clarity and efficiency of the proofs.

The novelty of this work also lies in our use of the Coq proof assistant. We present a formalization of Brzozowski's algorithm within Coq, showcasing the tactics and tools it offers that distinguish it from other proof assistants. This formalization not only provides a rigorous proof of the algorithm but also demonstrates the effectiveness of Coq's features for automata theory. We hope that this project inspires others to explore and produce research related to automata theory by adopting the methodology proposed in this study.

3 Formalization in Coq

We start from the standard definition of a NFA as the tuple

$$\langle Q, \Sigma, \delta, I, F \rangle \tag{1}$$

where Q is the finite set of states, Σ is the finite set of symbols (alphabet), $I \subseteq Q$ is the set of start states, $F \subseteq Q$ is the set of final (accepting) states, and $\delta: Q \times \Sigma \to 2^Q$ is the transition function. The alphabet is the set of symbols that can compose the strings to be read by the automaton. By definition, a finite automaton has exactly one start state [7]. For simplicity, let us consider the possibility of having more start states or none at all. Since all start states can be collapsed into one—keeping all their in and out-transitions—, or a disconnected state be constructed when none exists, there will always be an equivalent automaton with exactly one start state.

In this work, we choose to represent automata using lists instead of other data structures due to several advantages. The Coq library offers an extensive collection of propositions, lemmas and functions specifically designed for lists. This allows us to leverage existing tools without requiring any extensions. Additionally, using lists facilitates the application of induction directly on the automaton, simplifying the proof process by reducing the need to manage complex predicates. This approach not only accelerates the development of proofs about finite automata but also ensures that the underlying concepts remain intuitive and straightforward to reason about. Thus, lists provide a natural and efficient framework for this formalization. Other approaches were explored for this work—such as wrapping the automaton components in Coq's record types—but none facilitated the induction proof processes as effectively as using a single list. We formalize NFAs as lists of the non-recursive type NFA_comp:

```
Context {State Symbol : Type}.

Variant NFA_comp := state (q:State) | symbol (a:Symbol) |
  start (q:State) | accept (q:State) |
  transition (q1:State) (a:Symbol) (q2:State).

Variable Element : Type.
Definition ListSet := list Element.

Definition NFA := ListSet NFA_comp.
```

The type constructors represent, respectively, intermediate states, input symbols, start states, accepting states, and transitions between states. This approach effectively combines all elements of the tuple (1) into a finite list. The automaton in Fig. 1 can be represented as [symbol 0; symbol 1; start 0; state 1; accept 2; transition 0 1 1; transition 1 0 2; transition 2 0 2] or [start 0; accept 2; transition 0 1 1; transition 1 0 2; transition 2 0 2]. The existence of multiple representations for an NFA ensures the well-formedness of this formalization. Notably, there are numerous alternative list representations for this particular automaton; however, in the context of this formalization, the syntactic distinction of different automata is irrelevant since our correctness proofs focus on whether they recognize the same language.

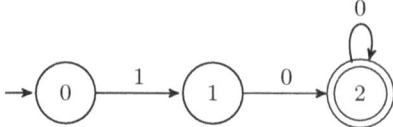

Fig. 1. State diagram for a simple finite automaton.

Our implementation of δ is the following function `transitionf`, which takes an automaton g, a list of states s, a symbol a, and returns all the states resulting from the transition from $q \in Q$ reading a:

```
Fixpoint transitionf (g:NFA) s a := match g with
 | transition q1 b q2::g => (if In_dec State_eq_dec q1 s
   then if Symbol_eq_dec b a then [q2] else nil
   else nil) ++ transitionf g s a
 | _::g => transitionf g s a
 | nil => nil
 end.
```

The above `match` command is applied for pattern matching over constructors. Moreover, `In_dec` is a decision procedure that tests whether a term is in a given list, and `State_eq_dec` and `Symbol_eq_dec` are the equality deciders of the types of states and symbols respectively. For convenience in some lemmas and definitions, we use a list of states as the second argument instead of a single state. The function `ext_transitionf` is the extended transition function that applies the transition function recursively throughout a string of symbols:

```
Fixpoint ext_transitionf (g:NFA) s w := match w with
 | a::w => ext_transitionf g (transitionf g s a) w
 | nil => s
 end.
```

We represent the transitions of a NFA as a function rather than an inductive predicate, primarily because this is how we perform computations over the automata. To compute the automaton's response to a given input, we defined a function that applies the transition function recursively: the extended transition function. From another perspective, while this functional approach is well-suited for direct computations, there are scenarios where reasoning about paths within the automaton is more intuitive using inductive predicates. For this reason, throughout this paper, we also employ different inductive types in some propositions, depending on the specific nature of the proof at hand. This dual approach allows us to adapt to the most effective method for each case.

We formalize DFAs as the following predicates about NFAs:

```
Variable nfa : @NFA State Symbol.

Definition start_singleton := ∃ q, In q (start_sts nfa) ∧
∀ q1 q2, In q1 (start_sts nfa) → In q2 (start_sts nfa) → q1 = q2.

Definition transitionf_det := ∀ q a q1 q2,
let s := transitionf [q] a in In q1 s → In q2 s → q1 = q2.

Definition is_dfa := start_singleton ∧ transitionf_det.
```

where, it should be noted, the syntax sign @ serves to deactivate implicit arguments. Here, `start_sts` computes all the start states from the given NFA. We limit the start states to be exactly one. Furthermore, the transition function `transitionf`, when applied to any single state, results in a list containing at most one distinct state. This means that a DFA can have a start state list with more than one element, provided all elements in this list are equal.

4 Brzozowski's Algorithm

As introduced earlier, Brzozowski's algorithm minimizes a DFA in two stages. The first stage involves reversing the transitions and swapping the set of start states with the set of final states, followed by converting the resulting possibly non-deterministic automaton into a DFA. The second stage repeats these steps with the resulting automaton. Notably, if the first stage results in a minimal DFA, then the entire algorithm will also yield a minimal DFA.

Besides proving the resulting automaton is minimal, it is also necessary to prove that the language recognized by the original automaton is preserved in the minimized DFA. The goal of this work is to demonstrate that all the states resulting from the first stage of Brzozowski's algorithm are distinguishable and that, after applying the reversal and determinization again, the original language remains intact. Besides, we must ensure the constructed automaton is deterministic.

The algorithm's implementation in Coq divides the steps of reversal and determinization, further subdividing the latter due to its complexity. Initially, any given finite automaton g is reversed to obtain g^R, altering the components of g as follows:

1. `start q1` becomes `accept q1`;
2. `accept q2` becomes `start q2`;
3. `transition q3 a q4` becomes `transition q4 a q3`.

When we apply this transformation to the DFA in Fig. 1, we obtain the non-deterministic finite automaton in Fig. 2. Following this, the determinization of any NFA g' is performed in four steps. Given I, the list of start states of g', a new automaton g'' is generated in the first step. This step prepends the start

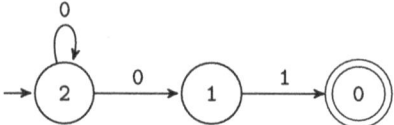

Fig. 2. The automaton from Fig. 1 reversed.

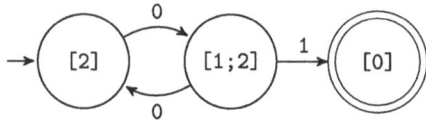

Fig. 3. The automaton from Fig. 2 determinized.

state `start I` to the transitions `transition Q a` (`transitionf g' Q a`) for every symbol `a` in the alphabet of `g'` and every state `Q` in the powerset of the states of `g'`.

The second step is list normalization. Lists differ from mathematical sets in that the order and repetition of elements matter. We can call lists with the same elements equivalent and replace all equivalent lists so that they all become equal. For instance, [1; 2; 3] and [3; 3; 1; 2] both represent the set $\{1, 2, 3\}$. Normalization, as we can denote this step of the algorithm, ensures that such lists are treated as equal. It shall be applied to all states of `g''`, as they represent sets of states from the original automaton `g'`. For every state `Q` in `g''`, the algorithm searches for the first equivalent list in the automaton and replaces it with that list.

The third step appends the accepting states to `g''`—they are obtained by the search of states that contain accepting states from `g'`. Finally, in the forth step, the unreachable states must be removed, given that it is useless to keep them. A state is unreachable when no possible input string leads to it. They are figured using a decision procedure that tests each state `Q` to see if there exists a path of length n from the start state `I` to `Q`, where n is the length of the list of states in `g''`. This involves recursively testing all transitions up to a depth of n.

Figure 3 shows the automaton in Fig. 2 converted into deterministic after going through the steps above. The sink state `[]` has been removed from this representation, although it is generated by the algorithm. We call `det` this sequence of four steps.

5 Proof of Brzozowski's Algorithm

In order to prove the correctness of Brzozowski's algorithm, we need to show that the generated automaton is a DFA, minimal and equivalent to the original automaton in recognizing the same language. A DFA is minimal if all its states are reachable and distinguishable [3,9]. Assuming the state and symbol types of the automaton have decidable equality, we can compare states and symbols during the transformations and proofs that follow.

To demonstrate that the language of the automaton remains unchanged after the transformations, we need to prove the reversed automaton g' recognizes the reverse language of the original automaton g:

$$L(g') = \{w^R | w \in L(g)\}$$

Refer to lemma `rev_language` in the code repository.

Furthermore, we must prove that the language is preserved in g", the automaton obtained after the determinization of g'. By applying the reversal and determinization again, the minimized automaton g_{min} will evidently recognize the same language as g, since

$$L(g_{min}) = \{(w^R)^R | w \in L(g)\}$$

where $(w^R)^R$ is equal to w by inductive proof in lemma `rev_twice`. For further details, please refer to theorem `same_language` in the code repository.

The proof of the language of the reversed automaton uses the following inductive predicate **path** to represent sequences of successive transitions:

```
Inductive path (g:NFA) : State → State → Word → Prop :=
  | path_nil q : path g q q nil
  | path_trans q1 q2 q3 a w : In (transition q1 a q2) g →
    path g q2 q3 w → path g q1 q3 (a::w).
```

This definition is useful for other proofs in this work and allows us to infer properties about the paths of finite automata using induction. From this definition, we obtain the following essential property:

$$\text{path g q1 q2 w} \Leftrightarrow \text{path g' q2 q1 } w^R$$

Therefore, if q1 and q2 are any start and final states of g respectively, the relation between q1 and q2 will be reversed in g', showing that w is accepted by g if and only if w^R is accepted by g'.

So as to ensure the reverse language is maintained in the DFA g", we also use induction on the paths of the automaton to prove the next two lemmas referred to as `det_exists_ext_transitionf1` and `det_exists_ext_transitionf2`, which are later used in the correctness of Brzozowski's algorithm.

Lemma 1. *For any state Q of g", any list $s \subseteq Q$ and any state q of g':*

$$q \in ext\_transitionf \ g' \ s \ w \Rightarrow$$
$$\exists Q', Q' \in ext\_transitionf \ g'' \ [Q] \ w \wedge q \in Q'$$

Proof. There exists some $q_0 \in s \subseteq Q$ such that path g' q_0 q w. For any path g' q_0 q_1 [a], we know that path g" Q Q_1 [a] is also true for some state $Q_1 \ni q_1$ of g". Then, inductively on w = a::w', we obtain path g" Q Q' (a::w') for some Q' ∋ q. Given the correspondence between `ext_transitionf` and `path`:

$$Q' \in \text{ext\_transitionf g'' [Q] w}$$

Lemma 2. *Similarly, for any states Q and Q' of g'' and any state $q \in Q'$ of g':*

$Q' \in ext\_transitionf\ g''\ [Q]\ w \Rightarrow$
$$\exists q', q \in ext\_transitionf\ g'\ [q']\ w \wedge q' \in Q$$

Proof. The proof is analogous to proof of Lemma 1.

Thus, we can easily demonstrate that the language of g'' is the same as g', since applying the lemmas above yields, for every state Q' of g'',

$Q' \in \text{ext\_transitionf g'' (start\_sts g'') w} \Leftrightarrow$
$$q \in \text{ext\_transitionf g' (start\_sts g') w}$$

where q is some state of g' in Q'.

The proof that the final automaton is deterministic follows from the definition of the construction function. It essentially involves showing that only one start state is generated at the beginning of the construction and that all transitions are deterministic, as

$$\text{transitionf g'' [Q1] a} = \text{[Q2; ...; Q2]}$$

where Q1 is any state of g'' and Q2 denotes a state as a normalized list representing the set of states listed by `transitionf g Q1 a`. It should be noted that Q2 might be empty (`[]`). Hence, in the new automaton, starting from a state Q1, we reach exactly one distinct state Q2 on reading any symbol a, as required for theorem `brzozowski_is_dfa`.

Demonstrating the correctness of Brzozowski's algorithm requires that all states resulting from the determinization are reachable (`all_reachable`). For this purpose, a new path definition `path'` was developed. This new definition encompasses the states traversed by the path and is equivalent to `path`, as proved by induction in Coq. Thus, as one can refer to lemma `path'_correct`,

$$\text{path g'' q1 q2 w} \Leftrightarrow \text{path' g'' [q1; ...; q2] w}$$

for any states q1 and q2 and string w. In addition to this new definition, the well-known pumping lemma for regular languages was applied in the proof of lemma `reachable_state_dec` to show that we only need to descend to level n in the automaton's search to determine if a state is reachable—where n is the number of states in the automaton. The pumping lemma shows that any path taking more than n states has a loop, so no further search is necessary. The pumping lemma was proven through the pigeonhole principle from the Logical Foundations text book [10].

To prove that the minimized automaton is indeed minimal—i.e., all states are distinguishable—we show that, after reversal and determinization, we obtain a minimal DFA g''. Reapplying these two transformations will noticeably produce a minimum DFA as well.

Lemma 3. *For any states q of g and Q of g", if*

$$\exists q', q' \in \texttt{ext\_transitionf } g \ [q] \ w^R \wedge q' \in Q \tag{2}$$

then, there exists Q' such that

$$Q' \in \texttt{ext\_transitionf } g" \ [Q] \ w \wedge q \in Q' \tag{3}$$

Starting from equation (3) for any Q', it is also true what is stated in (2).

Proof. These inferences are easily proven using Lemmas 1 and 2, and they were based on the answer from Jan [8] on the Stack Exchange website. They are referred to as `basic_observation1` and `basic_observation2` in the code repository.

Theorem 1. *Any indistinguishable states Q_1 and Q_2 of g" are equal.*

Proof. The states Q_1 and Q_2 are said to be indistinguishable if, for every string w, w reaches a final state of g" from Q_1 if and only if the same occurs from Q_2. We know that the final states of g" are those containing a start state of g. Hence, using the observation from Lemma 3, we obtain

$$\exists q'_1, q'_1 \in \texttt{ext\_transitionf } g \ [q0_1] \ w^R \wedge q'_1 \in Q_1 \Leftrightarrow$$
$$\exists q'_2, q'_2 \in \texttt{ext\_transitionf } g \ [q0_2] \ w^R \wedge q'_2 \in Q_2$$

where $q0_i$ is a start state of g reached from Q_i by w (for $i = 1, 2$). Assuming g is deterministic, we get

$$q0_1 = q0_2$$

and, consequently,

$$q'_1 = q'_2$$

Therefore, we conclude that every reachable state of g belongs to Q_1 if and only if it belongs to Q_2. Assuming g only has reachable states, then Q_1 and Q_2 represent the same set. Since we normalized the lists,

$$Q_1 = Q_2$$

as we wanted to show for theorem `all_distinguishable`.

The above proof relies on two assumptions about the reversed and determinized automaton. However, these assumptions are not necessary when we apply the entire algorithm in this way:

$$\texttt{det}(\texttt{det } g^R)^R$$

since `det` g^R is, as we have already demonstrated, a deterministic finite automaton without unreachable states.

This section summarized the reasoning used in Coq to demonstrate the correctness of Brzozowski's algorithm. By ensuring the full transformation preserves the language and that the resulting automaton is deterministic and minimal, we validated the effectiveness of the algorithm in producing a minimal DFA equivalent to the original.

6 Conclusion

We have successfully proved the correctness of Brzozowski's algorithm using definitions and lemmas from the standard Coq library, along with those we developed without installing extensions to the assistant. The entire formalization has approximately 2400 lines of proofs, and 580 lines of specifications. Additionally, we generalized the types for states and symbols to types with decidable equality. The primary goal of this work was to demonstrate that the automaton generated by the algorithm is deterministic, equivalent to the original automaton and minimal—having only reachable and distinguishable states. We have shown that the algorithm is effective not only for deterministic finite automata but also for non-deterministic ones, even if they have multiple start states or none at all.

Although some aspects of the formalization in this work were inspired by paper proofs, the present proof of Brzozowski's algorithm was entirely developed within Coq's formal language. This transition to Coq's environment provided a level of precision and rigor in the proof process that was initially challenging to achieve on paper. Coq also made it possible to develop a simpler proof of the correctness of the algorithm. The tools and tactics offered by Coq allowed us to construct detailed induction proofs with greater ease and reliability, guiding the process through its well-defined syntax and step-by-step procedures. This capability not only made complex proofs more manageable but also highlighted the advantages of using Coq for formalizing automata theory, reinforcing its value as a tool for advancing developments in this field.

The approach used in this work involves concepts that are accessible to computer science students without requiring in-depth knowledge of relatively advanced mathematics, such as coalgebras. Along these lines, this work introduced a straightforward method for representing automata, particularly finite automata. This representation allows the computation of these automata using well-established data structures in programming, which facilitates further demonstrations in the Coq proof assistant.

Future work could explore other proofs concerning automata theory, leveraging the definition of an automaton as a list of components. Additionally, future research could focus on optimizing the determinization algorithm—to prevent state explosion—and proving its correctness. This optimization is necessary for the practical applicability of Brzozowski's algorithm in various computational contexts.

Acknowledgments. This work was partially supported by Fundação de Amparo à Pesquisa e Inovação do Estado de Santa Catarina - FAPESC.

References

1. Athalye, A.: CoqIOA: a Formalization of IO Automata in the Coq Proof Assistant. Ph.D. thesis, Massachusetts Institute of Technology (2017). https://dspace.mit.edu/handle/1721.1/112831

2. Bertot, Y., Castran, P.: Interactive Theorem Proving and Program Development: Coq'Art The Calculus of Inductive Constructions, 1st edn. Springer Publishing Company, Incorporated (2010)
3. Bonchi, F., Bonsangue, M.M., Rutten, J.J., Silva, A.: Brzozowski's algorithm (co) algebraically. In: Logic and Program Semantics, pp. 12–23. Springer (2012), https://link.springer.com/chapter/10.1007/978-3-642-29485-3_2
4. Braibant, T., Pous, D.: Deciding Kleene algebras in Coq. Logic. Methods Comput. Sci. **8**, (2012). https://lmcs.episciences.org/1043
5. Cassandras, C.G., Lafortune, S.: Introduction to Discrete Event Systems, 2nd edn. Springer Science+Business Media, New York (2008)
6. Doczkal, C., Kaiser, J.O., Smolka, G.: A constructive theory of regular languages in Coq. In: International Conference on Certified Programs and Proofs. pp. 82–97. Springer (2013). https://link.springer.com/chapter/10.1007/978-3-319-03545-1_6
7. Hopcroft, J.E., Motwani, R., Ullman, J.D.: Introduction to Automata Theory, Languages, and Computation, 3rd edn. Pearson/Addison Wesley, Boston (2006)
8. Jan, H.: Proof of Brzozowski's Algorithm for DFA Minimization (2019). https://cs.stackexchange.com/questions/105574/proof-of-brzozowskis-algorithm-for-dfa-minimization
9. Paulson, L.C.: A formalisation of finite automata using hereditarily finite sets. In: International Conference on Automated Deduction, pp. 231–245. Springer (2015). https://link.springer.com/chapter/10.1007/978-3-319-21401-6_15
10. Pierce, B.C., et al.: Logical Foundations, vol. 1, 6.6 edn. UPenn CIS, Pennsylvania (2024)
11. Ramos, F.: Prova da minimização de autômatos finitos determinísticos pelo algoritmo de brzozowski assistida por computador (2021). https://pergamumweb.udesc.br/acervo/152736. supervisors: Karina Girardi Roggia, Rafael Castro G. Silva

Soundness-Preserving Fusion of Modal Logics in Coq

Miguel Alfredo Nunes[1](✉)[iD], Karina Girardi Roggia[2][iD], and Paulo Henrique Torrens[3][iD]

[1] Instituto de Filosofia e Ciências Humanas, Universidade Estadual de Campinas (Unicamp), Campinas, SP, Brazil
miguel.alfredo.nunes@gmail.com
[2] Departamento de Ciência da Computação, Universidade do Estado de Santa Catarina (UDESC), Joinville, Santa Catarina, Brazil
karina.roggia@udesc.br
[3] University of Kent, Kent, UK
paulotorrens@gnu.org

Abstract. This work presents the formal verification of the concept of fusion of modal logics in the Coq proof assistant, along with a proof of the preservation of soundness. Our formalization is based on previous work by da Silveira et al. that formalizes several normal modal systems using Coq and proves their soundness and weak completeness. We give a high level description of the base library, how we modified it to fit our needs, how we defined fusion and how we proved the transfer of soundness. Our definition allows for the fusion of any normal modal logics, with any amount of modalities, requiring no changes to the definitions in the library.

Keywords: Coq Proof Assistant · Modal Logic · Combining Logics

1 Introduction

Modal logics, and modal languages in general, are powerful and well established tools; their applications are far reaching: philosophers, mathematicians and also computer scientists all make use of modal logics for various tasks [6]. Yet, modal logics with a single modal operator are still the most well known and most used kinds of modal logics, something that philosopher Dana Scott [31, pp. 161] was already dissatisfied by half a century ago:

"Here is what I consider one of the biggest mistakes of all in modal logic: concentration on a system with just *one* modal operator."

Indeed, modal logics with a single modal operator are far less expressive than modal logics with several modal operators. One may consider, for instance, epistemic logics with a single modal operator. A logic of this kind is capable of representing the knowledge of a single agent, however, it is not capable of much more than that. It cannot, for instance, represent the knowledge of multiple agents nor represent how their knowledge may interact. Beyond that, knowledge is something fluid, it changes over time; a logic system that intends to faithfully represent the knowledge of agents would, ideally, be able to represent this change. Going even further in this direction, real world agents don't exist in an isolated vacuum where everything stays the same all the time, they exist in an evolving world where changes happen and they may reason and hold beliefs about those evolutions and changes of the world; wouldn't a logical system that is capable of formalizing those concepts too be desirable?

Although this may be a simple and perhaps ambitious example, it represents the idea motivating the use of *multimodal logics* and, more broadly, the notion of combinations of logics. Multimodal logics are logics that have multiple distinct modal operators, each of which may represent completely different concepts, such as, e.g., knowledge and time, and their interaction represents how these concepts interact, say, how knowledge evolves over time. To combine logics is, simply, to use some kind of method to obtain complex logic systems given simpler ones. We refer the reader to van Benthem in [34], who gives a similar account.

Indeed, combining logics is an easier way of obtaining multimodal logics when compared to defining them manually, as combining two logics with a single modality each will yield a logic with two modalities that has most (if not all) of the relevant properties of each base logic, whereas defining up a logic with two modalities from the ground not only requires considerable effort to define its basic components (such as language, semantics and syntax) but also to prove any relevant properties of said logic (such as soundness or completeness), things that might be derived from the combination.

Combining logics, still, is not such an easy task. It requires not only understanding of the logics being combined and also of the method, and all its technical details, being utilized. As such, one needs to take great care to be sure that they have not forgotten some important detail for a definition or an elusive step in a proof while using such combination methods. This suggests that proof assistants may be useful tools to use when attempting to combine logics, because if a combination procedure is properly detailed in a proof assistant, a logician who whishes to combine logics won't need to worry about forgetting any of these technical details that can be dealt with by the proof assistant, and will be able to focus on what they want to represent instead.

In order to investigate the use of proof assistants for combining modal logics, we present in this work an implementation of the method of fusion of modal logics in the Coq proof assistant. This method allows the combination of arbitrary normal modal logics, while also preserving their soundness, that is, if all logics being combined are sound, then so is the resulting combined logic [18]. Our work is based on the previous work on a library of modal logic in Coq which allows the definition of arbitrary modal logics [10], thus allowing us to represent the fusion of a large class of modal logics. The source code is publicly available online at https://github.com/funcao/LML under a permissive free software license.

1.1 Related Work

Proof assistants have been widely used to represent and reason with or about logics and their combinations, although the former is far more common than the latter. We found that the works which are most closely related to ours can roughly be divided in three main areas: proving metaproperties of modal logics in proof assistants and automated theorem provers; formalizing argumentation and reasoning with proof assistants and automated theorem provers, and formalizing the combination of logics in proof assistants.

Regarding the first area, we've found that the formalization of a proof of completeness for the modal logic S5 is the focus of the work of Bentzen [3], where the author models the Kripke semantics and axiomatic system of the logic through deep embedding[1] in the Lean proof assistant, focusing mostly on the completeness result (soundness is proven but details are omitted). Similarly, Maggesi and Brogi [26] prove, in the HOL-Light proof assistant, the soundness and completeness of modal logic GL (also known as Gödel-Löb logic or provability logic), modelling the syntax, as an axiomatic system, and the semantics, as Kripke semantics, of the logic through deep embedding.

Regarding the second area we've found that, with the goal of formalizing complex natural language arguments, Fuenmayor and Benzmüller [14] combine quantified dyadic deontic logic and the logic of indexicals in the Isabelle proof assistant, the logic systems are represented as shallow semantic embeddings with Kripke and neighborhood semantics and are used to model Chisholm's Paradox and Gewirth's Principle of Generic Consistency. Fuenmayor and Benzmüller [13] focus on utilizing Isabelle to reason about ethical arguments, in a similar way to the previous work, also utilizing shallow semantic embeddings, but combining alethic modal logics, dyad deontic logics and the logics of indexicals to represent and reason about ethical theories, specifically, to more accurately model the Principle of Generic Consistency and to make deductions of new formulas given this principle as a base theory. Lastly, we have the work of Benzmüller, Parent and van der Torre [5], in which the authors proposed a framework and a methodology for the design and engineering of normative systems and deontic logics for use in intelligent systems, in this framework ethical and legal theories are modelled as deontic logics combined with other, more complex logics depending on the context of the application, all of which are represented as shallow semantical embeddings in Isabelle and in the LEO-III automated theorem prover.

Lastly, regarding the third area, we've found that Benzmüller [4] proposes the combination of many different kinds of modal logics in simple type theory, representing the syntax of the logics as λ-terms and using this framework to reason with and about the combined logics, while also importing these representations into automated theorem provers and model checkers to verify that they are correct representations of the logics in question. The work of Rabe [30] has a more general goal, where it models logics, translations between logics and combinations of logics in a language for the representation of mathematical facts

---

[1] See [1] or Sect. 3 for a proper definition.

based on type theory know as M_{MT}, wherein logics are described both by means of category theory and type theory, combinations of logics are describe by categorial operations and some examples of combinations of logics are given, together with indications of implementations on proprietary provers. Finally, we have the work of Lescanne and Puisségur [23], which models, through deep embedding, dynamic logic of common knowledge in Coq, which is a combination of epistemic logic of common knowledge with dynamic logic, representing the logic syntactically as an axiomatic system and giving proofs in this representation of the muddy children puzzle.

It is worthy noting that, of all works analyzed, none attempted to tackle methods of combining logics per se, that is, the works analyzed present logics resulting from combination but did not attempt to combine them in the tools utilized nor did they attempt to show the preservation of properties, as such, to the best of the authors' knowledge, we believe our main result to be a novel approach as we aim at the fusion of arbitrary modal logic systems.

2 Core Concepts

2.1 The Coq Proof Assistant

The Coq proof assistant is a popular proof assistant, based on the Calculus of (co)Inductive Constructions (CIC) [32], which is a logical system based on intuitionistic type theory with type abstractions, dependent types, and that allows for primitive inductive and coinductive definitions. In Coq, proof verification amounts to type checking: propositions are types and proofs are λ-terms[2] (i.e., terms in the λ-calculus), so to verify a proof it is sufficient to check whether the λ-term of the proof has the same type as the proposition it is proving [29].

Coq is widely used for applications both in computer science, as a tool to verify software, and as a tool to formalize logical systems. As an example of its use to verify software we have the case of [22], where a C Compiler was developed and fully checked in Coq. As an example of its use to formalize logical systems we have the case of [28], where temporal logic was embedded in Coq.

An important aspect in this work is that the proofs being formalized, while not novel and already known to be true, are given in the literature through set theory. Some work is thus required to adapt those result to Coq's type theory, which we further elaborate on Sects. 3 and 4, but which are done in a standard way. For example, we use Coq's type of propositions to model set theoretical sets.

2.2 Modal and Multimodal Logics

Modal logic is a family of non-classical logics that deal with the concept of *modalities*: those are, according to [17], logical operators that qualify truths

---
[2] This relation between logical propositions and types in typed λ-calculi is known as the Curry-Howard correspondence.

about propositions. For example, modal logic allows us to state that a certain proposition *must* be true, that it *can* be true, that it *will always* be true, that it will *eventually* be true, amidst many others. The name "modal logic" may refer to a logic containing any positive number of modal operators, regardless of the relationship between them and their interpretations. Whenever necessary, the term "monomodal" will be used to refer to logics that have a single modality, "bimodal" will be used to refer to logics that have two distinct modalities, and "multimodal" will be used to refer to logics that have more than one modality[3] which are distinct among themselves.

According to [6], the study of modal logic as a mathematical discipline began with the works of Lewis [24,25]. In the former, the author created two modalities, the unary modality $\mathbf{I}$ meaning "it is impossible that" and the binary modality $\varphi \prec \psi$ meaning "φ strictly implies ψ", which is interpreted as $\mathbf{I}(\varphi \wedge \neg \psi)$, i.e. "it is impossible that φ is true and ψ is not true". In the latter work, the author further develops those ideas, replacing the modality $\mathbf{I}$ for the modality $\Diamond$, meaning "it is possible that", and redefining $\varphi \prec \psi$ to be $\neg \Diamond(\varphi \wedge \neg \psi)$. Additionally, five axiomatic systems where created, $\mathbf{S1} - \mathbf{S5}$, where $\mathbf{S1}$ is equivalent to the system of the first work and only $\mathbf{S4}$ and $\mathbf{S5}$ are normal modal logics that are still studied to this day. In this work, we will study in particular normal modal logic systems. A modal logic is said to be normal if it is closed under *modus ponens* and necessitation, and it has both K and Dual as axioms [9], all of which will be formally presented later.

The modern syntactical interpretation of modal logic is due to [16] and [27]. According to [15], both attempted to interpret intuitionistic logic by adding a new modal operator $\Box$ interpreted as "it is provable" in classical logic; in fact, Gödel recreated the system $\mathbf{S4}$ of Lewis in [16]. The modern semantics of modal logic, however, came many decades later with the works of Kripke [19,20]. His semantics, known nowadays as Possible Worlds semantics or Kripke semantics, gave a semantical interpretation of modal logic based on the concept of possible worlds and the relations between then, specifically, formulas with no modalities depend only on a "local" world, whereas formulas with modalities depend on the worlds that the local world is related to.

Multimodal logics do not have as clear a history as monomodal logics. E.g., according to [21], Aristotle and his commentators discussed arguments that could be interpreted as treating both time and necessity and, according to [7], the philosophers David Hume and Immanuel Kant presented problems that relied on distinct modes of thought. The likely first author to have considered multimodal logics with the same mathematical rigour as monomodal logics is M. Fitting in [12], who also presented an early form of the method of fusion of modal logics, which is the topic of this paper and will be discussed later.

---

[3] The use of different terms for logics with two modalities and logics with an arbitrary amount of modalities is somewhat traditional in the field of modal logic and, in many cases, is rather useful, as such the authors chose to make this distinction too, but it should be noted that it isn't necessary.

The language of modal logics is based on a countable set $\mathcal{P} = \{p_0, p_1, \ldots\}$ of propositional variables, together with a set $\mathcal{C} = \{\neg, \Box, \Diamond, \wedge, \vee, \rightarrow\}$ of connectives (respecting usual precedence), and the logical constants $\top$ and $\bot$, representing true and false respectively. As such, we have the grammar:

$$\varphi ::= p \mid \top \mid \bot \mid \neg\varphi \mid \Box\varphi \mid \Diamond\varphi \mid (\varphi_1 \wedge \varphi_2) \mid (\varphi_1 \vee \varphi_2) \mid (\varphi_1 \rightarrow \varphi_2)$$

In the above, $p \in \mathcal{P}$. For normal modal logics, the connectives $\Box$ and $\Diamond$ are dual and each instance $\Box\varphi$ (resp. $\Diamond\varphi$) may be replaced by $\neg\Diamond\neg\varphi$ (resp. $\neg\Box\neg\varphi$).

The semantics of modal logics treated here is defined as a Kripke semantics in the usual sense, where frames $\mathcal{F} = \langle \mathcal{W}, \mathcal{R} \rangle$ are defined as a 2-tuple of a set of worlds (which is possibly infinite) together with some accessibility relation between worlds, and models $\mathcal{M} = \langle \mathcal{F}, \mathcal{V} \rangle$ are defined as a 2-tuple of frames and a valuation function $\mathcal{V} : \mathcal{P} \rightarrow 2^{\mathcal{W}}$ (where $2^{\mathcal{W}}$ is the powerset of $\mathcal{W}$).

An usual formula satisfiability relation $\Vdash$, such as the ones defined in [6,9], is considered for our work. We will write $\mathcal{M}, w \Vdash \varphi$ if this relation holds (i.e., in model $\mathcal{M}$ and world w, the formula φ is satisfiable) and $\mathcal{M}, w \nVdash \varphi$ if it does not. We may also define a semantical entailment relation $\vDash$ in the usual manner, such as done by [6]: $\Gamma \vDash \varphi$ is defined if and only if $\forall \mathcal{M}, \Gamma \vDash_{\mathcal{M}} \varphi$. For this purpose, we first define entailment in a model $\Gamma \vDash_{\mathcal{M}} \varphi$ by considering only valuations in the specific model $\mathcal{M}$: $\forall w \in \mathcal{W}, (\forall \gamma \in \Gamma, \mathcal{M}, w \Vdash \gamma) \implies (\mathcal{M}, w \Vdash \varphi)$.

The syntactical entailment relation $\vdash$ for the modal logics treated here is defined as a Hilbert-style deductive system, with the usual rules for necessitation and *modus ponens*:

$$\frac{\vdash \varphi}{\Gamma \vdash \Box\varphi} \text{ Nec} \qquad \frac{\Gamma \vdash \varphi \rightarrow \psi \quad \Gamma \vdash \varphi}{\Gamma \vdash \psi} \text{ MP}$$

Along with those, we have the usual axioms of classical logic for the non-modal connectives of the language, such as the ones presented in [15]. For the modal connectives, we have the following axioms:

$$\Box(p_0 \rightarrow p_1) \rightarrow (\Box p_0 \rightarrow \Box p_1) \tag{K}$$

$$\Diamond p \leftrightarrow \neg\Box\neg p \tag{Dual}$$

Given these definitions, we can state then main metaproperties relevant to our work, those being soundness and completeness. A syntactical entailment relation is said to be sound with respect to a semantic entailment relation if, for any Γ and φ, Γ entails syntactically φ then Γ entails semantically φ, i.e. if φ is provable from Γ then φ is valid in any class of models where Γ is valid. Completeness is the inverse, i.e. if φ is valid in any class of models where Γ is valid then φ is provable from Γ. If $\Gamma = \emptyset$ then we have the weak soundness/completeness. We may represent this using the notation for the relations as:

$$\Gamma \vdash \varphi \underset{\text{Completeness}}{\overset{\text{Soundness}}{\rightleftarrows}} \Gamma \vDash \varphi$$

We proceed with the definitions for multimodal logics. They only require some simple extensions: the connectives $\Box$ and $\Diamond$ are each replaced by a list $\Box_1, \ldots, \Box_n$ and $\Diamond_1, \ldots, \Diamond_n$; frames are redefined to have multiple accessibility relations, where each relation is associated with a single modality; the rule of necessitation, the axioms K
and Dual are each replaced with n new instances, each one associated with a single modality. For simplification, we use natural numbers as indexes, but any countable set is applicable.

As such, we have the following grammar, where $i, n \in \mathbb{N}$ and $1 \leq i \leq n$:

$$\varphi ::= p \mid \top \mid \bot \mid \neg\varphi \mid \Box_i\varphi \mid \Diamond_i\varphi \mid (\varphi_1 \land \varphi_2) \mid (\varphi_1 \lor \varphi_2) \mid (\varphi_1 \to \varphi_2)$$

The frames have the form $\mathcal{F}_n = \langle \mathcal{W}, \mathcal{R}_1, \ldots, \mathcal{R}_n \rangle$ and models have the form $\mathcal{M}_n = \langle \mathcal{F}_n, \mathcal{V} \rangle$, satisfiability remains unchanged, except for the following two rules:

$$\mathcal{M}_n, w \Vdash \Box_i\varphi \text{ iff } \forall w' \in \mathcal{W}, (w\mathcal{R}_i w' \implies \mathcal{M}_n, w' \Vdash \varphi)$$
$$\mathcal{M}_n, w \Vdash \Diamond_i\varphi \text{ iff } \exists w' \in \mathcal{W}, (w\mathcal{R}_i w' \land \mathcal{M}_n, w' \Vdash \varphi)$$

The rule of necessitation is replaced by a generalized notion of necessitation:

$$\frac{\vdash \varphi}{\Gamma \vdash \Box_i\varphi} \text{ Nec}_i$$

And we have the following new axioms:

$$\Box_i(p_0 \to p_1) \to (\Box_i p_0 \to \Box_i p_1) \qquad (K_i)$$

$$\Diamond_i p \leftrightarrow \neg\Box_i\neg p \qquad (Dual_i)$$

2.3 Combining Logics

Combinations of logics is a relatively new topic in the field of modern logic [8]. It consists of methods to synthesize new logical systems from preexisting ones, whether through joining several distinct systems into a single one or through splitting a single system into several component systems [7].

The method of interest for this work is the method of fusion of modal logics, which, according to [15], is the simplest method to combine logics and, according to [8], was the first generic method to combine logics. Historically, the method and the name "fusion" were defined by [33], although [12] presented a similar method to combine some classes of logics.

According to [7], the fusion of modal logics is a binary operation defined on the class of modal logics semantically defined by Kripke semantics and syntactically defined by a Hilbert calculus. For two modal logics to be fused together, their languages must be defined over the same set $\mathcal{P}$ of propositional variables; they must each have a $\Box$ connective, a $\neg$ connective and a $\to$ connective defined in their respective languages; their deductive systems must each include an instance of the K axiom and the necessitation rule for their respective $\Box$ connectives, and their frames must all be defined over a fixed set $\mathbf{W}$ of worlds, i.e., they must be of the form $\mathcal{F} = \langle \mathbf{W}, \mathcal{R} \rangle$, with $\mathcal{R} \subseteq \mathbf{W} \times \mathbf{W}$.

If two logics $\mathcal{L}_1$ and $\mathcal{L}_2$ meet those requirements, they may be fused together into a new logic $\mathcal{L}_3$ that has two $\Box$ connectives, $\Box_1$ and $\Box_2$ respectively, two instances of the K axiom and the necessitation rule, one for each $\Box_i$, and all their frames will be of the form $\mathcal{F}_3 = \langle \mathcal{W}, \mathcal{R}_1, \mathcal{R}_2 \rangle$, where $\mathcal{R}_1$ is used to interpreted $\Box_1$ and $\mathcal{R}_2$ is used to interpret $\Box_2$. Simply put, the fusion of two monomodal logics will generate a bimodal logic. This definition may be generalized to an arbitrary number of modal logics in a straightforward way, something that [15] has show.

The fusion of modal logics, like many other methods of combining logics, preserves certain properties of the combined logics, that is, if any two (modal) logics $\mathcal{L}_1$ and $\mathcal{L}_2$ respect a certain property $\mathcal{P}$, then the logic $\mathcal{L}_3$ resulting from the fusion of $\mathcal{L}_1$ and $\mathcal{L}_2$ will also respect property $\mathcal{P}$ [18]. Some properties preserved by fusion are soundness, of particular interest for this work, but also completeness, finite model property, decidability and interpolation [15].

3 Modal and Multimodal Logics in Coq

To represent modal and multimodal logics in Coq, an earlier work [10] was utilized as a basis. In that work, the authors developed a modal logic library in Coq, in the style of a deep embedding, whose semantics was an implementation of Kripke semantics and syntax was an implementation of Hilbert calculus, with proofs of both soundness and weak completeness (i.e., completeness assuming that the context Γ is empty). We recall an embedding of a logic $\mathcal{L}_1$ inside another logic $\mathcal{L}_2$ is an encoding of the components of $\mathcal{L}_1$ in the language of $\mathcal{L}_2$, and it is separated into two kinds: *shallow* embeddings, which only encode the semantics and *deep* embedding which encodes both semantics and inference rules [1]. As such, the library defines $\Vdash$ by lifting the syntax of formulas into an equivalent type in Coq's type system.

This library allows for easy representation of modal formulas, due to the use of a custom notation, which allows the user to denote modal formulas in a rather intuitive way. For example, we may denote the formula $\Box p_0 \to (p_1 \wedge \Diamond p_2)$ as `[! []#0 -> (#1 / <> #2) !]`. Atoms are represented as natural numbers preceded by a hash symbol, and the use of delimiters `[!` and `!]` allows overloading of the usual Coq notation for the propositional connectives.

Evaluation of formulas and semantic entailment are simply defined as a direct translations into Coq's logic of the pen and paper definitions of these concepts, but, as with many other definitions in proof assistants, requiring more rigorous definitions. For example, it is common in pen and paper to use the symbol $\vDash$ to represent many different concepts, such as a set entailing a proposition in a model ($\Gamma \vDash_\mathcal{M} \varphi$), a formula being valid in a model ($\mathcal{M} \vDash \varphi$), or a formula being valid in a frame ($\mathcal{F} \vDash \varphi$). In Coq each of these concepts requires a different function to be properly defined.

The axiomatic system is, perhaps, the part of the library which is the least similar to usual pen and paper definitions, as the transition from informal set theory to type theory takes a heavy toll on the ease of defining concepts such as axiom systems. Instead of simply defining an axiom system as a set of formulas, the authors define a (small) type of axioms, which takes formulas as arguments in its constructors, a function that translates terms of the type of axiom into terms of the type of formulas, which, given an axiom constructed with some formulas (e.g. `ax1 f1 f2`), returns a more complex formula built with the formulas that constructed the axiom (e.g. `[! f1 -> (f2 -> f1) !]`), to then be able to define axiom systems as types that associate axioms with logical propositions.

This somewhat roundabout definition does have a positive side effect, it makes it impossible to deduce an instance of an axiom in a system where that axiom does not hold. For example, suppose we were to attempt to prove some formula in system K. We could erroneously deduce an instance of axiom T[4] which may go unnoticed until the proof is reviewed by ourselves or by another person at a later moment. This library makes it impossible to commit such a mistake, as the axiom T does not inhabit the type of axioms of system K, thus attempting to deduce it would trigger a type error.

Given this brief overview of the base library, we now shift our focus to the modifications made to it to allow for the definition of multiple modalities. Firstly, it is necessary to define some kind of index for the modalities of the language such that $\Box_i \neq \Box_j$ iff $i \neq j$. This was done by defining, in the root file of the library, a small type (i.e., an element of `Set`) of indexes as an implicit argument via the `Context` command, which then serves as a base to define a typeclass that represents the set of actual indexes, this simply being the characteristic function over the base type of indexes.

With this set of indexes, we then define an instance of this set of indexes as an implicit generalizing argument also as a `Context`[5]. Finally, we define a simple `Structure` that represents the actual indexes which will be used to build the modal formulas. This structure has two components, an index (i.e., an object that inhabits the base type of indexes) and a proof that this index is valid (i.e., a proof that it satisfies the conditions defined by the typeclass `modal_index_set`).

```
Context {I: Set}.
Class modal_index_set: Type := {
    C: I -> Prop (* C is a set of I, a small type. *)
}.

Context `{X: modal_index_set}.
Structure modal_index: Set := {
    index: I;
    index_valid: C index (* Proof index is an element of C. *)
```

---

[4] This axiom is defined as $\Box p \to p$ and it is correspondent to the class of reflexive frames, i.e. if $\mathcal{F}$ is a reflexive frame, then $\mathcal{F} \vDash \Box p \to p$, for more details see [9].

[5] Context definitions are nothing more than definitions of section specific variables that, in the case of typeclasses, allows for the implicit generalization of the type of the variable.

}.

This definition allows us to properly represent the grammar of multimodal logics, as shown in Sect. 2.2, by making some modifications to the definition of the grammar of modal logic in the base library, where the additional parameter in the clauses for Box and Dia represent the index of each modality.

```
Inductive formula: Set :=
   | Lit     : nat -> formula
   | Neg     : formula -> formula
   | Box     : modal_index -> formula -> formula
   | Dia     : modal_index -> formula -> formula
   | And     : formula -> formula -> formula
   | Or      : formula -> formula -> formula
   | Implies : formula -> formula -> formula.
```

This simple change, while using Coq's context mechanism, allows us to extend the base library to deal with multimodal logics, while also preserving the ability to reason about monomodal logics, by simply defining a singleton set as the index set. For example, consider the singleton set unit defined in the Coq Core Library as an index set. We may define an instance of the modal index typeclass over it by explicitly stating the type of the set over which this definition will be made. This is done by defining the type of the index as @modal_index_set unit (note that this requires an explicit definition of an implicit type, so we must precede it by a @). Given this definition, we may then define a modal index over it by providing the constructor tt of the unit type and the constructor I of the True type as arguments to the constructor of the modal_index structure, where we use True to represent a full set for the type unit. With those definitions we can represent formulas easily.

```
Instance unit_index: @modal_index_set unit := {|
   C x := True
|}.
Definition idx: modal_index :=
   Build_modal_index tt I.
```

To define the semantics of multimodal logics, it was also necessary to extend the definition of frames, so that a frame may have multiple accessibility relations. Given this extension, the rules for evaluating formulas containing modalities had to be updated to be able to handle formulas with multiple modalities.

```
Record Frame: Type := {
   W: Type;
   (* We quantify the relations over the set of valid indexes. *)
   R: modal_index -> W -> W -> Prop
}.
Fixpoint fun_validation (M: Model) (w: W (F M)) (f: formula): Prop :=
   match f with
   | Lit   x     => v M x w
   | Box   i f'  => forall w', R (F M) i w w' -> fun_validation M w' f'
   | Dia   i f'  => exists2 w', R (F M) i w w' & fun_validation M w' f'
```

```
(* Some lines omitted... *)
end.
```

These modifications are enough to represent the language and semantics of multimodal logics. More complex concepts, such as semantic entailment, were already defined and didn't need any modifications to be applicable to multimodal logics.

The basic notation of the library was also extended to better represent multimodal formulas. Modal formulas are written inside a [! !] block, as explained before, the connectives are written the same way as before, with the exception of the modalities, which are now indexed and written as [i] and <i>. For example, the formula $\Box_1 p_0 \to (p_1 \land p_2)$ may be written as [! [1]#0 -> (#1 /\ #2) !].

```
(* Some lines omitted... *)
Notation "[! m !]" := m
(at level 0, m custom modal at level 99, format "[! m !]").
Notation " p -> q " :=
(Implies p q) (in custom modal at level 13, right associativity).
(* Some lines omitted... *)
Notation " [ i ] p " := (Box i p)
(in custom modal at level 9, right associativity, format "[ i ] p").
Notation " < i > p " := (Dia i p)
(in custom modal at level 9, right associativity, format "< i > p").
Notation " # p " := (Lit p)
(in custom modal at level 2, no associativity, p constr at level 1,
    format "# p").
```

The axiomatic system also had to be extended to handle multiple modalities. This was done by adding the index of a modality as an additional parameter to the definition of the modal axioms of the system, which requires that the definitions of the axiomatic systems be quantified by the index as an additional parameter. Moreover, we have found it convenient to separate the propositional axioms from the base System K, as it was defined in the original library, given that the propositional axioms don't need a notion of index.

```
Inductive axiom: Set :=
| ax1: formula -> formula -> axiom (* Axiom 1: p -> q -> p. *)
(* Some lines omitted... *)
| ax10: formula -> axiom (* Axiom 10: ¬¬p -> p. *)
| axK:    modal_index -> formula -> formula -> axiom
| axDual: modal_index -> formula -> axiom
| axT:    modal_index -> formula -> axiom
(* Some lines omitted... *)
| axGL:   modal_index -> formula -> axiom.
```

Additionally, the definition of deduction had to be updated such that the necessitation rule works on indexed modalities. Note that systems are sets of axioms.

```
Inductive deduction (A: axiom -> Prop): theory -> formula -> Prop :=
(* Some constructors omitted... *)
```

```
| Nec: forall (t: theory) (f: formula) (i: modal_index),
    deduction A Empty f -> (* Necessitation works for any index. *)
    deduction A t [! [i]f !].

Inductive P: axiom -> Prop := (* Propositional logic, P. *)
| P_ax1: forall f g, P (ax1 f g) (* The axiom 1 is contained in P. *)
(* Some lines omitted... *)
| P_ax10: forall f, P (ax10 f). (* The axiom 10 is contained in P. *)

Variable idx: modal_index.
Inductive K: axiom -> Prop := (* Monomodal System K. *)
| K_P: forall f, P f -> K f (* K is a superset of P. *)
| K_axK: forall f g, K (axK idx f g) (* The axiom K is valid. *)
| K_axDual: forall f, K (axDual idx f). (* The axiom Dual is valid. *)
```

Minor changes were required in some other parts of the library, particularly in the proofs of some assorted useful theorems and definitions of Coq tactics, proofs of some logical equivalences, and in the proofs of the soundness of frame properties[6]. As these changes were so small, we omit further details in here.

The section of the library that dealt with soundness also had to undergo minor changes, but those represented a notable result: we were able to prove that all multimodal extensions of system K are sound. This soundness proof can be rather easily extended to other modal systems.

The major changes were in the section of the library that dealt with the proof of weak completeness. We were able to extend this proof to show that any normal multimodal axiomatic system is weak complete with respect to its Kripke semantics. It is worth noting that this proof is still a Henkin style proof, like the original proof in the base library. To do this extension, we had to split the axiomatic system K into it's propositional and modal components to allow us to adapt the many proofs of auxiliary lemmas and tactics to deal with multimodal logics. Similar results are found in the literature, in texts such as [9] and [15].

We must stress, however, that these results are not proofs of preservation of properties by fusion, they only show that (normal) multimodal logics weakly complete and that System K is sound, by adapting usual proofs of said results.

4 Combining Logics in Coq

To represent the fusion of modal logics it was first necessary to tackle the issue of how to represent the indexes of modalities that belong to modal systems resulting from the fusion of other systems. If we recall the definition of fusion from Sect. 2.3, we will see that the modalities of a system resulting from fusion is the disjoint union of the modalities of the base systems that were fused.

As such, to define the fusion of two logics, we had to first compute the disjoint union of their indexes, then define an instance of the modal_index_set typeclass,

---

[6] Those are proofs that if a frame has a certain condition then a certain axiom will be valid on all models built with that frame. For example, if a frame is reflexive then all models built with that reflexive frame will validate the axiom $\Box p \to p$.

and so we could define how to prove that an index belongs to the fusion index set, this being done by proving that it belongs to either set of base indexes.

```
Context {I1: Set}.
Context {I2: Set}.
Definition fusion: Set := I1 + I2. (* Disjoint union of types. *)

Context {X1: @modal_index_set I1}.
Context {X2: @modal_index_set I2}.
Instance fusion_index_set: @modal_index_set fusion := {|
    C i := (* Disjoint union of sets. *)
        match i with
        | inl a ⇒ @C I1 X1 a
        | inr b ⇒ @C I2 X2 b
        end
|}.
```

Notice that it is necessary to explicitly state the types of certain arguments that were previously defined as implicit. Given this definition, we defined some simple local notations to ease the development and readability of the following proofs. This notation was defined for indexes, formulas, frames, models and axioms. We only show here the case for indexes to avoid unnecessary repetition.

```
Local Notation modal_index1 := (@modal_index I1 X1).
Local Notation modal_index2 := (@modal_index I2 X2).
Local Notation modal_indexF := (@modal_index fusion fusion_index_set).
```

With those definitions, it was possible to represent the first concept related to fusions: the fusion of frames. Frames may be fused together if they have the same set of worlds. Should this condition be met, we can construct a new frame that has all the relations of both of the base frames. This is represented by a definition followed by a transparent proof that constructs a new frame with the relations of the base frames.

```
Definition join_frames (f1: Frame1) (f2: Frame2) (H: W f2 = W f1): FrameF.
Proof.
    (* Proof omitted. *)
Defined.
```

An additional technical detail, comparing to the standard pen and paper formulation, is that the types of formulas, axioms and judgements are indexed by the possible set of modal indexes, but we do not have a subtype relation in Coq's type theory: a formula may belong to two sets, but not to two types. To solve this issue, we defined a typeclass that "lifts" object from some basic type to a fused type, which is defined as a function from some type A to some type B. It should be noted that this definition precedes all the other ones presented so far, however we chose to present it now to make the reasoning behind it clearer.

```
Class lift_conv (A B: Type): Type := {
    lift: A -> B
}.
```

It was then necessary to prove that we may lift indexes, formulas and axioms from the basic indexes to the fusion indexes and also that lifting instances of axioms is the same as instantiating a lifted axiom (i.e. lifting and instantiating are well behaved as they commute). This is done by proving instances of this typeclass for each of these types. To avoid repetition, we present only the proofs of the instances of one of the logics which are combined.

```
Instance index_lift1: lift_conv modal_index1 modal_indexF.
Instance formula_lift1: lift_conv formula1 formulaF.
Instance axiom_lift1: lift_conv axiom1 axiomF.

Lemma instantiate_lift_inversion1:
    forall (p: axiom1) (f: formulaF),
    instantiate (lift p) = f ->
    f = lift (instantiate p).
Proof.
    (* Proof omitted. *)
Qed.
```

Following this, we proved that given a fusion frame/model, it was possible to recover the frames/models of the base logics that were fused (i.e. split the fusion model into its components) and that a split model could be lifted back up to a fusion model. These proofs served as a basis to show that fusion preserves evaluations, that is, if a formula φ is true/false in a model $\mathcal{M}_1$ that was split from a fusion model $\mathcal{M}_\mathcal{F}$, then φ lifted up to the fusion indexes will have the same truth value in the model $\mathcal{M}_\mathcal{F}$. Once again, we only present proofs of one of the relevant logics.

```
Lemma split_frame1: FrameF -> Frame1.
Lemma split_model1: ModelF -> Model1.
Instance lift_split_model1 M:
    @lift_conv (W (F (split_model1 M))) (W (F M)).

Lemma split_model1_coherence:
    forall M f w,
    fun_validation (split_model1 M) w f <->
    fun_validation M (lift w) (lift f).
Proof.
    (* Proof omitted. *)
Qed.
```

With all these basic properties, we were able to define the restrictions upon frames and the axiom systems of the fusion of logics. The restrictions upon frames of fusion is defined by the class of frames that this frame belongs, where a class of frames is a set containing all the frames that share a common restriction on their accessibility relation. The class of frames of fusion frames is defined by the classes of frames of the basic logics, that is, if the basic frames $\mathcal{F}_1, \mathcal{F}_2$ respectively belong to classes $\mathcal{C}_1$ and $\mathcal{C}_2$ (with corresponding restrictions $\mathcal{P}_1$ and $\mathcal{P}_2$) then the fusion frame $\mathcal{F}_f$ will belong to class $\mathcal{C}_f$ where relation $\mathcal{R}_1$ respects $\mathcal{P}_1$

and $\mathcal{R}_2$ respects $\mathcal{P}_2$. This may be generalized to an arbitrary amount of frames, depending on the logics that were fused together.

The axiom system of fusion is the system containing all axioms of the base logics, lifted up to the fusion indexes.

```
Variable P1: Frame1 -> Prop.
Variable P2: Frame2 -> Prop.

Definition PF: FrameF -> Prop :=
    (* Satisfy the frame condition from both logics. *)
    fun F => P1 (split_frame1 F) /\ P2 (split_frame2 F).

Variable A1: axiom1 -> Prop.
Variable A2: axiom2 -> Prop.

Inductive fusion_axioms: axiomF -> Prop :=
| fusion_axioms1: (* Include all axioms from system 1. *)
    forall p, A1 p -> fusion_axioms (lift p)
| fusion_axioms2: (* Include all axioms from system 2. *)
    forall p, A2 p -> fusion_axioms (lift p).
```

Finally, we achieve our goal: we were able to declare a generic definition of the property of soundness, as the definition in the base library was specific to System K, and give a proof that if axiom systems A_1 and A_2 are sound with respect to classes of frames $\mathcal{P}_1$ and $\mathcal{P}_2$, then the axiom system A_f resulting from the fusion of A_1 and A_2 is sound with respect to the class of frames $\mathcal{P}_f$, which is made up of fusion frames whose basic frames belong in $\mathcal{P}_1$ and $\mathcal{P}_2$. With this we then proved that soundness is transferred by fusion.

```
Definition entails_modal_class (G: theory) (p: formula): Prop :=
    forall M, P (F M) -> entails M G p.

Definition sound I '{X: @modal_index_set I} P A: Prop :=
    forall G p, (A; G |-- p) -> entails_modal_class P G p.

Theorem soundness_transfer:
    forall I1 '{X1: @modal_index_set I1} P1 A1,
    forall I2 '{X2: @modal_index_set I2} P2 A2,
    sound I1 P1 A1 ->
    sound I2 P2 A2 ->
    sound fusion (PF P1 P2) (fusion_axioms A1 A2).
```

We can then use this result to model a proper fusion of logics. For example, consider a system that fuses two distinct S4 logics, such as the one considered in [2]. To define it within the library, we first define the type (and set) of indexes:

```
Local Instance unit_index: @modal_index_set unit := {|
    C x := True (* Use the whole universe (i.e., unit). *)
|}.

(* The only possible index in the system. *)
```

```
Local Definition idx: modal_index :=
    Build_modal_index tt I.
```

And then we may define the new system itself to be the fusion:

```
(* We define X as the fusion of two copies of System S4 on idx. *)
Local Definition X :=
    fusion_axioms (S4 idx) (S4 idx).
```

This is enough to use the fusion for derivations. In order to prove its soundness, we also have to define the class of frames that we're interested in. In this case, we require that relations within frames are pre-order relations, since this is the case necessary for soundness in S4. Then, for the proof itself, it is enough to prove that its individual components are sound (which can be done by reusing the library we're extending).

```
(* Condition on frames for X: both need to be pre-orders. *)
Local Definition P: Frame -> Prop :=
    fun F => preorder_frame F idx.

(* We prove System X is sound from soundness of System S4 alone. *)
Goal (* Use P as the condition for both frames. *)
    sound fusion (PF P P) X.
Proof.
    apply soundness_transfer.
    - intros G p ? M ?.
      now apply soundness_S4 with (idx := idx).
    - intros G p ? M ?.
      now apply soundness_S4 with (idx := idx).
Qed.
```

This concludes our definition of fusion of modal logics in Coq. The above example has been checked within the developed library and shown to be sound, with the proof containing no holes (i.e., proofs are complete and no axioms were used, aside from the excluded middle which needs to be added in Coq's type theory).

5   Conclusions

In this work we presented a implementation of the fusion of modal logics in the Coq proof assistant, together with a proof that fusion preserves the property of soundness. The modal logic library upon which we've developed our work is highly expressive and allows us to define arbitrary normal modal logics, even nonalethic ones, and has proofs of soundness and weak completeness for the K system, with little effort required to extend those proofs to other modal systems.

At the moment of writing, we know of no other implementation of fusion in a proof assistant, let alone one that proves soundness preservation. As for future work, we intend to carry on improving the base library, adding the possibility to express bridge principles of fusion, thus allowing the addition of new axioms only to fused systems, which would allow treating interesting problems such as the representation of products of topologies as fusions of S4 with itself presented in [2]. Another point of improvement is to prove the preservation of (at least weak) completeness by fusion, which may be done via the method of stepwise construction of multimodal models presented by [11], this, however, would require an adaptation of the original proof due to differing definitions of a logical system, as well as considerable effort due to the complexity of the original proof. Another interesting avenue for future work is to implement different methods of combination, such as fibring [7].

Acknowledgements. This work was partially developed with funding from Conselho Nacional de Desenvolvimento Científico e Tecnológico (CNPq) grant number 409707/2022-8 and from Fundação de Amparo à Pesquisa e Inovação do Estado Santa Catarina (FAPESC).

References

1. Azurat, A., Prasetya, W.: A survey on embedding programming logics in a theorem prover. Tech. rep., Utrecht University: Institute of Information and Computing Sciences, Utrecht (2002)
2. Benthem, J.V., Bezhanishvili, G., Cate, B.T., Sarenac, D.: Multimodal logics of products of topologies. Stud. Logica. **84**(3), 369–392 (2006)
3. Bentzen, B.: A Henkin-style completeness proof for the modal logic S5. In: Baroni, P., Benzmüller, C., Wáng, Y.N. (eds.) CLAR 2021. LNCS (LNAI), vol. 13040, pp. 459–467. Springer, Cham (2021). https://doi.org/10.1007/978-3-030-89391-0_25
4. Benzmüller, C.: Combining logics in simple type theory. In: Dix, J., Leite, J., Governatori, G., Jamroga, W. (eds.) CLIMA 2010. LNCS (LNAI), vol. 6245, pp. 33–48. Springer, Heidelberg (2010). https://doi.org/10.1007/978-3-642-14977-1_6
5. Benzmüller, C., Parent, X., van der Torre, L.: Designing normative theories for ethical and legal reasoning: logikey framework, methodology, and tool support. Artif. Intell. **287**, 103348 (2020). https://doi.org/10.1016/j.artint.2020.103348, https://www.sciencedirect.com/science/article/pii/S0004370219301110
6. Blackburn, P., De Rijke, M., Venema, Y.: Modal Logic, vol. 53. Cambridge University Press, Cambridge (2001)
7. Carnielli, W., Coniglio, M., Gabbay, D.M., Gouveia, P., Sernadas, C.: Analysis and Synthesis of Logics: How to Cut and Paste Reasoning Systems, vol. 35. Springer Science & Business Media, Netherlands (2008). https://doi.org/10.1007/978-1-4020-6782-2
8. Carnielli, W., Coniglio, M.E.: Combining logics. In: Zalta, E.N. (ed.) The Stanford Encyclopedia of Philosophy. Metaphysics Research Lab, Stanford University, Stanford, Fall 2020 edn. (2020)
9. Carnielli, W.A., Pizzi, C., Bueno-Soler, J.: Modalities and Multimodalities, vol. 20. Springer (2008). https://doi.org/10.1007/978-1-4020-8590-1
10. Da Silveira, A.A., Ribeiro, R., Nunes, M.A., Torrens, P., Roggia, K.: A sound deep embedding of arbitrary normal modal logics in coq. In: SBLP 2022: XXVI Brazilian Symposium on Programming Languages, pp. 1–7. Association for Computing Machinery, New York, NY, USA (2022). https://doi.org/10.1145/3561320.3561329
11. Fine, K., Schurz, G.: Transfer theorems for multimodal logics. Logic and Reality: Essays on the Legacy of Arthur Prior 169–213 (1996)

12. Fitting, M.: Logics with several modal operators. Theoria **35**(3), 259–266 (1969)
13. Fuenmayor, D., Benzmüller, C.: Harnessing higher-order (meta-)logic to represent and reason with complex ethical theories. In: Nayak, A.C., Sharma, A. (eds.) PRICAI 2019: Trends in Artificial Intelligence, pp. 418–432. Springer International Publishing, Cham (2019). https://doi.org/10.1007/978-3-030-29908-8_34
14. Fuenmayor, D., Benzmüller, C.: Mechanised assessment of complex natural-language arguments using expressive logic combinations. In: Herzig, A., Popescu, A. (eds.) FroCoS 2019. LNCS (LNAI), vol. 11715, pp. 112–128. Springer, Cham (2019). https://doi.org/10.1007/978-3-030-29007-8_7
15. Gabbay, D.: Many-dimensional Modal Logics: Theory and Applications. Studies in logic and the foundations of mathematics, North Holland Publishing Company, Amsterdam (2003)
16. Gödel, K.: An interpretation of the intuitionistic propositional calculus. Collect. Works **1**, 301–303 (1986)
17. Goldblatt, R.: Mathematics of Modality. Center for the Study of Language and Information Publications, Stanford (1993)
18. Kracht, M., Wolter, F.: Properties of independently axiomatizable bimodal logics. J. Symbolic Logic **56**(4), 1469–1485 (1991)
19. Kripke, S.A.: A completeness theorem in modal logic. J. Symbolic Logic **24**(1), 1–14 (1959)
20. Kripke, S.A.: Semantical analysis of modal logic i normal modal propositional calculi. Math. Log. Q. **9**(5–6), 67–96 (1963)
21. Kuhn, S.: Modal Logic, vol. 10. Routledge, London, 1 edn. (1998)
22. Leroy, X.: The CompCert C verified compiler: documentation and user's manual. Ph. D. thesis, Inria (2021)
23. Lescanne, P., Puisségur, J.: Dynamic logic of common knowledge in a proof assistant. arXiv preprint arXiv:0712.3146 (2007)
24. Lewis, C.I.: A Survey of Symbolic Logic. University of California press, Berkeley (1918)
25. Lewis, C.I., Langford, C.H.: Symbolic Logic, vol. 170. Dover Publications New York, New York (1932)
26. Maggesi, M., Perini Brogi, C.: A formal proof of modal completeness for provability logic. In: Cohen, L., Kaliszyk, C. (eds.) 12th International Conference on Interactive Theorem Proving (ITP 2021). Leibniz International Proceedings in Informatics (LIPIcs), vol. 193, pp. 1–18. Schloss Dagstuhl – Leibniz-Zentrum für Informatik, Dagstuhl, Germany (2021). https://doi.org/10.4230/LIPIcs.ITP.2021.26, https://drops.dagstuhl.de/entities/document/10.4230/LIPIcs.ITP.2021.26
27. Orlov, I.E.: The calculus of compatibility of propositions mathematics of the USSR. Sbornik **35**, 263–286 (1928)
28. Paiva, N., Caleiro, C.: Temporal logic in Coq. Projeto de diplomaÃ§Ão, Licenciatura em Matemática Aplicada e Computação – Instituto Superior Técnico (1998)
29. Paulin-Mohring, C.: Introduction to the calculus of inductive constructions. In: Paleo, B.W., Delahaye, D. (eds.) All about Proofs, Proofs for All, Studies in Logic (Mathematical logic and foundations), vol. 55. College Publications, London (2015)
30. Rabe, F.: How to identify, translate and combine logics? J. Log. Comput. **27**(6), 1753–1798 (2017)
31. Scott, D.: Advice on Modal Logic, pp. 143–173. Springer Netherlands, Dordrecht (1970).https://doi.org/10.1007/978-94-010-3272-8_7
32. Team, T.C.D.: The Coq Reference Manual. France (2022)

33. Thomason, R.H.: Combinations of tense and modality. In: Handbook of Philosophical Logic, pp. 135–165. Springer, Dordrecht (1984). https://doi.org/10.1007/978-94-009-6259-0_3
34. van Benthem, J.: Epistemic logic and epistemology: the state of their affairs. Philos. Stud. **128**(1), 49–76 (2006)

Formally Verified Implementation of the K-Nearest Neighbors Classification Algorithm

Bernny Velasquez, Jessica Herring, and Nadeem Abdul Hamid[(✉)]

Berry College, Mount Berry, GA 30149, USA
{bernny.velasquez,jessica.herring}@vikings.berry.edu, nadeem@acm.org

Abstract. Classification, one of the most commonly applied algorithmic techniques in data mining, involves assigning a class label to observations based on previously seen data. Among the most ubiquitous and well-known approaches to classification is K-nearest neighbor (KNN) search, which predicts the class label for a query by determining the plurality class of its K-nearest data points. In this paper, we present a mechanically verified implementation of a K-nearest neighbors classification algorithm in the Coq proof assistant, a powerful formal verification tool. Formally certifying the implementation, by proving that it meets its specification, provides a strong guarantee and high confidence that the classifier actually produces results in the expected manner. Given the conceptually simple nature of the KNN algorithm, this serves as a good baseline for developing specification and verification techniques for machine learning implementations.

Keywords: nearest neighbors classification · machine learning · formal verification · coq

1 Introduction

As the use of machine learning (ML) algorithms permeates safety critical sectors such as healthcare, finance, transportation, and energy, how does one know if the *implementation* of a particular algorithm is free of coding defects? Traditional testing methods alone cannot provide high-assurance guarantees of correctness and other security properties. The paradigm shift in ML software development, where the behavior of a system emerges from the data provided to it (rather than rules provided in program code), makes it intrinsically challenging to test and verify such systems [8].

The inadequacy of traditional testing and validation methods, coupled with scalability issues and unknown use cases, poses a significant challenge when these models are applied to safety-critical systems like medical devices, smart grids, and autonomous vehicles [20]. One particular source of error (among many) is the implementation of an ML algorithm itself. The mechanics of moving from the mathematical model of an ML algorithm to its realization as (often highly-optimized) program code presents a large gap across which the translation happens. It thus becomes important to test that the code implementation accurately reflects the algorithmic intent [8].

Contribution. The main contribution of the work presented in this paper is a mechanically verified implementation of the K-nearest neighbors (KNN) classification algorithm in the COQ proof assistant. Given the conceptually simple nature of the KNN search algorithm, this serves as a good baseline for developing specification and verification techniques for ML implementations. The significant portions of the verification effort described in this paper involved integrating a previously verified KNN search algorithm ([16], see Sect. 2) with a certified Map data structure (Sect. 3.3) and a verified implementation of a plurality function (Sect. 3.2). The code repository for this project is available at: https://github.com/nadeemabdulhamid/knn-classify-sbmf24.

Outline. In the following section, we provide background on the COQ proof assistant and a discussion on work related to the KNN search algorithm. Following that, Sect. 3 includes a walk-through and presentation of our implementation in COQ, with an overview of its formal specification and verification in Sect. 4. Section 5 concludes with a discussion of overall results and future work.

2 Background and Related Work

COQ Proof Assistant. COQ [1,7] is an interactive theorem prover based on the Calculus of Inductive Constructions (CIC), a higher-order predicate logic extended with inductive data types. The COQ system provides a language that supports defining data types and functions in a functional programming paradigm while writing rich logical specifications and constructing proofs, all in a single unified framework. This allows the user to write executable code, state mathematical theorems about the code, and interactively develop proofs of the theorems, which are machine verified by a proof-checker kernel. Like many proof assistants, COQ offers some degree of proof automation, including proof search *tactics* and the ability for users to write their own tactic scripts. This is an important feature that seeks to balance the tension between the undecidability of many non-trivial properties about programs and the flexibility and usefulness of the framework. As noted by [21], the COQ infrastructure has enabled a wide variety of formally verified work in computer science and mathematics, including a fully-verified optimizing compiler for C [18], certified concurrent OS kernels [14], and an environment for reasoning about the security of cryptographic algorithms [5].

Nearest Neighbor Search. The essential idea of a KNN-based classification algorithm is straightforward and intuitive. Given a labeled set of data points, to predict the classification for a query point, the algorithm searches the entire data set for the K nearest neighbors to the query. The most frequent label of that set of neighbors is produced as the predicted label for the query. Since the initial work of Cover and Hart in 1967 [9], there exists a wide-ranging and immense amount of literature on KNN methods, for example, as surveyed by [25]. Variations encompass exact and approximate methods, heuristics to automatically choose an optimal K value, choice of "distance" metrics, and the data structure and algorithm used to search efficiently for neighbors [10].

In terms of analysis and verification of properties of the KNN-based classification, the initial published work [9] established bounds on the algorithm's probability of error. Other work has focused on computational complexity [10] and, more recently, robustness in the presence of adversarial scenarios [11,12,24]. All existing analyses, to our knowledge, are done "on paper" or using methods like abstract interpretation and focus on theoretical properties of the algorithm. The work presented in this article, by contrast, is a machine-checked proof of an actual concrete implementation providing a guarantee that the implementation meets its basic specification of desired properties in terms of how it generates output from the input data.

For our work, we build on a formally verified implementation [16] of KNN search that uses a standard k-d tree[1] structure [6,13] to efficiently search a multi-dimensional space. A k-d tree is a binary tree structure, with k-dimensional data points as nodes, that enables a branch-and-bound search technique, resulting in sub-linear search complexity. The primary results of the prior work in [16] are formally verified implementations of two primary functions:[2]

```
build_kdtree (k:nat) (data:list datapt) : kdtree
knn_search (D:datapt -> datapt -> nat) (K:nat)
           (k:nat) (tree:kdtree) (query:datapt) : list datapt
```

The first, `build_kdtree`, constructs a k-d tree structure from a list of k-dimensional data points. The second, `knn_search`, produces the K nearest neighbors[3] to the `query` point among all the points in the `tree`. Section 4 discusses the specification and verified properties of these implementations and how they are integrated into the results described in this paper.

Formal Verification in ML and AI. The application of formal methods to verification and validation of ML, or AI systems in general, is a relatively recent area of research. Seshia *et al.* [23] and Luckcuck *et al.* [19] survey the current state of the art and outline challenges from several different perspectives. Our

---

[1] Throughout the paper, lowercase k denotes the number of dimensions of the data points and uppercase K is the number of nearest neighbors that are sought.
[2] The Coq syntax we use for function headers is: ($ident_{\text{function}}$ ($ident_{\text{param}}$: $type_{\text{param}}$) $\cdots$ ($ident_{\text{param}}$: $type_{\text{param}}$) : $type_{\text{return}}$) representing a named function with explicitly-typed parameters.
[3] As part of our work for the implementation of this paper, we abstracted the distance metric, D, used by `knn_search` - an improvement over [16]. For space reasons, we omit any further discussion about it throughout the rest of this paper.

motivation and work is similar to Selsam et al. [22], who claim to present the first application of formal proof techniques to detect implementation errors in ML systems. However our framework is different and we chose to focus on a KNN-based approach for its ubiquity and familiarity.

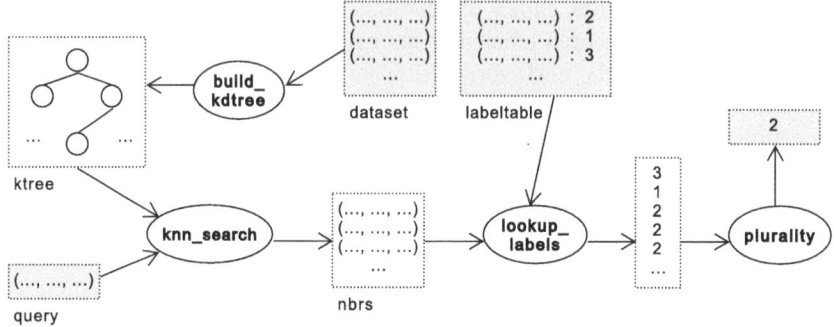

Fig. 1. Workflow of the classifier implementation.

3 KNN Classifier Implementation

The overall architecture of our implementation is diagrammed in Fig. 1, corresponding to the top-level COQ function definition of `classify` in Fig. 2(a). The shaded blue boxes are the provided data. The "2" in the green box is the final output: a predicted class label for the *query*.

3.1 Classify

The `classify` function in Fig. 2(a) receives two "hyperparameters" for the classification algorithm: the distance metric (D) and the number of neighbors to search for (K). It further takes the dimensionality of the data (k), the data set itself, a map (`LabelTable`) of data points to class indices (represented as natural numbers), and the query point. It first builds a k-d tree from the data set, then uses `knn_search` to identify the K nearest neighbors of the query point within the k-d tree. Once those neighbors are found, the `plurality` function is used to determine the predicted label for the query based on the labels of its neighbors. The result of `classify` is an *option* value, representing either Some label that is the plurality, or None. The latter is produced if there is not a strict plurality value among the nearest neighbors.

The `lookup_labels` function looks up in the label table each key from the list of neighbors to produce a list of the values that the keys are mapped to. If a key is not found in the map, the value 0 is used. For example, in pseudo-code, the following results in the list [3, 2, 3]:

    lookupLabels({ d : 3, g : 1, h : 3, b : 1, i : 2 }, [d, i, h]).

3.2 Plurality

The `classify` function relies on a helper, `plurality`, Fig. 2(b), to determine the most frequently occurring label from a given list of labels. The function returns a pair of a potential label (`option nat`) and the maximum frequency count of any label in the list of values. The reason for returning the pair with the count value is that at some point in the recursive evaluation of the function, there might be a tie in the counts of some elements (resulting in `None` being returned as the maximum frequency element), but as the recursive evaluation unfolds back through the list, then the count of one element may eventually exceed that count value and result in the restoration of `Some` maximal element. For the `plurality` function, COQ's `Function` command [4] is used, which not only enforces syntactic restrictions to guarantee termination of recursive calls, but also defines induction principles that enable reasoning about the definition.

```
Definition classify (D : datapt -> datapt -> nat) (* dist metric *)
                    (K : nat) (* number of neighbors *)
                    (k : nat) (* dimensions of all points *)
                    (dataset : (list datapt))
                    (labeltable : LabelTable)
                    (query : datapt)
                    : option nat :=
  let ktree := (build_kdtree k dataset) in
  let nbrs := knn_search D K k ktree query in
  fst (plurality (lookup_labels labeltable nbrs)).
```

(a)

```
Function plurality (vals : list nat) : option nat * nat :=
  match vals with
  | nil    => (None, 0)
  | h :: t => match (plurality t) with
              | (None, c) => let c' := (1 + count t h) in
                             if c <? c' then (Some h, c') else (None, c)
              | (Some x, c) => let c' := (1 + count t h) in
                               if c =? c'      then (None, c)
                               else if c <? c' then (Some h, c')
                               else            (Some x, c)
              end
  end.
```

(b)

Fig. 2. Implementation of the `classify` and `plurality` functions.

3.3 Map Data Structure

An important supporting data structure for the `classify` function is the label table: a *map* from data points (lists of naturals) to class labels (also naturals). We used a module in the COQ standard library that provides an efficient functional implementation of maps using AVL trees (`FMapAVL`).[4] The standard library module abstracts over both the type of keys and values of the map. However, unlike mainstream programming languages, it requires satisfaction of a rich set of constraints on the type of keys in order to be instantiated with it. In particular, the key must satisfy the requirements of being an *order relation*.[5] Thus, we needed to specify the notion of an *order* on lists of naturals (our data points). We did this through an inductively-defined proposition in COQ that represents lexicographic ordering on lists of naturals. This process took some effort to understand what was expected by the `FMapAVL` library, as the COQ standard library contains duplicate and deprecated modules and interfaces due to its evolution, and uses different notations and styles of specification across modules.

---

[4] https://coq.inria.fr/doc/v8.16/stdlib/Coq.FSets.FMapAVL.html.
[5] https://coq.inria.fr/doc/v8.16/stdlib/Coq.Structures.Orders.html.

3.4 Application

Appendix B presents a small application of our implementation to the well-known Iris flower data set [2]. We split the data set into conventional 80/20 training/test sets and build a classifier using the Manhattan distance metric and $K = 5$. At least for some permutations of the training/test data, there are no mis-classified data points. However, it should be noted that *correctness* of the mechanics of the algorithm implementation (as formalized in this work) does not imply that the algorithm will necessarily produce *accurate* classifications for data points. It could well be that the correct plurality vote of the K nearest neighbors is different from the actual label of a query point.

Theorem 1 (Classify_correct).
```
  ∀ K D k data labels query c,
1   dist_metric_wf D -> 0 < K -> 0 < k -> length data >= K ->
2   (forall v' : datapt, List.In v' data -> length v' = k) ->
3   (forall d : datapt, List.In d data -> FMap.In d labels) ->
4   (exists c near far classes,
5       classify D K k data labels query = Some c /\
6       Permutation data (near ++ far) /\
7       length near = K /\
8       all_in_leb (D query) near far /\
9       ClassesOf labels near classes /\
10      IsPlurality c classes)
11  \/
12  (classify D K k data labels query = None /\
13   ~exists c, IsPlurality c (lookup_labels labels
14                (knn_search D K k (build_kdtree k data) query))).
```

Fig. 3. Specification of the `classify` function.

4 Verification

In this section, we present our formalized specification of correctness and outline the process of building the certified proof. For the purposes of exposition, results are presented here in top-down order. In actual proof scripts, the various intermediate properties must be established before they can be used in the final theorem certifying correctness. (See Appendix A for a full summary.)

Ultimately, when executed, (`classify K k data labels query`) produces either (`Some c`) or `None`. In the former case, of the K nearest neighbors of `data` to `query`, more of them should have classification c in the `labels` table than any other label. In the latter case, it must be that a plurality value does not exist amount the labels of the nearest neighbors. The formal specification (Fig. 3) breaks this down precisely and elaborates some necessary premises.[6] Theorem 1

---

[6] Conventionally, in COQ theorem statements, a conjunction of premises is written as a string of implication clauses (... -> ... -> ...).

requires (line 1) that, in additional to well-formedness of the distance metric, both the number of neighbors sought and dimension k of the data points are strictly positive. Also, there must be at least K data points to begin with, and (line 2) every data point must properly be a list of k values. Line 3 relates data to labels: every point in the data must be assigned a label.

```
Inductive ClassesOf (LT : LabelTable) : list datapt -> list nat -> Prop :=
  | classesOf_nil : ClassesOf LT nil nil
  | classesOf_cons : forall k v ks vs,
      MapsTo k v LT -> ClassesOf LT ks vs -> ClassesOf LT (k::ks) (v::vs).

Definition IsPlurality (m:nat) (ns:list nat) : Prop :=
  List.In m ns /\ (forall m', m' = m \/ count ns m' < count ns m).
```

Fig. 4. The ClassesOf and IsPlurality predicates.

In that case, the result of (line 5) applying the classify function is to (4,6) induce a partition of the data into two lists, near and far. The length of near will be exactly K (line 7): these are the K nearest neighbors. The all_in_leb proposition (8) states that with respect to the distance metric anchored at the query point, every data point in the near list is less than or equal to the distance value to every point in the far list. Line 9 specifies that the data points in near map to the labels in classes, based on labels. ClassesOf is an inductively defined proposition that relates a list of data points to a list of labels, over a fixed label table (Fig. 4). Finally, (line 10) the predicted class c must be the mode of the class labels (classes) of the near data points. The IsPlurality predicate states that m is *the* plurality element of ns when m ∈ ns and the count of anything (other than m itself) in ns is strictly less than the count of m in ns.

The proof of the first disjunct (the Some c result) of Theorem 1 (lines 4–10 in the theorem statement) is divided into two main parts. The first involves the nearest neighbors (lines 6–8) and the second deals with certifying the plurality class. For the former, the work in this paper applies the results of [16], which culminated in a certified proof of the KNN search itself.

We are then left with establishing (lines 9 and 10 of Fig. 3) the correspondence of the classes labels to the near points, and c as the plurality value of those. Essentially, this involves proving that ClassesOf and IsPlurality are specifications of the behavior of lookup_labels and plurality, respectively. Theorem 2 in Fig. 5 is proved through straightforward induction. The premise requires that every key k in the list of keys ks is present in the label table. For Theorem 3, we establish three separate lemmas - one for each condition 2–4. In each lemma, the proof proceeds by structural induction on the list ns. Since we define the plurality function using the COQ *Functional Induction* library,[7] we use the generated induction principle to reason about the function. When applied, the principle generates 6 cases to be handled: one for each possible "execution" path of the plurality function (Fig. 2b, Sect. 3.2).

---

[7] https://coq.inria.fr/refman/using/libraries/funind.html.

Theorem 2 (lookup_labels_correct).
∀ LT ks vs,
1   (forall k, List.In k ks -> In k LT) ->
2   lookup_labels LT ks = vs -> ClassesOf LT ks vs.

Theorem 3 (plurality_correct).
∀ ns m c,
1   plurality ns = (Some m, c) -> (* if m is plurality with count c, *)
2   List.In m ns /\
3   count ns m = c /\
4   (forall m', m' = m \/ count ns m' < count ns m).

Fig. 5. Specifications of `lookup_labels` and `plurality`.

5 Conclusions and Future Work

This paper has presented a complete, functional, formally verified implementation of a standard KNN classification algorithm. "Formally verified" means that the code is associated with a mechanically-checked theorem establishing its correctness properties. We have focused on specifying and proving properties of the result that the implementation produces, rather than theoretical properties of KNN classification algorithm itself (e.g. time efficiency, or error rate for a given distribution of data).

As is the case with proofs "on paper," the process of developing a specification and proving was iterative and took many rounds of revision, both the code and the proof. In fact, at one point, our formulation of Theorem 1 was buggy: lines 9 and 10 were expressed directly in terms of `lookup_labels` (as opposed to using `ClassesOf` to specify it), which meant the conclusion could be trivially satisfied by a bogus implementation of `lookup_labels`. This reinforces the point that mechanized formal verification is not a magic bullet [15,17]. It only transfers the onus of correctness from the code to the specification. In most cases though, specifications are simpler than the code itself and thus it is easier for a human to read and be convinced of the correctness of a specification than of a complicated and/or subtle code implementation. (Contrast the implementation of `plurality` in Fig. 2b with the definition of `IsPlurality` in Fig. 4.)

In its current state, the work described in this paper consists of approximately 450 non-blank lines of code, specifications, and proof scripts. The proof scripts and organization of the proofs themselves (e.g. into lemmas) were significantly improved through repeated revision and refactoring. While we did not use any COQ extensions beyond its standard library, the use of our own user-defined tactics cut down the length of proof scripts by a factor of four in places.

There are many opportunities and directions for extending and building on this work. There are numerous variants of the "standard" KNN algorithm that are used in practice. Cunningham and Delany [10], for example, discuss three factors that result in significant variations of the algorithm: alternate similarity (or distance) measures, speedup techniques through data structures other than a k-d tree or by adopting approximate methods, and dimension reduction. In addition to verifying only input-output behavior, it would eventually also be useful to incorporate certification of properties such as probabilities of error, robustness to adversarial attacks, or time complexity in the formal proofs.

There still remains a considerable gap between the applicability of formal verification tools like COQ and languages actually used by ML researchers. Thus, we hope to continue with "porting" our verification of the KNN algorithm to an implementation in a mainstream language such as C, using a framework like the Verified Software Toolchain [3]. Finally, in the long term, we look forward to investigating and validating the use of formal methods in a broader variety of machine learning algorithms, developing a toolkit of proof techniques and specification approaches to help facilitate widespread adoption of such technology.

A Summary of COQ Developments

A.1 Implementations

```
Definition unwrap (opt : option nat) : nat :=
    match opt with
        | Some value => value
        | None => 0
    end.

Fixpoint count(vals : list nat) (num: nat) : nat :=
    match vals with
    | nil => 0
    | h :: t => if h =? num
                then S (count t num)
                else count t num
    end.

Fixpoint lookup_labels (LT : LabelTable) (keys : list datapt)
    : (list nat) :=
    match keys with
        | nil => nil
        | h :: t => unwrap (find h LT) :: lookup_labels LT t
    end.

Function plurality (vals : list nat) : option nat * nat :=
  match vals with
  | nil     => (None, 0)
  | h :: t => match (plurality t) with
              | (None, c) => let c' := (1 + count t h) in
                  if c <? c' then (Some h, c') else (None, c)
              | (Some x, c) => let c' := (1 + count t h) in
                  if c =? c'      then (None, c)
                  else if c <? c' then (Some h, c')
                  else                 (Some x, c)
```

```
                      end
   end.

Definition classify (dist_metric : datapt -> datapt -> nat)
                    (K : nat) (* number of neighbors *)
                    (k : nat) (* dimensions of all points*)
                    (dataset : (list datapt))
                    (labeltable : LabelTable)
                    (query : datapt)
                    : option nat :=  (* predicted label *)
    let ktree := (build_kdtree k dataset) in
    let nbrs := knn_search dist_metric K k ktree query in
        fst( plurality (lookup_labels labeltable nbrs) ).
```

A.2   Specifications

```
(* 'ClassesOf LT ks vs' is a inductively defined proposition
   representing, "LT maps the elements of ks, pairwise,
   to elements of vs" *)
Inductive ClassesOf (LT : LabelTable)
    : list datapt -> list nat -> Prop :=
    | classesOf_nil : ClassesOf LT nil nil
    | classesOf_cons :
        forall k v ks vs,
        MapsTo k v LT ->
        ClassesOf LT ks vs ->
        ClassesOf LT (k::ks) (v::vs).

(* 'IsPlurality m ns' is a proposition representing,
   "m is the plurality element of ns" which is to say,
     "m is an element of ns, and the count of anything in ns
     (that is not already m) is strictly less than the count
     of m in ns." *)
Definition IsPlurality (m:nat) (ns:list nat) : Prop :=
  List.In m ns
  /\ (forall m', m' = m \/ count ns m' < count ns m).
```

A.3   Proof Statements

```
(* ClassesOf is a specification for lookup_labels *)
Theorem lookup_labels_correct : forall LT ks vs,
    (forall k', List.In k' ks -> In k' LT) ->
    lookup_labels LT ks = vs -> ClassesOf LT ks vs.

(* Lemmas for plurality_correct *)
(* plurality element must be a member of the list *)
Lemma plurality_in_list :
```

```
    forall ns m c, plurality ns = (Some m, c) -> List.In m ns.

(* the plurality count cannot be a tie between two
   distinct values *)
Lemma eq_plurality_impossible :
    forall ls m' m c,
        m' <> m -> (count ls m') = c -> (count ls m) = c ->
            forall x, plurality ls <> (Some x, c).

(* the result of plurality must be consistent with count *)
Lemma plurality_some_count :
    forall ls m c,
        plurality ls = (Some m, c) -> count ls m = c.

(* the count of the plurality element is strictly
   greater than every other element *)
Lemma plurality_all_lt :
    forall ns m c,
        plurality ns = (Some m, c) ->
        forall m', m' = m \/ count ns m' < count ns m.

(* specification of plurality *)
Lemma plurality_correct :
    forall ns m c,
    plurality ns = (Some m, c) ->
        List.In m ns /\
        count ns m = c /\
        (forall m', m' = m \/ count ns m' < count ns m).

(* IsPlurality is a specification for plurality *)
Theorem plurality_is_plurality :
    forall ns m, fst (plurality ns) = Some m -> IsPlurality m ns.

(* Final specifications: correctness of classify *)
Theorem classify_correct_some :
    forall dist_metric, dist_metric_wf dist_metric ->
    forall K k data labels query c,
    0 < K -> 0 < k -> length data >= K ->
    (forall v' : datapt, List.In v' data -> length v' = k) ->
    (forall d : datapt, List.In d data -> FMap.In d labels) ->
    classify dist_metric K k data labels query = Some c ->
    exists near far classes,
        Permutation data (near ++ far) /\
        length near = K /\
        all_in_leb (dist_metric query) near far /\
        ClassesOf labels near classes /\
        IsPlurality c classes.

Theorem classify_correct :
    forall dist_metric, dist_metric_wf dist_metric ->
```

```
forall K k data labels query,
0 < K -> 0 < k ->
length data >= K ->
(forall v' : datapt, List.In v' data -> length v' = k) ->
(forall d : datapt, List.In d data -> FMap.In d labels) ->
(exists c near far classes,
    classify dist_metric K k data labels query = Some c /\
    Permutation data (near ++ far) /\
    length near = K /\
    all_in_leb (dist_metric query) near far /\
    ClassesOf labels near classes /\
    IsPlurality c classes)
\/
(classify dist_metric K k data labels query = None /\
 ~exists c, IsPlurality c (lookup_labels labels
                (knn_search dist_metric K k
                    (build_kdtree k data) query))).
```

B Sample Application: Iris Dataset

To test our implementation on actual data, we applied it to the well-known Iris flower data set [2]. The data set contains measurements (in cm, to one decimal point precision) of four different attributes for 50 iris flowers from each of 3 different species (a total of 150 data points). We preprocess the data set to multiply the values by 10 (to convert to integers) and then render the data set and its classifications in Coq syntax, as a randomly shuffled list of data points and their classifications:

```
Definition IRIS_DATASET : (list datapt) :=
    [ [62; 28; 48; 18]; [58; 26; 40; 12];  ...  [51; 38; 15; 3] ].

Definition IRIS_LABELTABLE : LabelTable :=
    (add [62; 28; 48; 18] 2
    (add [58; 26; 40; 12] 3
     ...
     (add [51; 38; 15; 3] 1 (empty nat)))).
```

We then split the data set into conventional 80/20 training/test sets and build a classifier using the Manhattan distance metric and $K = 5$.

```
Definition TRAINING := firstn 120 IRIS_DATASET.
Definition TEST := skipn 120 IRIS_DATASET.

Definition CLASSIFIER : datapt -> option nat :=
  classify manhattan_dist 5 4 TRAINING IRIS_LABELTABLE.
```

Some spot checks of its behavior:

```
Compute (CLASSIFIER [50; 30; 12; 2]).    (*  =  Some 1 *)
Compute (CLASSIFIER [67; 31; 56; 24]).   (*  =  Some 2 *)
```

We can now run each test data point through the classifier, pair it with the actual classification in the label table, and filter out pairs where there is a discrepancy:

```
Compute List.filter pair_diff
        (List.map (fun t => (find t IRIS_LABELTABLE, CLASSIFIER t))
              TEST).
```

In this case, at least for this permutation of the training/test data, there are no mis-classified data points.[8]

References

1. The Coq proof assistant, v8.16 (2022). https://coq.inria.fr/
2. Anderson, E.: The species problem in Iris. Ann. Mo. Bot. Gard. **23**(3), 457–509 (1936). http://www.jstor.org/stable/2394164
3. Appel, A.W.: Verified software toolchain. In: Barthe, G. (ed.) Programming Languages and Systems, pp. 1–17. Springer, Berlin Heidelberg, Berlin, Heidelberg (2011). https://doi.org/10.1007/978-3-642-19718-5_1
4. Barthe, G., Forest, J., Pichardie, D., Rusu, V.: Defining and reasoning about recursive functions: a practical tool for the coq proof assistant. In: Hagiya, M., Wadler, P. (eds.) Functional and Logic Programming, pp. 114–129. Springer, Berlin Heidelberg, Berlin, Heidelberg (2006). https://doi.org/10.1007/11737414_9
5. Barthe, G., Grégoire, B., Zanella Béguelin, S.: Formal certification of code-based cryptographic proofs. In: POPL '09: Proceedings of the 36th Annual ACM SIGPLAN-SIGACT Symposium on Principles of Programming Languages, pp. 90–101. Association for Computing Machinery, New York, NY, USA (2009). https://doi.org/10.1145/1480881.1480894
6. Bentley, J.L.: Multidimensional binary search trees used for associative searching. Commun. ACM **18**(9), 509–517 (1975). https://doi.org/10.1145/361002.361007
7. Bertot, Y., Castran, P.: Interactive Theorem Proving and Program Development: Coq'Art The Calculus of Inductive Constructions. Springer Publishing Company, 1st edn. (2010). https://doi.org/10.1007/978-3-662-07964-5
8. Braiek, H.B., Khomh, F.: On testing machine learning programs. J. Syst. Softw. **164**, 110542 (2020). https://doi.org/10.1016/j.jss.2020.110542
9. Cover, T., Hart, P.: Nearest neighbor pattern classification. IEEE Trans. Inf. Theory **13**(1), 21–27 (1967). https://doi.org/10.1109/TIT.1967.1053964
10. Cunningham, P., Delany, S.J.: K-nearest neighbour classifiers - a tutorial. ACM Comput. Surv. **54**(6), 1–25 (2021). https://doi.org/10.1145/3459665

---

[8] Note, that *correctness* of the mechanics of the algorithm implementation (as formalized in this work), does not imply that the algorithm will necessarily produce *accurate* classifications for data points. It could well be that the correct plurality vote of the K nearest neighbors is different from the actual label of a query point.

11. Fan, A.Z., Koutris, P.: Certifiable robustness for nearest neighbor classifiers. In: Olteanu, D., Vortmeier, N. (eds.) 25th International Conference on Database Theory, ICDT 2022, March 29 to April 1, 2022, Edinburgh, UK (Virtual Conference). LIPIcs, vol. 220, pp. 1–20. Schloss Dagstuhl - Leibniz-Zentrum für Informatik (2022). https://doi.org/10.4230/LIPICS.ICDT.2022.6
12. Fassina, N., Ranzato, F., Zanella, M.: Robustness certification of k-nearest neighbors. In: Proceedings of the 23rd IEEE International Conference on Data Mining (ICDM'23) (2023)
13. Friedman, J.H., Bentley, J.L., Finkel, R.A.: An algorithm for finding best matches in logarithmic expected time. ACM Trans. Math. Softw. **3**(3), 209–226 (1977). https://doi.org/10.1145/355744.355745
14. Gu, R., Shao, Z., Chen, H., Wu, X., Kim, J., Sjöberg, V., Costanzo, D.: Certikos: an extensible architecture for building certified concurrent OS kernels. In: OSDI'16: Proceedings of the 12th USENIX Conference on Operating Systems Design and Implementation, pp. 653–669. USENIX Association, USA (2016)
15. Hall, J.A.: Seven myths of formal methods. IEEE Softw. **7**(5), 11–19 (1990)
16. Hamid, N.A.: (Nearest) neighbors you can rely on: formally verified k-d tree construction and search in Coq. In: SAC '24: Proceedings of the 39th ACM/SIGAPP Symposium on Applied Computing, pp. 1684–1693. Association for Computing Machinery, New York, NY, USA (2024). https://doi.org/10.1145/3605098.3635960
17. Kneuper, R.: Limits of formal methods. Form. Asp. Comput. **9**(4), 379–394 (1997). https://doi.org/10.1007/BF01211297
18. Leroy, X.: Formal verification of a realistic compiler. Commun. ACM **52**(7), 107–115 (2009). https://doi.org/10.1145/1538788.1538814
19. Luckcuck, M., Farrell, M., Dennis, L.A., Dixon, C., Fisher, M.: Formal specification and verification of autonomous robotic systems: a survey. ACM Comput. Surv. **52**(5), 1–41 (2019). https://doi.org/10.1145/3342355
20. Namiot, D., Ilyushin, E., Chizhov, I.: On a formal verification of machine learning systems. Int. J. Open Inf. Technol. **10**(05), 30–34 (2022)
21. Pierce, B.C., et al.: Logical Foundations, Software Foundations, vol. 1. Electronic textbook (2023). http://softwarefoundations.cis.upenn.edu, version 6.5
22. Selsam, D., Liang, P., Dill, D.L.: Developing bug-free machine learning systems with formal mathematics. In: ICML'17: Proceedings of the 34th International Conference on Machine Learning, vol. 70, pp. 3047–3056. JMLR.org (2017)
23. Seshia, S.A., Sadigh, D., Sastry, S.S.: Toward verified artificial intelligence. Commun. ACM **65**(7), 46–55 (2022). https://doi.org/10.1145/3503914
24. Sitawarin, C., Kornaropoulos, E.M., Song, D., Wagner, D.: Adversarial examples for k-nearest neighbor classifiers based on higher-order voronoi diagrams. In: Beygelzimer, A., Dauphin, Y., Liang, P., Vaughan, J.W. (eds.) Advances in Neural Information Processing Systems, vol. 34. Curran Associates Inc, Red Hook, NY (2021)
25. Syriopoulos, P.K., Kalampalikis, N.G., Kotsiantis, S.B., Vrahatis, M.N.: kNN classification: a review. Ann. Math. Artif. Intell. 1–33 (2023). https://doi.org/10.1007/s10472-023-09882-x

Formal Methods for Security and Privacy

Formal Verification of Forward Secrecy and Post-Compromise Security for TreeKEM

Alex J. Washburn[(✉)] [iD] and Subash Shankar

Hunter College, New York, NY 10065, USA
academia@recursion.ninja, subash.shankar@hunter.cuny.edu

Abstract. The TreeKEM protocol is the preeminent implementation candidate for the Message Layer Security standard. Prior work analyzed TreeKEM by defining the Continuous Group Key Agreement security game, which facilitated proof of some security guarantees and also identified protocol deficiencies which were subsequently remedied. This work extends such applications by formalizing the Continuous Group Key Agreement security game through multiple soundness preserving abstractions. The model is parameterized by N, representing an unbounded protocol duration among N distinct participants. Once formalized, the game is encoded within Promela and essential security guarantees are verified for $N \leq 16$ via the model checker Spin. This represents a notable achievement, both in practical security terms for the TreeKEM protocol, as well as demonstrating scalability techniques for non-trivial parameter bounds when modeling a complex, concurrent protocol.

Keywords: Cryptographic Protocols · Formal Verification · Linear Temporal Logic · Model Checking · Promela · Spin

1 Introduction

Secure and asynchronous communication channels between two parties, known as Secure Messaging (SM) [24], have become increasingly commonplace [13,21,25]. The natural extension of SM requires the expansion of the security guarantees to communication between *more* than two parties, known as Secure Group Messaging (SGM) [11]. To be considered a SGM protocol [4], the Internet Engineering Task Force (IETF) s states the following operations must exist for each participating member:

1. Create a new communication group consisting of a set of known members
2. Broadcast a message to all members in the group
3. Receive a message from a member in the group
4. Add a new member to the group
5. Remove an existing member from the group
6. Instruct all group members to use a new shared key via an update algorithm

Furthermore, the IETF defines Message Layer Security (MLS) [14], a standardization specification within which SGM protocols can be defined. MLS describes the SGM protocol environment in which protocol agents interact. The Internet threat model (ITM) of RFC3552 [19] is the context within which the MLS specifies its security guarantees. Additionally, an Authentication Service (AS) [16] exists from which a messenger can request a fresh public key for a specified contact that can be immediately used within the MLS protocol. Similarly, the existence of a Delivery Service (DS) is stipulated. The DS can receive messages addressed to any contact and stores them until the contact polls for new messages. The ability to query AS and DS third-parties simplifies the asynchronicity requirement, mediating potential protocol synchronization issues between participants. The MLS specification also specifies Forward Secrecy *with Updates* (FSU) [14] and Postcompromise Security (PCS) [9] as security guarantees of the protocol, amongst others. Both Forward Secrecy (FS) and PCS have been researched with respect to SM, producing provably secure as well as efficient constructions, but for SGM were previously open problems in cryptographic protocols. The recentness of research regarding SGM informed our choice of verifying FS and PCS

The TreeKEM protocol [5] was (informally) conceived in 2018, and formally described in 2019 [15]. The IETF along with many other corporate and government sponsors have put their support behind the TreeKEM protocol. TreeKEM provides functionality for achieving each of the six operations to be considered a SGM protocol (discussed further in Sect. 2.1). Additionally TreeKEM aims to satisfy both the efficiency goals and security guarantees of the MLS specification, addressing the previously open problems of FS and PCS for SGM. Conformance with both of these definitions is a result of TreeKEM's construction.

The essence of TreeKEM is a protocol to generate continuous, fresh, shared, and secret random keys for use by group members. This generation process is based on a left-balanced binary tree (LBBT) [3] shared by all participants, with nodes decorated by public keys [22]. Leaf nodes of the LBBT contain the public key uniquely corresponding to a group member, and each internal node contains a constructed public key, with a private key shared by each group member in that sub-tree. Hence the root node's key material is known to all group members and used for symmetric encryption of messages. The TreeKEM LBBT of key material evolves over time, delineated by discrete "communication epochs," in such a way that all group members maintain continuous agreement of the shared LBBT and secret root key.

Correspondingly, the TreeKEM protocol is temporally delineated into discrete quanta referred to as "communication epochs," representing a collection of messages sent using the same secret root key. To create a new communication epoch, any group member may broadcast a control message for distribution via the DS, instructing the other group members how to evolve the shared LBBT and associated key material to arrive at the shared symmetric key of the new epoch. Figure 1 depicts a simple case of communication epoch progression. New encryption "epochs" are created by a member broadcasting a control message for one of the following operations:

- Add a member to the group
- Remove a member from the group
- Update their continuously agreed upon symmetric key

This work presents two primary verification goals for the TreeKEM protocol; the security guarantees of AbrevFSU and PCS specified by MLS. The former offers protection in the case that a protocol's long-term secret key(s) are compromised [6]. The latter ensures that no matter how many compromises of key material occur among the group members previously, once no new compromises occur, the group members will eventually reestablish secrecy through continued protocol usage [10].

Prior work has analyzed TreeKEM through a security game [2], which will be further elaborated on and utilized below in Sect. 2. The resulting analysis yielded a mathematical proof, via graph theory, of the security guarantees FSU and PCS for TreeKEM. In contrast, this paper presents a mechanical verification of the same security guarantees for TreeKEM, up to some parameterized bound, by utilizing model checking.

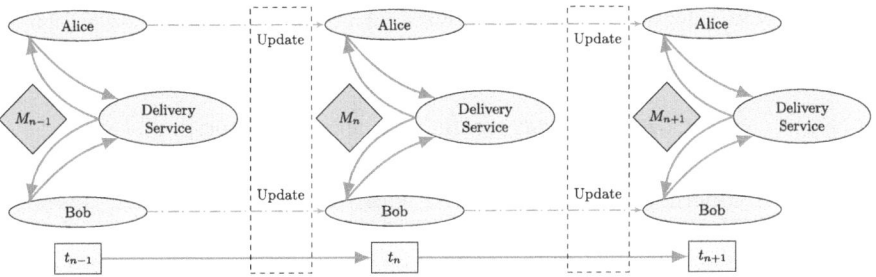

Fig. 1. SGM Timeline depicting the progression of SGM communication epochs t_{n-1}, t_n, and t_{n+1} between Alice and Bob. The participants exchange (mediated by the DS) sets of messages M_{n-1}, M_n, and M_{n+1} during epochs t_{n-1}, t_n, and t_{n+1}, respectively.

2 Formalization and Abstractions

Formalizing the model under verification is always an important and detailed process. The verification methodology chosen by the authors utilizes explicit state model checking. For this reason, it is important to rigorously control the size of the model's state-space in order to avoid state-space explosion. To that end, the authors developed multiple abstractions (discussed later in this section) that progressively reduce the model's state-space. Without these abstractions, the model is not verifiable for even modestly sized parameters.

Table 1. Description of CGKA security game oracles and their corresponding $\ulcorner$**CGKA**$\lrcorner$ algorithms.

CGKA security game Oracle Name and Inputs	Corresponding $\ulcorner$**CGKA**$\lrcorner$ Algorithm	Brief description of Oracle Semantics
init()	init	Begins the CGKA security game.
create-group($\vec{\text{ID}}^n$)	create	Initialize a group with n members.
add-user(ID, ID$'$)	add	ID initiates adding ID$'$ to the group.
remove-user(ID, ID$'$)	rem	ID initiates removing ID$'$ from the group.
send-update(ID)	upd	ID initiates updating the group's shared key.
deliver(ID, ID$'$)	proc	DS delivers a message to ID$'$ from ID.
no-del(ID)	—	ID stops deleting keys upon epoch changes.
corr(ID)	—	$\mathcal{A}$ learns the current state of ID.
reveal(t)	—	$\mathcal{A}$ learns the group's current shared key.
chall(t)	—	$\mathcal{A}$ ends the CGKA security game.

2.1 Continuous Group Key Agreement

In the two-party case, a general notion of Continuous Key Agreement has been used to provide robust security guarantees such as forward secrecy and post-compromise security [1,17,18]. For SGM, this same notion has been extended as Continuous Group Key Agreement (CGKA), which is used as an abstraction for reasoning about the MLS security guarantees [2]. A continuous group key-agreement scheme $\ulcorner$**CGKA**$\lrcorner$ is an abstract collection of algorithms used to maintain secure communications between a group of two or more participants, each algorithm being known and performed locally by participants:

$$\ulcorner\textbf{CGKA}\lrcorner = \{\text{ init, create, add, rem, upd, proc }\}$$

Additionally, an oracle-based security game for CGKA is also defined by [2]. The authors inherit the definitions along with the assumptions from this work and provide the most contextually relevant details herein. Each oracle is defined in terms of one or more of the algorithms from the $\ulcorner$**CGKA**$\lrcorner$ definition. The CGKA security game defines these oracles, as listed in Table 1. An adversary can query all ten of the game's oracles and through the sequence of queries use the oracles to direct the execution of the CGKA protocol. The group members can only call the six $\ulcorner$**CGKA**$\lrcorner$ algorithms above, while the adversary can only query the ten oracles. However, there exists one oracle which corresponds to each of the six $\ulcorner$**CGKA**$\lrcorner$ algorithms, effectively giving the attacker comparable options to any group member in addition to the options provided by the remaining four oracles.

These oracles define a security game [23] which emulates the ITM. Such security games are a common analysis tool made by cryptographers, where the "game moves" representing protocol semantics, and the objective is to show that the probability of an adversary $\mathcal{A}$ breaking a given security property by playing this game is negligible. Within the CGKA security game, an adversary $\mathcal{A}$ is parameterized by (T, C, N). The T value indicates that the protocol runs in at most T epochs, during which time $\mathcal{A}$ can make at most C "challenge queries" to the reveal() or chall() oracles, and the total unique group members of the protocol can never exceed N. The goal of $\mathcal{A}$ is to infer information about the shared TreeKEM root key. Within the security game, this is modeled by $\mathcal{A}$ ending the game via a challenge query to the chall() oracle, and subsequently demonstrating non-negligible advantage. We model the TreeKEM protocol in terms of the CGKA security game as the initial abstraction.

Advantage is formally defined by [2], but a brief definition follows. A bit b, hidden from $\mathcal{A}$, is flipped uniformly at random. If $b = 1$ then the real TreeKEM protocol is used in the security game, otherwise when $b = 0$ the security game simulates TreeKEM with the encrypted messages beteween entities replaced by bit-strings of equal length to the replaced message sampled uniformly at random from $\{0, 1\}^*$. $\mathcal{A}$ demonstrates advantage if and only if they can guess the value of b with probability $\varepsilon > \frac{1}{2}$. Since $\mathcal{A}$ can distiguish between random bit-strings and encrypted data, the princile of indistinguishability is violated and the protocol is not secure.

2.2 Abstraction: Adversarial Direction

While both the adversary $\mathcal{A}$ and each group member can initiate a new epoch within the CGKA security game, modeling this explicitly complicates the model unnecessarily. Recall that within the ITM, $\mathcal{A}$ controls the network. This is modeled within the CGKA security game by messages sent from any source only being delivered if $\mathcal{A}$ permits it by querying deliver(). Because the verification methodology will explore all possible interleaving of concurrent actions within the CGKA security game, simulating nondeterministic computation, this can be utilized to form an additional simplifying abstraction.

Suppose for a given epoch e_i that the non-empty set M consists of all "epoch advancing messages" originating from calls to algorithms *add*, *rem*, and *upd* by group members. By the rules of the CGKA security game, $\mathcal{A}$ selects some message $m \in M$ sent by group member j and queries deliver(g_j, g_k) to propagate delivery of m to the group members and advance to the next communication epoch. Without loss of generality, rather than group member j creating and sending m by calling either algorithm *add*, *rem*, or *upd*, the adversary $\mathcal{A}$ equivalently queries the corresponding add-user(g_j, g_k), remove-user(g_j, g_k), or send-update(g_j, g_k) oracle, respectively. This operational equivalence permits the modeling of the CGKA security game to only consider $\mathcal{A}$–originating calls to algorithms *add*, *rem*, and *upd* via queries to the oracles add-user(), remove-user(), and send-update(), respectively. Consequently, the model does not need to consider any group member calls to *add*, *rem*, and *upd*, allowing these states to be safely removed from the model encoding without effecting protocol semantics. The model can explicitly track epoch progress by the adversary via t and c variables corresponding to epoch index and a binary indicator of a challenge query made within the current epoch, respectively.

2.3 End-To-End Encryption Concession

The verification of end-to-end encryption is beyond the scope of this model, as the objective is solely the FSU and PCS security properties. Recognizing this, one can assume that end-to-end encryption of messages between group members holds. By conceding this, it is not necessary to model the communication between group members, as $\mathcal{A}$ will not gain any advantage by observing messages between group members. This simplifying abstraction removes the need to maintain message queues as well as model the processing order of messages by the DS. Furthermore, the explicit modeling of the DS becomes entirely superfluous. Instead of explicitly modeling the message processing semantics of the DS, the consistent message delivery requirement of the DS is *implicitly* modeled by the actions available to $\mathcal{A}$ at a given protocol state.

2.4 Abstraction: Parameterized Bounds of T, C, and N

Another important simplifying abstraction is the explicit bounding of the T, C, and N parameters of the (T, C, N) Adversary $\mathcal{A}$. The model will be parameterized by T and N and entail all possible starting group sizes $s \in [2, N]$ and all possible sequences of oracle queries consisting of T or fewer epochs. This provides a partial bound for the model, though not a finite bounding, as idempotent or cyclic query sequences are permitted. Interestingly, with this abstraction C does not need to be explicitly parameterized.

Recall that a challenge query is made to either `chall()` or `reveal()`. A query to the former ends the security game. A query to the latter reveals the group's shared secret key, so a subsequent query to `reveal()` within the same epoch would result in the same model state. Furthermore, a query to `reveal()` then `chall()` within the same epoch would trivially result in $\mathcal{A}$ ending the game with knowledge of the secret key. Consequently, CGKA security game limits $\mathcal{A}$ to at most one challenge query per epoch.

Suppose one were to fix the number of epochs T. Then necessarily $C \in [1, T]$, as $\mathcal{A}$ can only perform *one* challenge query per epoch. Within the formalized security game, during each epoch $\mathcal{A}$ has the option to make either zero or one challenge query. Given the exhaustiveness of model checking methodology, all possible choices are explored. Therefore, without any loss of generality, verification of a model parameterized by a fixed T also implicitly verifies $\forall C \in [1, T]$, allowing for the specification of C to be elided from the model parameters.

2.5 Abstraction: Required Progression

A fundamental simplifying abstraction in the presented model is a restriction imposed on $\mathcal{A}$, allowing only "non-redundant" moves within the CGKA security game. Redundancy, in this context, refers to the situation where $\mathcal{A}$ chooses to query an oracle in such a way that the security game enters a state that has already been reached within the same epoch. Put simply, each query made by $\mathcal{A}$ must lead to a unique and previously unseen state, which will be referred to as a "fresh" state within the epoch. It is worth noting that this constraint does not sacrifice any expressiveness in the model; it simply eliminates cycles in the model's state transition graph. The application of this constraint has a significant impact by bounding the model's state-space.

Let us consider the oracles that drive the game. A query to add-user(), remove-user(), or send-update() advances the epoch, ensuring that it always results in a fresh state, specifically the first state of the *next* epoch. Additionally, querying chall() ends the game, and since the game has not ended before this query, it necessarily leads to a fresh state. These "epoch-ending" queries do not limit the moves available to $\mathcal{A}$ in the epoch prior to the query, as the previous epoch is no longer relevant to the "non-redundant" constraint after the query.

To query corr() or no-del(), there must be an applicable member ID. Furthermore, there exist binary indicators g_i and h_i for each member ID corresponding to whether the ID associated with i is corrupted and whether they are deleting old key values, respectively. For convenience, let $\top$ denote the positive value and $\bot$ the negative. After such a query, the state of the group member is consistently changed from $\top$ to $\bot$. To change the state of a group member from $\bot$ to $\top$, $\mathcal{A}$ must query either remove-user() or send-update(). However, querying either of these oracles results in a new epoch, which means that querying corr() or no-del() subsequently leads to a fresh state. Since this query alters the state of the group member from $\top$ to $\bot$, there is no way the state of a group member could have been changed from $\bot$ to $\top$ during the current epoch.

Furthermore, considering corr() and no-del(), one can recall that the number of unique group members is bounded by N. Although $\mathcal{A}$ can query both oracles multiple times during an epoch, due to the "non-redundant" constraint, each query monotonically decreases the available moves for $\mathcal{A}$. Eventually, since N is finite, there will no longer be an option to make a "non-redundant" query to corr() or no-del() because the state of all group members will be $\bot$. Similarly, querying reveal() can only occur at most once per epoch, resulting in a fresh state and decreasing the available moves for $\mathcal{A}$ by one, as the "non-redundant" constraint prevents querying reveal() again in the current epoch.

Analyzing the relationship of the oracles in the CGKA security game state, one can observe that imposing the "non-redundant" constraint causes the available moves for $\mathcal{A}$ in the current epoch to monotonically decrease with each query. Eventually, this leads to a point where no "non-redundant" moves are available that would result in the same epoch, requiring $\mathcal{A}$ to advance the game to the next epoch. Consequently, utilizing this can be considered a "Required Progression" abstraction which fully bounds the model's state-space by the parameters T and N. This is apparent by observing that the number of queries $\mathcal{A}$ can make in each epoch is constrained by N and the total number of epochs is constrained by T.

If one considers a function $f : \mathsf{LTS} \mapsto 2^{|s|}$ where LTS are the labeled transition system states of the model and $|s|$ is the state-vector length, then this abstraction reduces the cardinality disparity between the codomain of f and the image of f by decreasing $|s|$. It is worth noting that SPIN has the capability through stutter extension of the model and verification of stutter invariant properties to perform this same abstraction without manually encoding it into the model. However, utilization of stutter extension capabilities of SPIN does not reduce the state-vector length, only modifying the transitions between states and therefore does not decrease the *representational* difference of the codomain and the image of f during the verification process. In contrast, the manual encoding of this abstraction appreciably reduces the state-vector length, and consequently the memory requirements of verification process since these vectors are added to the DFS stack and accumulated in a hashtable for efficient memoization. Hence it is sometimes useful, as in this case, to manually reason through the application of a manually encoded abstraction layer to improve the tractability of verification. This can be especially important as model parameter sizes grow.

2.6 Abstraction: Markovian Property

The final abstraction to be utilized in the modeling of TreeKEM protocol is the observation that, in its currently simplified form, the model can be viewed as a Markov Process. Consider $\mathcal{A}$ entering a CGKA security game state s_i. How the TreeKEM protocol evolved prior to s_i does not inform the moves available to $\mathcal{A}$, rather the current game state s_i solely informs this. Furthermore, how the knowledge accumulated by $\mathcal{A}$ prior to s_i was obtained does not further inform $\mathcal{A}$ of the TreeKEM protocol's CGKA key; instead all $\mathcal{A}$ knowledge is deduced from s_i. Phrased differently, state s_{i-1} has no unique information which informs state transitions from s_i, and state transitions from s_i are determined solely from the information contained within s_i.

Applying this abstraction has a profoundly important impact on model verification. Because the model can be encoded as a Markov process, it can become "memoryless" and not require the encoding of the current epoch number within the game state. Consequently, the model applying this "Markovian Property" abstraction elides the specification of T from the model parameters. The resulting model is parameterized only by N, yet verifying all $t \in [1, \infty)$ and $c \in [1, t]$.

3 Model Instantiation

3.1 Promela and Spin

Let $^{2}\mathcal{M}_{\text{CGKA}}\langle N \rangle$ denote the TreeKEM model encoding with parameter N, for the model derived by composing the abstractions described in Sect. 2. The encoding implementation of $^{2}\mathcal{M}_{\text{CGKA}}\langle N \rangle$ utilized the Protocol Meta Language (Promela) [12], which is the modeling language for the Spin model checker. The key language feature of Promela is that *all* branches – conditional execution, looping, and randomness – are evaluated non-deterministically, making it a natural choice for encoding the model. The Promela encoding [27] of $^{2}\mathcal{M}_{\text{CGKA}}\langle N \rangle$ produces all possible states and transitions of TreeKEM, and this representation is then supplied to a model checker for verification.

The explicit state model checker Spin [12] was chosen as the verification tool for this work. As an explicit-state model checker, Spin utilizes a representation of all possible model states as a Finite State Machine (FSM) [8], with transitions corresponding to possible changes in model state. Spin then verifies a user-specified property by traversing through all transitions of the FSM, and checking that a property holds at each model state. The principle drawback of explicit state model checking is the immense state-space resulting as the model complexity grows [7]. As a venerable tool, Spin does much to address this [20] but the authors' own encoding adaptations which further mitigate the state-space explosion are detailed below in Sects. 3.2 and 3.3. Additionally, Spin supports numerous compile time directive which alter the state-space representation, search trajectories, and time-memory trade-offs (see Table 2).

Table 2. Spin performance options used for verification.

Compilation Directives:		Runtime Flags
HC4	PMAX=2	-a
JOINPROCS	QMAX=0	-A
MEMLIM=204800	SC	-m20000000
MURMUR	SEPQS	-v
NOBOUNDCHECK	SFH	-w32
NOFAIR	SPACE	-x
NOFIX	VECTORSZ=101	

3.2 Encoding of Bit-Arrays

In the default Promela type system, an array of bits is encoded as an array of bytes at runtime, resulting in each "bit value" requiring 8 bits during verification. This encoding inflates the state-vector size unnecessarily by 7 bits additional bits and causes the model checker to consider 256 states instead of the actual 2 binary states which are valid encodings (0x00 = TRUE, 0xFF = FALSE). Consequently, verification times are slower, and at least eight times more memory is required. To address this, bits within a fixed bit-width Promela type are manually toggled using C Pre-processor macros, reducing the state-vector size and improving runtime efficiency while minimizing memory usage.

3.3 Control Flow Elision via PopCount

An additional, significant Promela encoding technique within the presented work was the application of a bit-wise population count (PopCount) operation. PopCount returns the number of bits set in the value of a fixed bit-width type. Within the model encoding, due to the "Required Progression" abstraction (Sect. 2.5), it is necessary to count the number of set (or unset) bits to determine which queries are available for $\mathcal{A}$. This bit counting occurs multiple times within the model. The naive approach involves a counter along with a looping control flow structure to individually test each applicable bit value. In contrast, the PopCount operation returns the number of set bits without iteration.

The authors included PopCount as a small, inlined sequence of arithmetic and bit-wise operations which runs in $\mathcal{O}(1)$ time with no additional memory. Substituting PopCount in place of the naive iteration has two notable effects, reducing the state-vector length by removing the loop counter and reducing the number of state transitions by removing the entire control flow structure of the loop. For a bit-array of length n, the number of transitions encoded in the model by iteration increases exponentially with respect to n. This exponential transition encoding occurs because for each iteration of the bit counting loop, the set bit counter's value can either be incremented or maintained, hence 2^n transitions to count the number of set bits. Conversely, the PopCount macro derives a *constant* number of transitions independent of n.

3.4 LTL Properties

The security guarantees under verification are encoded in Linear Temporal Logic (LTL). LTL expressions are natively supported by Promela and Spin. Below are the English definitions of FSU and PCS with their corresponding LTL formulae.

Definition 1 (Forward Secrecy with Updates). *If the state of any group member is leaked during an epoch «1», the shared keys from all previous epochs remain hidden from the adversary «2».*

LTL Predicate (FSU) :

$$\Box(\underbrace{\texttt{CGKA@move\_corrupt}}_{«1»} \implies \underbrace{\texttt{learnedLegacyKey} = \bot}_{«2»})$$

The Promela model is named CGKA, and the state within the model at which $\mathcal{A}$ queries the oracle corr(targetID) is labeled move_corrupt. The term CGKA@move_corrupt will be true only when CGKA is in state move_corrupt. Additionally, the model contains a boolean flag learnedLegacyKey indicating when $\mathcal{A}$ has learned, during the *current* epoch, information about the shared group key of any *any previous* epoch. The LTL formula (FSU) is a direct translation of the natural language FSU description.

Definition 2 (Post-compromise Security). *After every group member whose state was leaked initiates an epoch update «2», and that update instruction message is processed by all group members «1», the shared key becomes confidential again «3».*

LTL Predicate (PCS) :

$$\Box\Big((\underbrace{\texttt{CGKA@start\_of\_epoch}}_{«1»} \wedge \underbrace{\texttt{memberKeys} = \vec{0}}_{«2»}) \implies \underbrace{\texttt{learnedActiveKey} = \bot}_{«3»}\Big)$$

The state within the model at which an epoch begins is labeled as start_of_epoch. The term CGKA@start_of_epoch will be true only when CGKA is in state start_of_epoch. The model contains a bit-vector memberKeys of length N indicating which group members have had their keys corrupted by $\mathcal{A}$. The expression memberKeys = $\vec{0}$ is true iff the bit-vector contains no set bits. Finally, the model contains a boolean flag learnedActiveKey indicated when $\mathcal{A}$ has infered information about the *current* shared group key. This LTL formula (PCS) translates the security guarantee in a fairly direct way.

4 Methodology

The methodology presented is two-fold. First, the performance is measured of the model $^{②}\mathcal{M}_{\text{CGKA}}\langle N \rangle$ described in this work and compared with the performance of a precursor model defined by [26] denoted as $^{①}\mathcal{M}_{\text{CGKA}}\langle N, T \rangle$. The comparison model $^{①}\mathcal{M}_{\text{CGKA}}\langle N, T \rangle$ is the same semantic encoding of $^{②}\mathcal{M}_{\text{CGKA}}\langle N \rangle$ *before* the abstractions described were applied, i.e.: ABSTRACTIONS($^{①}\mathcal{M}_{\text{CGKA}}\langle N, T \rangle$) = $^{②}\mathcal{M}_{\text{CGKA}}\langle N \rangle$. Therefore $^{①}\mathcal{M}_{\text{CGKA}}\langle N, T \rangle$ is a fitting comparative baseline from which the effects of the composed abstractions can be measured. Comparison of performance is made across several metrics, including state-vector length, runtime, memory usage, state-space size, and transition count. Both models performed verification of the (FSU) and (PCS) properties. Second, $^{②}\mathcal{M}_{\text{CGKA}}\langle N \rangle$ is utilized to verify (FSU) and (PCS) for parameters far beyond the capabilities of $^{①}\mathcal{M}_{\text{CGKA}}\langle N, T \rangle$. Subsequently, the authors provide brief contextual commentary on these verification results.

All verification runs of both $^{②}\mathcal{M}_{\text{CGKA}}\langle N \rangle$ and $^{①}\mathcal{M}_{\text{CGKA}}\langle N, T \rangle$ ran on AMD Opteron 6380 cores operating at 2500 MHz[1]. Each verification run utilized 2 cores and up to 200 GiB of RAM. All Spin performance tuning options used during verification are listed in Table 2. The performance observations of the verification runs are depicted in Table 5. Note that all run-times are "wall clock" time not "CPU time." All LTL properties for all models were successfully verified.

5 Results

5.1 Descriptive Power

The paramount result of this work is, perhaps unsurprisingly, the model $^{②}\mathcal{M}_{\text{CGKA}}\langle N \rangle$ itself. Note that the precursor model $^{①}\mathcal{M}_{\text{CGKA}}\langle N, T \rangle$ must *individually* verify each T parameter, limiting it's descriptive scope to a TreeKEM communication group which exists for a series of epochs less than or equal to the parameterized upper bound of T. In contrast, all verification runs of $^{②}\mathcal{M}_{\text{CGKA}}\langle N \rangle$ provide verification for an unbounded, finite series of communication epochs. Hence for the same N, the verification result of $^{②}\mathcal{M}_{\text{CGKA}}\langle N \rangle$ will provide infinitely more descriptive power than the verification results of $^{①}\mathcal{M}_{\text{CGKA}}\langle N, T \rangle$ for all $T \in [1, \infty)$.

---

[1] Performed on the American Museum of Natural History scientific computing cluster.

Since this leap in descriptive power was derived directly form the composed abstractions, the authors argue that the presented compositions constitute a meaningful contribution as a case study in combining multiple disparate formalization and encoding techniques which is, with some minor creativity, transferable to other modeling endeavors.

Table 3. Encoding efficiency comparison of the composed abstraction model with the work of [26].

②$\mathcal{M}_{CGKA}\langle N \rangle$			①$\mathcal{M}_{CGKA}\langle N, T \rangle$		②$\mathcal{M}_{CGKA}\langle N \rangle$			①$\mathcal{M}_{CGKA}\langle N, T \rangle$		②$\mathcal{M}_{CGKA}\langle N \rangle$			①$\mathcal{M}_{CGKA}\langle N, T \rangle$	
N	T	State Vector	T	State Vector	N	T	State Vector	T	State Vector	N	T	State Vector	T	State Vector
4	∞	56 B	4	192 B	7	∞	64 B	4	224 B	10	∞	88 B	4	260 B
			5	240 B				5	296 B				5	352 B
			6	248 B				6	304 B				6	352 B
			7	248 B				7	304 B				7	360 B
			8	268 B				8	316 B				8	372 B
5	∞	64 B	4	200 B	8	∞	68 B	4	236 B	11	∞	88 B	4	268 B
			5	264 B				5	312 B				5	368 B
			6	264 B				6	320 B				6	376 B
			7	264 B				7	320 B				7	376 B
			8	284 B				8	340 B				8	388 B
6	∞	64 B	4	216 B	9	∞	88 B	4	244 B	12	∞	88 B	4	276 B
			5	280 B				5	336 B				5	384 B
			6	280 B				6	336 B				6	392 B
			7	288 B				7	336 B				7	392 B
			8	300 B				8	356 B				8	412 B

Table 4. Performance comparison of the composed abstraction model with the work of [26].

Model	N	T	LTL	Runtime	Memory	States	Transitions
①$\mathcal{M}_{CGKA}\langle 7, 7 \rangle$	7	7	(FSU)	35,659s	1.325 GiB	2.159×10^7	3.163×10^7
	7	7	(PCS)	66,258s	21.218 GiB	3.019×10^8	3.050×10^7
②$\mathcal{M}_{CGKA}\langle 7 \rangle$	7	∞	(FSU)	6,230s	52.008 GiB	1.142×10^9	2.082×10^9
	7	∞	(PCS)	17,800s	110.001 GiB	2.060×10^9	3.462×10^9

Table 5. Performance measurements of composed abstraction model verification results for $N = 16$.

Model	N	T	LTL	Runtime	Memory	States	Transitions	Search Depth
$^{②}\mathcal{M}_{\text{CGKA}}\langle 16 \rangle$	16	∞	(FSU)	77,272s	156.382 GiB	3.034×10^9	6.591×10^9	2.598×10^9
	16	∞	(PCS)	79,552s	191.092 GiB	3.475×10^9	7.969×10^9	4.386×10^9

5.2 Comparative Scalability

Empirical comparison results of employing these abstractions in conjunction with the bit-packing and PopCount encodings impressively reduced the model complexity, model parameters, state-vector size, verification time, as well as the memory footprint! For comparison, Table 3 compares state-vector length of the model $^{②}\mathcal{M}_{\text{CGKA}}\langle N \rangle$ with $^{①}\mathcal{M}_{\text{CGKA}}\langle N, T \rangle$ from the work of [26], emphasizing the vast difference in model expressiveness and encoding efficiency. A cursory analysis of the data within Table 3 reveals state-vector length improvement of $^{②}\mathcal{M}_{\text{CGKA}}\langle N \rangle$ from the baseline $^{①}\mathcal{M}_{\text{CGKA}}\langle N, T \rangle$ which varies from $\approx 64\%$ to 80%. Even the least improvement measure is still remarkably significant.

Consequently, the verification performance of $^{②}\mathcal{M}_{\text{CGKA}}\langle N \rangle$ also differs drastically from the baseline $^{①}\mathcal{M}_{\text{CGKA}}\langle N, T \rangle$ due to this reduction of state-vector lengths. As depicted in Table 4, a modest time/memory tradeoff permits the abstracted model encoding to complete verification much faster than the work presented by [26]. Security guarantee verification not only concludes execution more quickly, but as noted in Sect. 5.1 the conclusion also literally produces an infinitely stronger result; $\forall T \in [1, \infty)$.

5.3 Meaningful Verification

Given the new range of tractable verification provided by $^{②}\mathcal{M}_{\text{CGKA}}\langle N \rangle$, verification was performed with model parameters which were previously untenable using $^{①}\mathcal{M}_{\text{CGKA}}\langle N, T \rangle$. Verification of FSU and PCS was conducted on the models $^{②}\mathcal{M}_{\text{CGKA}}\langle 16 \rangle$. Both models had a state-vector of 100B. Then verification results produced by $^{②}\mathcal{M}_{\text{CGKA}}\langle 16 \rangle$ for both properties were *positive*, affirming that the properties hold for the model. The positive verification of the LTL encodings for FSU and PCS given by $^{②}\mathcal{M}_{\text{CGKA}}\langle 16 \rangle$ are not surprising. Rather, it is consistent with the expectations shown by the previous ⌜**CGKA**⌝ abstraction formalization work [2]. While consistent, this is the first instance known to the authors which has modeled the TreeKEM protocol and verified FSU and PCS for all (T, C, N)–Adversaries, with $T \in [1, \infty)$, $C \in [1, T]$, and $N \in [2, 16]$. Formal verification for TreeKEM of this scope has not been done before.

5.4 Future Work

The authors hypothesize that the model $^{\textcircled{2}}\mathcal{M}_{\text{CGKA}}\langle\,N\,\rangle$ can scale to $N = 24$ on computing cluster hardware without further modification. Perhaps even $N \approx 32$ can be achieved with minor modifications. Similarly, additional properties of TreeKEM can be explored with this work's model encoding, such as exploring the relaxation of DS requirements, enabling TreeKEM with a less trusted third party.

6 Conclusion

This work presents a verification of FSU and PCS for TreeKEM; an important undertaking in establishing the security of and confidence in the protocol. Furthermore, an example of effective, and generally applicable model abstraction and model encoding techniques is illustrated. The authors believe that, though no abstraction in isolation is novel, this is the first work to compose these abstractions and encoding techniques in the combination presented. The exploration of combining these techniques has been shown necessary for achieving scalability when verifying a complex model such as the TreeKEM protocol. An unqualified improvement was obtained across each of the following measurable dimensions: model complexity, parameterization, state-vector length, and verification space as well as time. These improvements were essential to perform verification of the largest known TreeKEM group size to date. While the application and analysis of presented techniques herein was limited to TreeKEM, the techniques are not so bespoke that they apply only to modeling and verifying TreeKEM. Rather, it is probable that only minor creativity is require to transfer them to other modeling efforts.

References

1. Alwen, J., Coretti, S., Dodis, Y.: The double ratchet: security notions, proofs, and modularization for the signal protocol. In: Ishai, Y., Rijmen, V. (eds.) EUROCRYPT 2019. LNCS, vol. 11476, pp. 129–158. Springer, Cham (2019). https://doi.org/10.1007/978-3-030-17653-2_5
2. Alwen, J., Coretti, S., Dodis, Y., Tselekounis, Y.: Security analysis and improvements for the IETF MLS standard for group messaging. In: Micciancio, D., Ristenpart, T. (eds.) CRYPTO 2020. LNCS, vol. 12170, pp. 248–277. Springer, Cham (2020). https://doi.org/10.1007/978-3-030-56784-2_9
3. Bærentzen, J.A.: On left-balancing binary trees. Technical report, Technical University of Denmark, Technical report (2003)
4. Barnes, R., Beurdouche, B., Robert, R., Millican, J., Omara, E., Cohn-Gordon, K.: The messaging layer security (MLS) protocol. Internet-Draft draft-ietf-mls-protocol-14, Internet Engineering Task Force (2022). https://datatracker.ietf.org/doc/html/draft-ietf-mls-protocol-14, work in Progress
5. Bhargavan, K., Barnes, R., Rescorla, E.: TreeKEM: asynchronous decentralized key management for large dynamic groups a protocol proposal for messaging layer security (MLS). Research report, Inria Paris (2018). https://hal.inria.fr/hal-02425247

6. Boyd, C., Gellert, K.: A modern view on forward security. Comput. J. **64**(4), 639–652 (2021)
7. Burch, J.R., Clarke, E.M., McMillan, K.L., Dill, D.L., Hwang, L.J.: Symbolic model checking: 1020 states and beyond. Inf. Comput. **98**(2), 142–170 (1992)
8. Clarke, E.M., Emerson, E.A.: Design and synthesis of synchronization skeletons using branching time temporal logic. In: Kozen, D. (ed.) Logic of Programs 1981. LNCS, vol. 131, pp. 52–71. Springer, Heidelberg (1981). https://doi.org/10.1007/bfb0025774
9. Cohn-Gordon, K., Cremers, C., Garratt, L.: On post-compromise security. In: 2016 IEEE 29th Computer Security Foundations Symposium (CSF), pp. 164–178. IEEE (2016)
10. Cohn-Gordon, K., Cremers, C., Garratt, L.: On post-compromise security. In: 2016 IEEE 29th Computer Security Foundations Symposium (CSF), pp. 164–178 (2016). https://doi.org/10.1109/CSF.2016.19
11. Cohn-Gordon, K., Cremers, C., Garratt, L., Millican, J., Milner, K.: On ends-to-ends encryption: asynchronous group messaging with strong security guarantees. In: Proceedings of the 2018 ACM SIGSAC Conference on Computer and Communications Security, pp. 1802–1819 (2018)
12. Holzmann, G.J.: The Spin Model Checker: Primer and Reference Manual. Addison-Wesley Professional, hardcover edn. (2003)
13. Jahn, M.A., Porter, B.W., Patel, H., Zillich, A.J., Simon, S.R., Russ, A.L.: Usability assessment of secure messaging for clinical document sharing between health care providers and patients. Appl. Clin. Inform. **9**(02), 467–477 (2018)
14. Omara, B., Rescorla, I., Kwon, D.: The messaging layer security (MLS) architecture. In: Proceedings of Network Working Group. Internet Engineering Task Force (2020)
15. Omara, E., Beurdouche, B., Rescorla, E., Inguva, S., Kwon, A., Duric, A.: The messaging layer security (MLS) architecture. Internet-Draft draft-ietf-mls-architecture-03, Internet Engineering Task Force (2019). https://datatracker.ietf.org/doc/draft-ietf-mls-architecture/03/. work in Progress
16. Perlman, R.: An overview of PKI trust models. IEEE Netw. **13**(6), 38–43 (1999)
17. Perrin, T., Marlinspike, M.: Axolotl ratchet, p. 16 (2013). https://github.com/trevp/axolotl/wiki (visited on 2014-11-02)
18. Perrin, T., Marlinspike, M.: The double ratchet algorithm. GitHub wiki **112** (2016), M. Marlinspike and T. Perrin. The double ratchet algorithm (2016)
19. Rescorla, E., Korver, B.: RFC3552: Guidelines for Writing RFC Text on Security Considerations (2003)
20. Rudin, H., West, C., et al.: On limits and possibilities of automated protocol analysis. In: Protocol Specification, Testing, and Verification, VII: Proceedings of the IFIP WG 6.1 Seventh International Conference on Protocol Specification, Testing, and Verification, vol. 7, p. 339. North Holland (1987)
21. Schröder, S., Huber, M., Wind, D., Rottermanner, C.: When SIGNAL hits the fan: on the usability and security of state-of-the-art secure mobile messaging. In: European Workshop on Usable Security, pp. 1–7. IEEE (2016)
22. Shirey, R.W.: Internet Security Glossary, Version 2. RFC 4949 (2007). https://doi.org/10.17487/RFC4949. https://www.rfc-editor.org/info/rfc4949
23. Shoup, V.: Sequences of games: a tool for taming complexity in security proofs. cryptology eprint archive (2004)
24. Unger, N., et al.: SoK: secure messaging. In: 2015 IEEE Symposium on Security and Privacy, pp. 232–249. IEEE (2015)

25. Vaziripour, E., et al.: Is that you, alice? A usability study of the authentication ceremony of secure messaging applications. In: Thirteenth Symposium on Usable Privacy and Security (SOUPS 2017), pp. 29–47 (2017)
26. Washburn, A.J.: Formal Verification Applications for the TreeKEM Continuous Group Key Agreement Protocol. Master's thesis (2022)
27. Washburn, A.J., Shankar, S.: SPIN Model of TreeKEM: FSU & PCS (2024). https://doi.org/10.5281/zenodo.13893828

Formal Privacy Analyses for Open Banking

Luigi D. C. Soares[1,2(✉)], Mário S. Alvim[1], Di Bu[2], Natasha Fernandes[2], and Yin Liao[2]

[1] UFMG, Belo Horizonte, Brazil
contact@luigidcsoares.com, msalvim@dcc.ufmg.br
[2] Macquarie University, Sydney, Australia
{di.bu,natasha.fernandes,yin.liao}@mq.edu.au

Abstract. The term "Open Banking" describes a series of global initiatives to allow the sharing of customer data between financial companies to facilitate competition within their sector. In this paper, we formalise in the rigorous framework of quantitative information flow (QIF) relevant privacy risks in a concrete Open Banking scenario, namely: (i) transaction-history recovery and (ii) collateral attribute-inferences using external correlations. We provide extensive analyses of these risks in real-world data from Open Banking, supplied by a fintech in Australia. We show that the Open Banking system studied presents considerable privacy risks with respect to transactions, both in the presence and in the absence of demographic data. Finally, we exemplify potential real-world collateral attribute-inference attacks, in which we show how an attacker might leverage scientific correlations to infer individuals' level of neuroticism and self-control from their transaction history. We hope that this work may: (i) help financial customers in Australia make better-informed decisions about what kind of information, and how much of it, to share via Open Banking; (ii) raise awareness about the potential privacy risks of Open Banking in other countries; and (iii) foster the development of privacy regulation in digital finance and the open data economy.

Keywords: Open Banking · Privacy-Risk Analysis · Quantitative Information Flow

1 Introduction

The term "Open Banking" describes a series of global initiatives to allow the sharing of customer data between financial companies, such as banks or fintechs (i.e., financial technology companies), in order to facilitate competition within their sector. Under Open Banking, financial institutions provide access to customer banking information via an API.[1] Customers then provide consent for 3rd

---
[1] See https://standards.openbanking.org.uk/api-specifications/ or https://consumerdatastandardsaustralia.github.io/standards/#banking-apis.

parties to access all or some of their banking information. The advantage to the customer is that it (ideally) gives them control over the sharing of their financial data, facilitating access to new financial products or services. The advantage to the financial sector is that it encourages new business models and provides opportunities for smaller fintechs to evaluate customers without requiring negotiation with other banks or relying on customer-provided information.

In this work, we provide a thorough formal analysis of privacy risks associated with sharing de-identified data via Open Banking. This involves (i) *transaction data*, which is de-identified data released via Open Banking and includes details of individual transactions such as amount spent, vendor, location, and date, and (ii) in some cases, *demographic data*, which is de-identified personal data including details such as age, gender, zip code, and job. More precisely, we assess the sensitive information that can be inferred from the collected datasets by any entity with access to them (e.g., the financial institution that collected the data in the first place or any other 3rd party with whom the data is shared).

We formalise our attack models in the rigorous mathematical framework of *quantitative information flow (QIF)* [3]. A crucial advantage of the use of QIF is that it allows for great flexibility in privacy analyses, since variations of practical scenarios of interest can be seamlessly captured in the framework. We notice, however, that QIF is not a privacy guarantee that a system may satisfy (such as differential privacy or k-anonymity, for some proper choice of parameters), but it is rather a framework for quantifying the privacy provided by the system in terms of its resistance to inference attacks. This is a crucial advantage of QIF: its guarantees are presented in terms of threats, which are easier to interpret for data managers and consumers. In terms of scalability, QIF has been put to test in a thorough formal privacy analysis of the Official Educational Censuses in Brazil, covering over a decade of microdata for more than 65 million individuals [4], which led to concrete changes in data-release policies by the Brazilian government.[2] Moreover, QIF has been successfully applied to a wide variety of scenarios that can be modelled as some form of information flow, including privacy and security [1,5,10,13,17], machine learning [23,27], and fairness [6].

Contributions. We rigorously formalise and provide extensive analyses of privacy risks in real-world data from Open Banking, supplied by a fintech in Australia:

- **Transaction-history recovery:** Success in recovering all transactions provided by a customer is clearly a damaging scenario, since it may lead the adversary to infer sensitive attributes, such as customers' buying habits, stores visited, or income. The availability of demographic data can facilitate this process. Nevertheless, as we shall see, this attack remains possible even without any sort of personal information at the adversary's disposal.
- **Collateral attribute-inference:** A crucial novelty of our work is the assessment of a more subtle privacy risk: *collateral attribute-inference* (a.k.a., *Dalenius attacks* in QIF [2,3]). In this case, the goal is not to infer individuals'

---

[2] In Portuguese: https://www.gov.br/inep/pt-br/assuntos/noticias/institucional/nota-de-esclarecimento-divulgacao-dos-microdados.

attributes that are explicitly present in the dataset, but to exploit *known correlations* between *attributes in the dataset* with *sensitive information not explicitly present in the dataset*. Such correlations have been used in, e.g., the Cambridge Analytica scandal to sway voters during elections, with dire consequences.[3] We exemplify a possible real-world collateral-inference attack, where we demonstrate how to leverage external, known correlations to infer individuals' personality traits from their financial activities.

Moreover, we set up a rigorous framework that can be used to model other Open Banking scenarios in the future, and analyze the corresponding privacy threats.

Related Work. Early privacy concerns about Open Banking focused on phishing attacks designed to lure consumers into handing over consent to their data [14]. The potential privacy risks of demographic data have been well-known since at least Sweeney's seminal work with the US Census [25]. Detailed transactions have also been shown to be problematic: four data points in credit card transaction data are enough to re-identify 90% individuals out of 1.1 million people [18]. However, in contrast to our work, these privacy analyses are deterministic.

More recently, studies have found correlations between people's spending behaviours and personal traits, which have been exploited to predict such traits. Examples of correlations range from people's lifestyles and preferences [12] to (possibly) harmful correlations such as individuals' psychological conditions [15,26] —knowing someone's personality traits might, for instance, bear influence on hiring decisions, either for good or bad [7,9,16,19]. Nevertheless, to the best of our knowledge, no previous work has formally quantitatively evaluated collateral-inference types of information leaks from financial data due to known correlations. Our analyses are in line with those of Alvim et al. [4] on educational data, but we incorporate collateral-inferences and consider Open Banking data.

Ethical Disclosure. The demographic and transaction datasets used in this work have been provided to us by a financial institution for the purposes of this research and are not publicly available. Consent was provided by customers for use of this data, and our use of the data has been ethically reviewed by our organisation. No real information about individuals has been revealed in this paper, as our examples use dummy names and values in place of true data. Moreover, no real re-identification or inference was performed in our analyses, since we, as researchers, lack the auxiliary knowledge that we assume the adversary has about customers to complete the attacks.

Plan of the Paper. The remainder of this paper is organised as follows. Section 2 provides necessary background on quantitative information flow (QIF). In Sect. 3, we formalise our attack models in QIF. In Sect. 4, we analyse the first kind of privacy risk, transaction-history recovery, both in the presence and absence of

---

[3] Information obtained from https://www.theguardian.com/news/2018/may/06/cambridge-analytica-how-turn-clicks-into-votes-christopher-wylie.

demographic data. In Sect. 5, we consider the more refined scenario in which the adversary explores a correlation to infer sensitive information not immediately available in the database. Finally, Sect. 6 concludes this work.

2 Preliminaries: QIF

In this section, we review fundamental concepts from quantitative information flow (QIF) that we use to formalise privacy risks. Our model assumes a Bayesian adversary who makes an optimal guess by combining their prior knowledge of the data-sharing mechanism with some auxiliary information.

Secrets, Prior Knowledge, and Prior Vulnerability. A *secret* X models the information sought by the adversary; the set of possible secrets is denoted by $\mathcal{X}$. The adversary's prior knowledge about the secrets can be modelled as a distribution $\pi \in \mathbb{D}\mathcal{X}$, where $\mathbb{D}\mathcal{X}$ denotes the set of all probability distributions over the values in $\mathcal{X}$. We write π_x for the probability assigned by π to secret value x.

In this work, we adopt as a privacy measure the *Bayes vulnerability*, which is closely related to Rényi min-entropy and Bayes risk [8,21,24]. It represents the adversary's probability of guessing the secret value correctly in one try. (See Appendix A for a deeper discussion on privacy measures in QIF.) The *prior Bayes vulnerability* can be computed as

$$V(\pi) = \max_{x \in \mathcal{X}} \pi_x. \qquad (1)$$

Channels, Posterior Knowledge, and Posterior Vulnerability. The secret value is fed into and processed by a system (modelled as a channel) that produces some observable behaviour that the adversary can use to launch an attack. Formally, an *information-theoretic channel* $C : \mathcal{X} \to \mathbb{D}\mathcal{Y}$ takes an input (secret) $x \in \mathcal{X}$ and produces an output (observation) $y \in \mathcal{Y}$ according to some distribution in $\mathbb{D}\mathcal{Y}$. When $\mathcal{X}$ and $\mathcal{Y}$ are discrete, we write C as a matrix whose element $C_{x,y}$ is the probability of producing output $y \in \mathcal{Y}$ when the input is $x \in \mathcal{X}$. Rows in C are distributions over $\mathcal{Y}$; if C is deterministic, every entry in C is 0 or 1, and each row contains exactly one value 1. By combining the prior $\pi : \mathbb{D}\mathcal{X}$ on secrets with knowledge of the channel $C : \mathcal{X} \to \mathbb{D}\mathcal{Y}$ representing how the system works, the adversary can compute a joint distribution $\pi \triangleright C : \mathbb{D}(\mathcal{X} \times \mathcal{Y})$:

$$(\pi \triangleright C)_{x,y} = \pi_x C_{x,y}, \text{ for every } x \in \mathcal{X} \text{ and } y \in \mathcal{Y}. \qquad (2)$$

Now, from the joint $\pi \triangleright C$, the adversary can perform Bayesian reasoning to update their knowledge about the secret from the prior π to a revised knowledge consisting of: (i) a marginal distribution on possible values of y obtained as

$$p(y) \stackrel{\text{def}}{=} \sum_{x \in \mathcal{X}} (\pi \triangleright C)_{x,y}, \qquad (3)$$

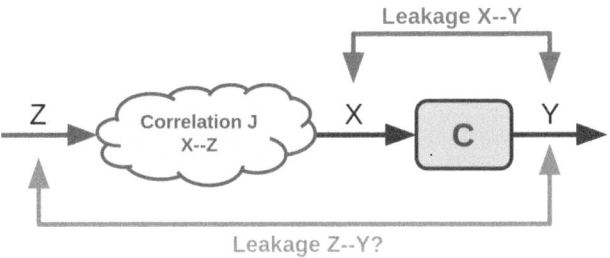

Fig. 1. Collateral-inference leakage: a channel C maps X to Y, but the secret of interest is another value Z correlated with X. Observations of the output Y of C can leak information about Z, given the correlation between X and Z.

and (ii) for each observation y, a posterior distribution δ^y on set $\mathcal{X}$ obtained as the conditional probability $p(x \mid y)$, i.e.,

$$\delta_x^y \stackrel{\text{def}}{=} \frac{(\pi \triangleright C)_{x,y}}{p(y)}, \quad \text{for each } x \in \mathcal{X}. \tag{4}$$

The *adversary's posterior knowledge* is denoted by $[\pi \triangleright C]$, and consists of the distribution on the output values $y \in \mathcal{Y}$ together with each corresponding posterior distribution δ^y on secret values (that is, each δ_x^y is the updated probability of secret value x given that output value y was observed). We consider two possible definitions of *posterior Bayes vulnerability* in this paper:

– *Dynamic* posterior Bayes vulnerability, which corresponds to the adversary's maximum probability of guessing the secret value correctly for a fixed observation y. It is defined as

$$V^y[\pi \triangleright C] \stackrel{\text{def}}{=} V(\delta^y). \tag{5}$$

– *(Expected/static)* posterior Bayes vulnerability, which corresponds to the expected maximum probability of the adversary guessing the secret correctly, weighted over all possible values y that the observation can take. It is

$$V[\pi \triangleright C] \stackrel{\text{def}}{=} \sum_{y \in \mathcal{Y}} p(y) V^y[\pi \triangleright C] = \sum_{y \in \mathcal{Y}} \max_{x \in \mathcal{X}} (\pi \triangleright C)_{x,y}. \tag{6}$$

Information Leakage. Finally, we can compute *channel leakage* as the ratio between posterior and prior vulnerabilities. This corresponds to the multiplicative factor by which the observation of the system increases the adversary's maximum probability of guessing the secret value correctly. In the context of this paper, this captures to how much the customers' privacy risk has increased.

Collateral-Inference Leakage (a.k.a., Dalenius-Scenarios Leakage). Up to this point, we have computed the leakage of secret X caused by a channel C. But now assume that there is another secret Z from a set $\mathcal{Z}$ that: (i) apparently has

Table 1. Relevant fields from each dataset in our attacks. Fields marked as "QID" were considered as the adversary's auxiliary knowledge, whereas fields tagged as "Secret" are the sensitive information that adversaries seek to learn.

	Field	Description	Role
Demographic	Age	Customer's exact age	QID
	Employment	Part/full-time, unemployed, student, etc	QID
	Gender	Customer's gender (male or female)	QID
	Zip Code	Location where the customer lives	QID
	User ID	Customer's identification number	Secret
Transaction	Amount	Total amount paid or received	QID
	Category	Transaction's category (e.g., groceries)	QID
	Date	Year, month and day that the transaction took place	QID
	Payee	To whom the transaction was paid (e.g., Aldi)	QID
	Description	Detailed description of the transaction	Secret
	User ID	Customer's identification number	Secret

nothing to do with C, but (ii) is correlated with X via some joint distribution $\Pi : \mathbb{D}(\mathcal{Z} \times \mathcal{X})$ known to the adversary. In this case, we can quantify how much C (surprisingly) teaches the adversary about Z, as in Fig. 1.

Notice that the joint $\Pi : \mathbb{D}(\mathcal{Z} \times \mathcal{X})$ must induce the marginal distribution π on $\mathcal{X}$ that is the prior to channel C. Π also induces a prior $\rho : \mathbb{D}\mathcal{Z}$ representing the adversary's knowledge about Z. Moreover, we can express the joint Π as the result of combining the prior $\rho : \mathbb{D}\mathcal{Z}$ with a channel $B : \mathcal{Z} \to \mathbb{D}\mathcal{X}$. More precisely: (i) $\rho_z B_{z,x} = \Pi_{z,x}$ for all $z \in \mathcal{Z}$ and $x \in \mathcal{X}$, and (ii) each row $B_{z,-}$ of B is found by normalising row $\Pi_{z,-}$. Now, it can be shown [2,3] that the conditional probability $p(y \mid z)$ for each $y \in \mathcal{Y}$ and $z \in \mathcal{Z}$ from Fig. 1 is equal to $(BC)_{z,y}$, where BC is just the ordinary matrix multiplication of matrices B and C, i.e., $(BC)_{z,y} = p(y \mid z)$. This leads to the following definitions:

– The *prior* collateral Bayes vulnerability of Z is

$$\mathcal{D}V(\Pi) \stackrel{\text{def}}{=} V(\rho). \tag{7}$$

– The dynamic and expected collateral Bayes vulnerabilities are, respectively,

$$\mathcal{D}V^y[\Pi \triangleright C] \stackrel{\text{def}}{=} V^y[\rho \triangleright BC] \tag{8}$$

$$\mathcal{D}V[\Pi \triangleright C] \stackrel{\text{def}}{=} V[\rho \triangleright BC] \tag{9}$$

3 Formalisation of Attacks Under Open Banking

Table 1 describes the relevant information from the demographic and the transaction datasets used in our attacks. Table 2a and 2b provide examples of such datasets. Each individual has a unique, artificially created ID value, which is attached to all of their transactions. Figure 2 provides an overview of our model for Open Banking attacks, whose components we describe in detail below.

Table 2. Example of demographic and transaction data for five individuals.

(a) Demographic dataset.

User ID	Age	Gender
1	46	M
2	21	M
3	46	Female
4	23	Female
5	23	Female

(b) Transaction dataset.

User ID	Payee	Description
1	Red Rooster	Chicken Burger
1	Clinic	Fertility Treatment
2	Aldi	Groceries
3	Uber	23 minutes trip
3	Lakeside Hotel	One night
3	Clinic	Skin-Cancer Treat.
4	Uber	13 minutes trip
5	Uber	25 minutes trip

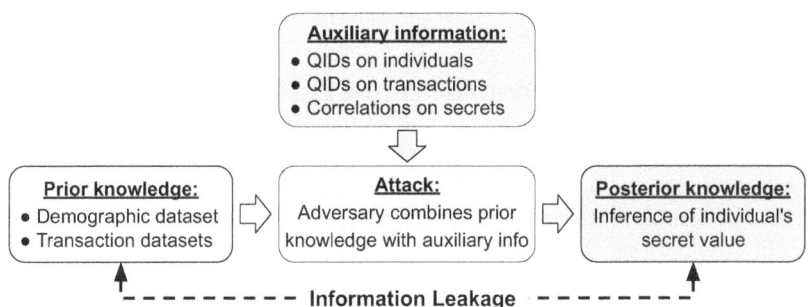

Fig. 2. Overview of attack model.

In our model, the secret X could be, for instance, an individual's employment status in the demographic dataset or the maximum amount spent by a given individual in the transaction dataset. It could even be information not explicitly present in the datasets, such as a person's personality trait (which may be correlated to buying habits), in the case of collateral-inference attacks.

We consider that the adversary has a particular target and has access to the database D of interest (be it the demographic dataset, the transaction dataset, or a combination of both). This gives them a prior π over transaction histories, and their goal is to identify which transaction history belongs to their target — thus recovering all of their target's transactions — or infer some sensitive information correlated to their target's financial activities (i.e., a collateral inference).

In all of our attacks, a crucial element is the use of *quasi-identifiers (QIDs)*, which are attributes that, although not unique in themselves, may be combined to (almost) uniquely identify a record in a dataset [11,20,22,25]. For instance, Sweeney has famously shown that 87% of the population in the USA Census of 1 990 could be uniquely re-identified using only three QIDs: date of birth, gender, and zip code [25]. In this work, we exemplify how QIDs can be used in attacks to Open Banking systems in which we are interested.

Finally, the system C is composed of the demographic and/or transaction datasets, associating secret values X with observable QID values Y. For instance, in Example 1 (Sect. 4.1), the observation Y corresponds to the combination of two QIDs: a customer's age and gender. With access to the database D, the adversary can compute the channel $C : \mathcal{X} \to \mathbb{D}\mathcal{Y}$ mapping secrets to QIDs as

$$C_{x,y} = \frac{\#rows\ with\ secret\ x\ and\ QIDs\ y\ \text{in database}\ D}{\#rows\ with\ secret\ x\ \text{in database}\ D}. \tag{10}$$

The channel C encodes the probability of the adversary learning a particular information $y \in \mathcal{Y}$ under the assumption that the secret is $x \in \mathcal{X}$, i.e., $p(y \mid x)$. Then, once an observation $y \in \mathcal{Y}$ is made from C — or, in other words, upon learning some QIDs y — the adversary can update their knowledge about the secret X via Bayesian reasoning to compute a posterior distribution, as per (4).

4 Quantification of Transaction-History Recovery Risks

In this section, we explore the first kind of privacy risk described in Sect. 1. We start by analysing in Sect. 4.1 the scenario in which the adversary has access to both the demographic and the transaction datasets. Then, in Sect. 4.2 we assess the privacy risks that remain even when the access to demographic data is removed. Each risk is presented with a simple and concrete example of attack, which is then modelled using the formalism from Sect. 3. We then provide experimental analyses of these attacks in real Open Banking data.

We consider as adversary any entity with access to the collected data, be it the original institution or any 3rd party with which the data is shared. We personify such an adversary as Charlize, a data analyst working for a fintech F, whose job is to assess customers' transactions to help them find suitable investment plans. We also assume that Charlize knows that her target is a client of fintech F.

4.1 Transaction-History Recovery via Demographic QIDs

Consider the case where the fintech F collects both demographic and financial data from customers, and let Alex be a client of F. In this scenario, Charlize has access to the demographic dataset from Table 2a as well as to the transaction dataset from Table 2b, and her goal is to recover Alex's financial data in the Open Banking system. Given that no two customers have the exact same transaction history in Table 2b, Charlize's objective reduces to determining Alex's ID.

Example 1. Assume that Charlize learns some (perhaps seemingly innocuous) QIDs about Alex: that she is a 46-year-old woman. Using this knowledge, Charlize can query the demographic dataset of Table 2a and discover that there is only one person with such QIDs in the dataset, thus learning that Alex's ID in the Open Banking system must be 3. Then, Charlize can retrieve Alex's financial history from the transaction dataset and learn all of Alex's transactions details, which includes a transaction to a skin-cancer clinic!

Instantiating the Example Using QIF. In the attack above, the secret X is Alex's transaction history, which, for this example, can be seen as Alex's user ID. Therefore, the secret X takes values in the set $\mathcal{X} = \{1, 2, 3, 4, 5\}$ of five possible IDs. Although Charlize knows that Alex is in the dataset, before the attack she does not have any reason to believe that any ID is more likely than any other to be Alex's. Hence, Charlize's prior knowledge π on Alex's ID is a uniform distribution $\pi = (1/5, 1/5, 1/5, 1/5, 1/5)$ over $\mathcal{X}$. A rational strategy allows her to guess any secret as the correct one, so the corresponding prior Bayes vulnerability is $V(\pi) = 1/5$, meaning that her probability of correctly re-identifying Alex in the Open Banking system assuming no auxiliary information is 20%.

But, since Charlize has access to the demographic dataset, she can employ (10) to build the channel $C^{\text{Re-id}}$ below representing the mapping from user IDs to QIDs in the Open Banking system. Then, she can combine her uniform prior π on IDs with channel $C^{\text{Re-id}}$ to obtain a joint $\pi \triangleright C^{\text{Re-id}}$, as per (2):

$$\pi \quad C^{\text{Re-id}} \; (46,\text{M}) \; (21,\text{M}) \; (46,\text{F}) \; (23,\text{F}) \qquad \pi \triangleright C^{\text{Re-id}} \; (46,\text{M}) \; (21,\text{M}) \; (46,\text{F}) \; (23,\text{F})$$

$$\begin{array}{c}1\\2\\3\\4\\5\end{array}\begin{bmatrix}\frac{1}{5}\\\frac{1}{5}\\\frac{1}{5}\\\frac{1}{5}\\\frac{1}{5}\end{bmatrix} \triangleright \begin{array}{c}1\\2\\3\\4\\5\end{array}\begin{bmatrix}1 & 1 & 0 & 0 & 0\\0 & 1 & 0 & 0\\0 & 0 & 1 & 0\\0 & 0 & 0 & 1\\0 & 0 & 0 & 1\end{bmatrix} = \begin{array}{c}1\\2\\3\\4\\5\end{array}\begin{bmatrix}\frac{1}{5} & 0 & 0 & 0\\0 & \frac{1}{5} & 0 & 0\\0 & 0 & \frac{1}{5} & 0\\0 & 0 & 0 & \frac{1}{5}\\0 & 0 & 0 & \frac{1}{5}\end{bmatrix}$$

From $\pi \triangleright C^{\text{Re-id}}$, Charlize can perform Bayesian reasoning to update her prior knowledge about Alex's ID to some posterior, revised knowledge $[\pi \triangleright C^{\text{Re-id}}]$:

$$[\pi \triangleright C^{\text{Re-id}}] \; \begin{array}{cccc} p(y_1) = \frac{1}{5} & p(y_2) = \frac{1}{5} & p(y_3) = \frac{1}{5} & p(y_4) = \frac{2}{5} \\ (46,\text{M}) & (23,\text{M}) & (46,\text{F}) & (23,\text{F}) \end{array}$$

$$\begin{array}{c}1\\2\\3\\4\\5\end{array}\begin{bmatrix}1 & 0 & 0 & 0\\0 & 1 & 0 & 0\\0 & 0 & 1 & 0\\0 & 0 & 0 & \frac{1}{2}\\0 & 0 & 0 & \frac{1}{2}\end{bmatrix}$$

The first row of $[\pi \triangleright C^{\text{Re-id}}]$ represents Charlize's updated knowledge about the probability of QIDs. Each column under a combination of values for QIDs represents the conditional probability of the corresponding ID being the right one, given these QIDs values. For instance, the column under QIDs $y_4 = (23, \text{F})$ indicates that, given these QIDs, there is a 50% probability that the individual in question has ID $x = 4$ and a 50% probability that the individual has ID $x = 5$.

Now, the attack itself starts when Charlize learns some auxiliary information about Alex: her age (46) and gender (Female). Using these two QIDs, Charlize can filter the demographic dataset and find that there is a unique record matching the criteria: that of user ID 3. Formally, Charlize's posterior knowledge (after learning the QIDs) is updated from a uniform prior on all IDs to a posterior distribution assigning all probability to the ID $x = 3$, as indicated in $[\pi \triangleright C^{\text{Re-id}}]$ above. Now, Charlize's rational strategy is to guess that Alex's ID is 3, and she would be right with probability 1. Hence, the *dynamic* posterior Bayes vulnerability with respect to the observation $y_3 = (46, \text{F})$ is $V^{y_3}[\pi \triangleright C^{\text{Re-id}}] = 1$, as per (5), which is five times higher than the prior Bayes vulnerability.

Notice that, although Alex's QIDs were unique enough to single her out with certainty in the demographic dataset, this may not always be the case. As the column under QIDs $y_4 = (23, \text{F})$ in $[\pi \triangleright C^{\text{Re-id}}]$ indicates, if Charlize's target is a 23-year-old female, the re-identification can happen with only 50% accuracy. Therefore, it may be relevant to assess the expected leakage *over all possible individuals that can be chosen as targets*. In the above scenario, the *expected* posterior Bayes vulnerability, according to (6), is $V[\pi \triangleright C] = 1/5 + 1/5 + 1/5 + 1/5 = 4/5$. This, in turn, means that the expected leakage is $(4/5)/(1/5) = 4$, indicating that Charlize's expected chance of correctly re-identifying Alex upon learning her age and gender is four times higher than Charlize's initial chance of success.

Results. To evaluate the transaction-history recovery risks when demographic data is available, we considered a database with 17 206 customers, who together made 10 223 473 transactions. Table 3 summarises the privacy risks for the four combinations of demographic QIDs that yielded the highest Bayes vulnerabilities, along with the highest outcome when zip code is unknown. Since the demographic dataset contains 17 206 users, the prior Bayes vulnerability is $5.8 \cdot 10^{-5}$. Assuming that the adversary knows their targets' age, gender, zip code, and employment status, the adversary's expected probability of recovering their target's financial activities is 90%. In the absence of the target's employment status, the adversary's expected chance of success of re-identification decreases to 83%. Notice that lack of knowledge about the target's zip code brings the adversary's posterior success rate down to only 3%.

4.2 Transaction-History Recovery via Transaction QIDs

The risks analysed in Sect. 4.1 consider an adversary that has access not only to the transaction dataset, but also to the demographic dataset, which contains revealing QIDs (such as zip code and age) that can be exploited in attacks. In this section, we consider privacy risks that remain even when demographic data is not available. Thus, in the examples below we still consider Charlize, an employee of fintech F, as the adversary, but we assume that the fintech does not maintain demographic data anymore. Charlize's target is now her acquaintance Bob. Furthermore, to investigate how transaction QIDs can be composed as transaction histories grow, we consider Charlize acting in a longitudinal scenario in

Table 3. Risks of transaction-history recovery using the demographic dataset. Results are rounded to three decimal places. The first row corresponds to the case of an adversary whose auxiliary information does not include the target's zip code. The remaining rows correspond to the four combinations of demographic QIDs that resulted in the largest Bayes vulnerabilities, sorted in ascending order. Recall that $V(\pi)$ represents the prior Bayes vulnerability of the secret (i.e., the adversary's probability of guessing the secret correctly before observing the output of the system) and $V[\pi \triangleright C]$ represents the expected posterior vulnerability of the secret (after observing the output of the system). The prior is the same for all cases, and the leakage of information in each case is given by the ratio between posterior and prior vulnerabilities.

QIDs	$V(\pi)$	$V[\pi \triangleright C]$
Age, Gender, Employment	$5.8 \cdot 10^{-5}$	0.034
Gender, Zip Code, Employment		0.368
Age, Gender, Zip Code		0.835
Age, Zip Code, Employment		0.851
Age, Gender, Zip Code, Employment		0.905

which the transaction dataset is updated monthly with the corresponding novel activities performed by customers. We start with a simple motivating example:

Example 2. Charlize learned through some social media platform that Bob has recently eaten at Red Rooster. Using this information, she queries the transaction dataset (Table 2b) and finds that the only compatible transaction belongs to user ID 1. Consequently, Charlize can recover Bob's whole transaction history, which includes a transaction related to a fertility treatment!

Instantiating the Example Using QIF. Here, again, the secret X is Bob's transaction history, which can be seen as the set $\mathcal{X} = \{1, 2, 3, 4, 5\}$ of possible IDs. Before the attack is performed, Charlize has no reason to believe that any value of X is more likely than any other, so she considers a uniform prior π on $\mathcal{X}$. Hence, the prior Bayes vulnerability of the secret is $V(\pi) = 1/5$.

Charlize can build, from the transaction dataset, the channel $C^{\text{Hist.}}$ mapping transaction histories to QIDs, as per (10). Then, by combining the uniform prior $\pi = (1/5, 1/5, 1/5, 1/5, 1/5)$ on IDs with channel $C^{\text{Hist.}}$, Charlize can obtain the joint $\pi \triangleright C^{\text{Hist.}}$, as per (2), and, from that, compute the posterior knowledge $[\pi \triangleright C^{\text{Hist.}}]$:

$$[\pi \triangleright C^{\text{Hist.}}] \begin{array}{c} \\ 1 \\ 2 \\ 3 \\ 4 \\ 5 \end{array} \begin{array}{c} p(y_1) = \frac{1}{10} \\ \text{Red Rooster} \\ \left[\begin{array}{c} 1 \\ 0 \\ 0 \\ 0 \\ 0 \end{array} \right. \end{array} \begin{array}{c} p(y_2) = \frac{1}{6} \\ \text{Clinic} \\ \frac{3}{5} \\ 0 \\ \frac{2}{5} \\ 0 \\ 0 \end{array} \begin{array}{c} p(y_3) = \frac{1}{5} \\ \text{Aldi} \\ 0 \\ 1 \\ 0 \\ 0 \\ 0 \end{array} \begin{array}{c} p(y_4) = \frac{7}{15} \\ \text{Uber} \\ 0 \\ 0 \\ \frac{1}{7} \\ \frac{3}{7} \\ \frac{2}{7} \end{array} \begin{array}{c} p(y_4) = \frac{1}{15} \\ \text{Lakeside} \\ 0 \\ 0 \\ 1 \\ 0 \\ 0 \end{array} \left. \begin{array}{c} \\ \\ \\ \\ \\ \end{array} \right]$$

The attack is actually executed when Charlize uses Bob's transaction payee (y_1 = Red Rooster) as a QID to identify that the corresponding posterior distribution in $[\pi \triangleright C^{\text{Hist.}}]$ (the column below y_1) assigns all probability to $x = 1$. Hence, the posterior *dynamic* Bayes vulnerability is $V^{y_1}[\pi \triangleright C^{\text{Hist.}}] = 1$, which means that, by using as QID the transaction's payee, Charlize's probability of recovering Bob's whole transaction history increased five-fold. The corresponding expected posterior Bayes vulnerability, as per (6), is $V[\pi \triangleright C^{\text{Hist.}}] = 1/10 + 1/10 + 1/5 + 1/5 + 1/15 = 2/3$. Consequently, the expected leakage is $(2/3)/(1/5) = 10/3$.

Table 4. Transaction dataset (second month).

User ID	1	2	3	3	4	5
Payee	Uber	Transfer	Uber	Red Rooster	Uber	Transfer

Now, suppose that Charlize gains access to a second month of transaction data, summarised in Table 4. Charlize can construct a channel $D^{\text{Hist.}} : \mathcal{X} \to \mathbb{D}\mathcal{Y}'$ similar to $C^{\text{Hist.}}$, but for the second month of data. Then, due to independence of the observations, she can compose the two channels into the following channel $C^{\text{Hist.}} \parallel D^{\text{Hist.}} : \mathcal{X} \to \mathbb{D}(\mathcal{Y} \times \mathcal{Y}')$, where $\left(C^{\text{Hist.}} \parallel D^{\text{Hist.}}\right)_{x,(y,y')} = C^{\text{Hist.}}_{x,y} \cdot D^{\text{Hist.}}_{x,y'}$:

$C^{\text{Hist.}} \parallel D^{\text{Hist.}}$	(RR, Uber)	(Clinic, Uber)	(Clinic, RR)	(Aldi, Transfer)	...
1	$\frac{1}{2}$	$\frac{1}{2}$	0	0	...
2	0	0	0	1	...
3	0	$\frac{1}{6}$	$\frac{1}{6}$	0	...
4	0	0	0	0	...
5	0	0	0	0	...

Each output $(y, y') \in \mathbb{D}(\mathcal{Y} \times \mathcal{Y}')$ corresponds to one observation y in the first month and another y' in the second. In this case, the expected posterior Bayes vulnerability reaches $14/15$, and the corresponding expected leakage is $14/3$. Overall, the addition of only one extra month of data increased leakage by 40%.

Results. Table 5 shows the risks of transaction-history discovery for the four worst combinations of transaction QIDs (i.e., the four combinations that resulted in the largest Bayes vulnerabilities), in conjunction with the case when the exact amount is unknown to the adversary (i.e., the adversary knows only the transaction's date, payee, and category). We constructed the channel from the transaction dataset, as per (10), and considered a uniform prior on transaction histories. For this experiment, we considered four (consecutive) months of transactions. The database holds a total of 14 998 194 transactions (ranging from 3 037 108 to 5 121 799 per month) distributed into 42 073 financial histories. Consequently, the prior Bayes vulnerability is $1/42073 = 2.37 \cdot 10^{-5}$.

Table 5. Risks of re-identification and of transaction-history recovery without using the demographic dataset. Results are rounded to three decimal places. The first row corresponds to the case of an adversary whose auxiliary information does not include the transaction's exact amount. The remaining rows correspond to the four combinations of transaction QIDs that resulted in the largest Bayes vulnerabilities, sorted in ascending order accordingly to the last column, i.e., $n = 4$, where n is the number of months considered in the longitudinal setup. Recall that $V(\pi)$ represents the prior Bayes vulnerability of the secret (i.e., the adversary's probability of guessing the secret correctly before observing the output of the system) and $V[\pi \triangleright C_1 \parallel \cdots \parallel C_n]$ represents the expected posterior vulnerability of the secret (after observing the output of the system for n months). The prior is the same for all cases, and the leakage of information in each case is given by the ratio between posterior and prior vulnerabilities.

QIDS	$V(\pi)$	$V[\pi \triangleright C_1 \parallel \cdots \parallel C_n]$			
		$n=1$	$n=2$	$n=3$	$n=4$
Date, Payee, Category	$2.73 \cdot 10^{-5}$	0.053	0.292	0.609	0.836
Date, Amount		0.266	0.807	0.975	0.998
Date, Payee, Amount		0.521	0.911	0.992	0.999
Date, Amount, Category		0.437	0.917	0.994	1.000
Date, Payee, Amount, Category		0.544	0.936	0.996	1.000

Assuming that the adversary learns as QIDs the date, payee, amount, and category of one of their target's transactions, the expected chance of recovering their target's whole transaction history is 54%. Notice that the risk, although much smaller than the 90% found in Sect. 4.1 when the demographic dataset was also available, remains significant. It is worth noting that much of this risk comes from knowing the exact value of one transaction, given that the removal of the transaction's amount would significantly reduce the vulnerability, down to a 5% expected success rate. Nevertheless, as customers share more data over time, this risk increases considerably. A second month's worth of data raises the adversary's success rate to 93%. After a third month, the adversary can recover virtually every transaction history in the dataset, with 99.6% accuracy. And, even with no knowledge about the transaction value, a longitudinal attack over four months of financial activities can raise the adversary's success rate to 83%.

5 Quantification of Collateral Attribute-Inference Risks

In the previous section, we considered the risk of transaction-history recovery, which constitutes a privacy breach for individuals and can reveal very sensitive attributes present in the Open Banking database. In this section, we explore the more refined collateral attribute-inference attacks, where the adversary's goal is not to infer individuals' attributes *that are explicitly present in the Open Banking database*, but to exploit known correlations to infer sensitive information *not explicitly present in the Open Banking database.* To illustrate, consider the following correlation Π between number of transactions and neuroticism level: $\Pi = \{(\text{Low}, 1) : 2/5, (\text{Mid}, 1) : 1/5, (\text{Mid}, 2) : 1/5, (\text{High}, 3) : 1/5\}$. (Neuroticism is scored from 2 to 14, but for simplicity in this example we grouped the scores.)

Example 3. While examining Bob's transactions, Charlize recalls a scientific study that uncovers a strong correlation (the joint Π above) between buying habits and psychological traits. She then decides to apply this study to try to infer Bob's level of neuroticism. Charlize knows that Bob's transaction history is composed of two transactions. By linking this information with the correlation between number of transactions and neuroticism score, she can infer that Bob might have an intermediate level of neuroticism.

Instantiating the Example Using QIF. We want to quantify how much information channel $C^{\#\text{Tr.}} : \mathcal{X} \to \mathbb{D}\mathcal{Y}$ mapping customers' transaction counts X to transaction QIDs Y (indirectly) leaks about the individuals' neuroticism level Z, which takes values in $\mathcal{Z} = \{\text{Low}, \text{Mid}, \text{High}\}$. $C^{\#\text{Tr.}}$ can be constructed from an extension of the transaction dataset, which incorporates the number of transactions made by each individual. Then, we multiply $C^{\#\text{Tr.}}$ by channel B obtained from the joint Π. The result is the channel $BC^{\#\text{Tr.}}$ below:

$$B \begin{array}{c} \\ \text{Low} \\ \text{Mid} \\ \text{High} \end{array} \begin{bmatrix} 1 & 2 & 3 \\ 1 & 0 & 0 \\ \frac{1}{2} & \frac{1}{2} & 0 \\ 0 & 0 & 1 \end{bmatrix} \quad C^{\#\text{Tr.}} \begin{array}{c} \\ 1 \\ 2 \\ 3 \end{array} \begin{bmatrix} \text{RR} & \text{Clinic} & \text{Aldi} & \text{Uber} & \text{Lakeside} \\ 0 & 0 & \frac{1}{3} & \frac{2}{3} & 0 \\ \frac{1}{2} & \frac{1}{2} & 0 & 0 & 0 \\ 0 & \frac{1}{3} & 0 & \frac{1}{3} & \frac{1}{3} \end{bmatrix} = BC^{\#\text{Tr.}} \begin{array}{c} \\ \text{Low} \\ \text{Mid} \\ \text{High} \end{array} \begin{bmatrix} \text{RR} & \text{Clinic} & \text{Aldi} & \text{Uber} & \text{Lakeside} \\ 0 & 0 & \frac{1}{3} & \frac{2}{3} & 0 \\ \frac{1}{4} & \frac{1}{4} & \frac{1}{6} & \frac{1}{3} & 0 \\ 0 & \frac{1}{3} & 0 & \frac{1}{3} & \frac{1}{3} \end{bmatrix}$$

By combining channel $BC^{\#\text{Tr.}}$ with a prior distribution $\rho = (2/5, 2/5, 1/5)$ on neuroticism levels (also extracted from the correlation Π) and employing Bayesian reasoning, Charlize obtains the posterior knowledge

$$[\pi \triangleright BC^{\#\text{Tr.}}] \begin{array}{c} \\ \text{Low} \\ \text{Mid} \\ \text{High} \end{array} \begin{bmatrix} p(y_1) = \frac{1}{10} & p(y_2) = \frac{1}{6} & p(y_3) = \frac{1}{5} & p(y_4) = \frac{7}{15} & p(y_4) = \frac{1}{15} \\ \text{Red Rooster} & \text{Clinic} & \text{Aldi} & \text{Uber} & \text{Lakeside} \\ 0 & 0 & \frac{2}{3} & \frac{4}{7} & 0 \\ 1 & \frac{3}{5} & \frac{1}{3} & \frac{2}{7} & 0 \\ 0 & \frac{2}{5} & 0 & \frac{1}{7} & 1 \end{bmatrix}$$

Then, knowing that Bob went to Red Rooster, Charlize updates her knowledge to the posterior under column y_1. Hence, in this scenario she can be confident that Bob has an intermediate level of neuroticism. In the expected case, the adversary's chance of discovering someone's neuroticism level is $\mathcal{DV}[\Pi \triangleright C^{\#\text{Tr.}}] = 1/10 + 1/10 + 2/15 + 4/15 + 1/15 = 2/3$, as per (9), which is $5/3$ times higher than their prior chance of success $V(\rho) = 2/5$ (i.e., before learning any transaction QIDs).

Results. We now assess the privacy risks of collateral-inference contexts in a real-world dataset. The experimental setup is similar to that adopted in Sect. 4.1. We assess the information leaked from the Open Banking system about someone's psychological trait — neuroticism, scored from 2 to 14, and self-control, scored from 1 to 7 — due to a correlation with that person's spending behaviour. To characterise spending behaviour, we chose three of the metrics analysed by Tovanich et al. [26]: the total number of transactions (n_{tot}), the total amount (a_{tot}), and the average amount (a_{avg}) spent by each customer. We considered only the integer parts of a_{tot} and a_{avg}.

To construct the collateral-inference scenarios, we require a joint distribution between the psychological traits that the adversary seeks and the spending metrics. Tovanich et al. [26] did not provide the joint distributions that correspond to the data they used in their experiments. However, they provided some useful Pearson correlations, together with plots of the marginal distributions on the psychological traits scores. Using these, we determined the marginal distributions from the plots for neuroticism and self-control.

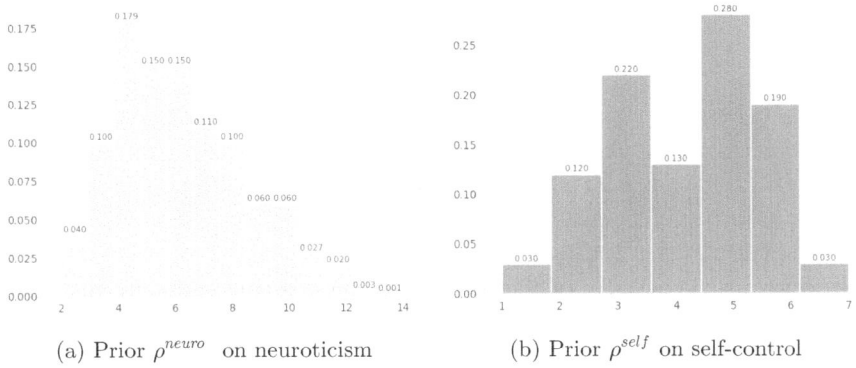

(a) Prior ρ^{neuro} on neuroticism (b) Prior ρ^{self} on self-control

Fig. 3. Prior distributions on psychological traits.

The derived prior (marginal) distributions ρ^{neuro} and ρ^{self} for, respectively, neuroticism and self-control are depicted in Fig. 3. In the absence of auxiliary knowledge, from the prior distribution ρ^{neuro} we conclude that the adversary's optimal guess for a random individual's neuroticism score is 4, the secret value that maximises prior Bayes vulnerability: $V(\rho^{neuro}) = 0.179$. Similarly, the a priori optimal guess for self-control is 5, with a corresponding prior Bayes vulnerability of $V(\rho^{self}) = 0.280$.

For the attack itself, we constructed synthetic datasets correlating the spending metrics and the personality trait scores. For that, we first generate scores for each user in the transaction dataset, following the prior distributions in Fig. 3. Then, we shuffle the trait scores and the metric values. After that, we iteratively randomly choose users (indices), sort the trait scores in ascending order if the target Pearson correlation is non-negative or in descending order otherwise, and sort the metric values in ascending order, until achieving a Pearson correlation as close as possible to the target. (See Appendix B for the pseudocode that was used in the construction of the joints and for the Pearson correlations.)[4]

Table 6 shows the posterior collateral Bayes vulnerability and the corresponding information leakage in our experiments. Knowledge of date, payee, amount, and category of one of their target's transactions and access to the customers' transaction count n_{tot} increases the adversary's probability of guessing their target's neuroticism and self-control score by a factor of, respectively, 1.114 and 1.038 (reaching a posterior success of about 19% and 29%, respectively).

Table 6. Information leakage about individuals' psychological traits, given correlations with their spending behaviour. Results correspond to the 95% confidence interval of 30 randomly constructed joints.

Trait	Metric	$V(\rho)$	$\mathcal{D}V[\Pi \triangleright C]$	Information Leakage
Neuroticism	n_{tot}	0.179	[0.198, 0.200]	[1.114, 1.119]
	a_{tot}		[0.600, 0.601]	[3.362, 3.364]
	a_{avg}		[0.597, 0.598]	[3.346, 3.348]
Self-control	n_{tot}	0.280	[0.290, 0.292]	[1.038, 1.041]
	a_{tot}		[0.616, 0.620]	[2.202, 2.214]
	a_{avg}		[0.641, 0.643]	[2.292, 2.294]

In constrast, knowledge of the total or average amount spent by customers incur on a much higher privacy risk. Access to the total amount spent by customers (a_{tot}) boosts the adversary's expected success by a factor of 3.362 for neuroticism and a factor of 2.202 for self-control. Finally, if the adversary knows the correlation between personality traits and the average amount spent by customers, their chance of identifying their target's trait correctly increases by a factor of 3.346 for neuroticism and by a factor of 2.292 for self-control. In all four scenarios, the posterior Bayes vulnerability reached around 60%.

6 Discussion and Conclusion

Our study has formalised and highlighted the risks of data sharing for consumers, for both transaction-recovery and indirect attribute-inference risks (via collateral-inference scenarios) in a real Open Banking system in Australia. Although our analysis focuses on the risks associated with customers who have

---

[4] We reinforce that the use of synthetic joints was due to the fact that we only had access to correlations in the form of Pearson correlations; the datasets from which these correlations were computed are not publicly available. Nevertheless, we do believe the synthetic data is illustrative of the kind of concrete threat we are considering.

provided consent to use their data, we argue that the onus should be on regulators to ensure that privacy-risk mitigation is inherent in the design of data-sharing protocols. Furthermore, we highlight the issue of accountability for privacy breaches and with whom responsibility lies. Moves to increase consumer controls over data amplify the chances that consumers will unwittingly expose themselves to privacy risks. It appears that consumer-controlled sharing exonerates institutions from obligations regarding private data sharing and forces consumers to absorb that risk. Our view is that it should be up to organisations and regulators to provide guidelines to assist consumers in making informed decisions.

On the Mechanisation of Our Approach. The QIF framework provides formulas according to which the leakage of sensitive information is measured (in terms of prior and posterior vulnerabilities) taking as input: (i) a prior distribution representing the adversary's prior knowledge and (ii) a channel representing the system's behaviour. To compute such formulas in practice, we need to first model the prior and the channel in each case of interest (often writing personalised code to extract the prior and the channel from the data), and then these parameters can be passed onto a QIF library that can compute leakage.

Analyses of Other Scenarios. We highlight that, although this work focused on the implementation of Open Banking in Australia, by analysing one particular dataset provided by a fintech company, the framework described can be used to quantify the privacy risks of any other similar Open Banking model. However, this requires access to other real-world datasets that reflect the specification of the Open Banking system that one wishes to analyse. Consequently, the results may vary according to the data.

Key Recommendations. Our research shows that the release of arbitrary text fields in transaction data leads to unnecessary privacy risks to customers, and privacy liabilities to small fintechs. To our knowledge, these fields are only used to identify transaction categories, and could be redacted to disclose far less information than they do at present. The transactions' payee field may also carry sensitive information, and thus should (at the very least) be treated before being shared. We also recommend to customers that no more than one month's worth of data is released to prevent longitudinal attacks, which are much more damaging with the release of additional data. However, it is unclear how much utility is lost to the fintech in this case (i.e., how much information they would require in order to make a reasonable financial judgement). We leave this investigation to future work. We also believe that the release of demographic data leads to unnecessary privacy invasions above what utility this information might provide, and we recommend that demographic data on individual users is not collected, or, at the least, not directly associated with the provided transaction data.

Future Work. We plan to extend our analysis to other collateral-inference scenarios (e.g., health issues, political preferences) and use the theory of QIF to limit the damage caused by such attacks over all possible correlations and gain functions using collateral (Dalenius) capacity [3]. We also want to study the trade-off between privacy and utility if different privacy mechanisms are employed.

Acknowledgments. Luigi D. C. Soares was supported by the Brazilian National Council of Scientific and Technological Development (CNPq), under grant number 140359/2022-2, and by Macquarie University, via the International Cotutelle Macquarie University Research Excellence Scholarship (Cotutelle "iMQRES").

A More Details on Quantitative Information Flow

The leakage measures used in Quantitative Information Flow (QIF) were developed by the security community in line with the principle that leakages should correspond with an adversarial attack, and if the leakage of a system increases, this increase should be *justifiable* by demonstrating an adversary who is able to learn more from the leakier system. However, leakages can be difficult to interpret in practice, and so we give here some toy examples to explain the leakage measures used in this paper and how to use them.

Let us say that we are given a dataset of 100 users in which one user is identifiable with certainty (using their QIDs) and every other user is identifiable with at most 50% probability. This could be depicted by the following channel:

$$
\begin{array}{c|cccccc}
C & Q_1 & Q_2 & Q_3 & \cdots & Q_{n-1} & Q_n \\
\hline
u_1 & 1 & 0 & 0 & \cdots & 0 & 0 \\
u_2 & 0 & 1 & 0 & \cdots & 0 & 0 \\
u_3 & 0 & 1 & 0 & \cdots & 0 & 0 \\
u_4 & 0 & 1 & 0 & \cdots & 0 & 0 \\
\vdots & \vdots & \vdots & \vdots & \vdots & \vdots & \vdots \\
u_{99} & 0 & 0 & 0 & \cdots & 0 & 1 \\
u_{100} & 0 & 0 & 0 & \cdots & 0 & 1
\end{array}
$$

Now, the risk to user u_1 of having their data breached is *not* the same as the leakage of the system. The risk to a user (with respect to an attack) is given by the posterior vulnerability; this measure focuses on the posterior knowledge of the adversary, i.e., that *after the attack*. The leakage of the system tells us how much the system itself contributes to the attacker's *gain in knowledge* with respect to the prior state, i.e., that *before the attack was performed*.

Let us denote the dynamic Bayes leakage of a system C, assuming a prior π and given an observation y, by $\mathcal{L}^y(\pi, C)$. In the above case, the dynamic posterior vulnerability for the individual user (using a uniform prior v) is $V^{Q_1}[v \triangleright C] = 1$, meaning that their probability of being re-identified given observation Q_1 is 1. The dynamic leakage of this system for user u_1 is $\mathcal{L}^{Q_1}(v, C) = 1/(1/100) = 100$. Hence, the adversary's knowledge has increased 100-fold.

Now consider a dataset of 10 000 users in which one is identifiable with 10% probability. This could be depicted by the channel

$$
\begin{array}{c|cccccc}
D & Q_1 & Q_2 & Q_3 & \cdots & Q_{n-1} & Q_n \\
\hline
u_1 & 1 & 0 & 0 & \cdots & 0 & 0 \\
\vdots & \vdots & \vdots & \vdots & \vdots & \vdots & \vdots \\
u_{10} & 1 & 0 & 0 & \cdots & 0 & 0 \\
u_{11} & 0 & 1 & 0 & \cdots & 0 & 0 \\
\vdots & \vdots & \vdots & \vdots & \vdots & \vdots & \vdots \\
u_{99} & 0 & 0 & 0 & \cdots & 0 & 1 \\
u_{100} & 0 & 0 & 0 & \cdots & 0 & 1
\end{array}
$$

Here the first 10 users share the same QIDs Q_1. Therefore, the probability of an adversary guessing user u_1 given the observation Q_1 (under a uniform prior v) is $V^{Q_1}[v \triangleright D] = 1/10$, as expected, and the dynamic leakage of this system for user u_1 and the observation Q_1 is $\mathcal{L}^{Q_1}(v, D) = (1/10)/(1/10000) = 1000$. Notice that this is higher than what we computed for channel C, which might be interpreted as indicating that this channel D is less safe for user u_1 than is channel C. However, the leakage between two systems operating on different secret spaces cannot be compared in this way, since the adversary has different priors on the different spaces (thus, we are not comparing apples with apples). If we were just considering user u_1, we would just compare posterior vulnerabilities, which implies that channel D is safer than channel C (for that user).

In terms of when to rely on leakages, let us consider now the channel C_2 below, which has the same secret space as C. However, this time no user is vulnerable to attack with certainty.

$$
\begin{array}{c|cccccc}
C_2 & Q_1 & Q_2 & Q_3 & \cdots & Q_{n-1} & Q_n \\
\hline
u_1 & 1 & 0 & 0 & \cdots & 0 & 0 \\
u_2 & 1 & 0 & 0 & \cdots & 0 & 0 \\
u_3 & 0 & 1 & 0 & \cdots & 0 & 0 \\
u_4 & 0 & 1 & 0 & \cdots & 0 & 0 \\
\vdots & \vdots & \vdots & \vdots & \vdots & \vdots & \vdots \\
u_{99} & 0 & 0 & 0 & \cdots & 0 & 1 \\
u_{100} & 0 & 0 & 0 & \cdots & 0 & 1
\end{array}
$$

Now we can compute the dynamic leakage of this system for user u_1 and observation Q_1 and compare it with the corresponding dynamic leakage of C. For C_2, we have $\mathcal{L}^{Q_1}(v, C_2) = (1/2)/(1/100) = 50$, meaning that the adversary's knowledge has increased 50-fold on C_2, compared with their 100-fold increase on C, indicating that C_2 is safer than C for user u_1.

Alternatively, we can compare the multiplicative leakages for the more general cases (expected and maximum gain of the adversary, where the max-case takes into account the "best" observation — in the adversary's perspective —

irregardless of its probability):

$$\mathcal{L}(v, C) = n \qquad \mathcal{L}(v, C_2) = n$$
$$\mathcal{L}^{max}(v, C) = 100 \qquad \mathcal{L}^{max}(v, C_2) = 50$$

This shows that channel C is not better than C_2 for any leakage measure, and is worse for the worst-case measures that we use.

B Construction of Joints from Pearson Correlations

As explained in Sect. 2, a collateral attribute-inference attack requires a joint Π representing a known correlation between secrets Z and X. However, as mentioned in Sect. 5, we only had access to correlations in the form of *Pearson correlations*; the datasets from which these correlations were computed are not publicly available. In view of this, we opted to construct synthetic joints from the Pearson correlations, using the transaction dataset we have available and the Pearson correlations and marginal distributions on the personality traits given in [26]. Algorithm 1 shows the pseudocode for the construction of such joints.

Table 7. Comparison between the Pearson correlations given in [26] and the correlations we obtained for the synthetically built datasets, when demographic information is available. Numbers correspond to the 95% confidence interval of 1 000 randomly constructed joints. The interval's lower and upper limits are rounded down and up to four decimal places.

Trait	Metric	Pearson [26]	Pearson achieved
Neuroticism	n_{tot}	−0.0735	[−0.0735, −0.0734]
	a_{tot}	−0.1644	[−0.1308, −0.1307]*
	a_{avg}	−0.1496	[−0.1496, −0.1495]
Self-control	n_{tot}	−0.0717	[−0.0717, −0.0716]
	a_{tot}	+0.0976	[+0.0975, +0.0976]
	a_{avg}	+0.1524	[+0.1523, +0.1524]

*Target correlation is not reachable with the data available

Table 7 shows the Pearson correlations from [26] between neuroticism/self-control and each of the chosen spending metrics, side by side with the Pearson correlations achieved in the synthetic joints that we constructed.

Algorithm 1. Pseudocode for generating synthetic joints, given two lists, Z and X, and a Pearson correlation between Z and X. The input Z here would be, e.g., a list of neuroticism scores, distributed according to a marginal distribution on neuroticism. And, X would be a list of people's total number of transactions, computed from the transaction dataset. Assume that *pearson* is an existing function that computes the Pearson correlation between two lists.

```
 1: function GENERATE_JOINT(Z, X, target_pcorr, ε)
 2:     // First, update target if original target is unreachable
 3:     if target_pcorr ≥ 0 then
 4:         upper_limit ← pearson_upper_limit(Z, X)
 5:         target_pcorr ← min(target_pcorr, upper_limit)
 6:     else
 7:         lower_limit ← pearson_lower_limit(Z, X)
 8:         target_pcorr ← max(target_pcorr, lower_limit)
 9:     end if
10:     // Then, shuffle data to get an initial joint
11:     Z ← shuffle Z
12:     X ← shuffle X
13:     curr_pcorr ← pearson(Z, X)
14:     n ← |Z| * 10/100
15:     // Finally, iteratively sort data at random
16:     while | curr_pcorr - target_pcorr | > ε do
17:         indices ← choose n indices at random
18:         if target_pcorr ≥ 0 then
19:             Z' ← Z, with Z[indices] sorted in ascending order
20:         else
21:             Z' ← Z, with Z[indices] sorted in descending order
22:         end if
23:         X' ← X, with X[indices] sorted in ascending order
24:         new_pcorr ← pearson(Z', X')
25:         // Due to sorting, pcorr always goes in one direction
26:         if | new_pcorr | ¡ | target_pcorr | + ε then
27:             Z ← Z'
28:             X ← X'
29:             curr_pcorr ← new_pcorr
30:         else
31:             n ← int(n/2)
32:         end if
33:     end while
34:     return (Z, X)
35: end function
```

References

1. Alvim, M.S., Andrés, M.E., Chatzikokolakis, K., Degano, P., Palamidessi, C.: On the information leakage of differentially-private mechanisms. J. Comput. Secur. **23**(4), 427–469 (2015). https://doi.org/10.3233/JCS-150528

2. Alvim, M.S., Chatzikokolakis, K., McIver, A., Morgan, C., Palamidessi, C., Smith, G.: Additive and multiplicative notions of leakage, and their capacities. In: Proceedings of CSF, pp. 308–322. IEEE (2014). https://doi.org/10.1109/CSF.2014.29
3. Alvim, M.S., Chatzikokolakis, K., McIver, A., Morgan, C., Palamidessi, C., Smith, G.: The Science of Quantitative Information Flow. Springer (2020)
4. Alvim, M.S., Fernandes, N., McIver, A., Morgan, C., Nunes, G.H.: Flexible and scalable privacy assessment for very large datasets, with an application to official governmental microdata. Proc. Priv. Enhancing Technol. **2022**(4), 378–399 (2022). https://doi.org/10.56553/popets-2022-0114
5. Alvim, M.S., Fernandes, N., McIver, A., Morgan, C., Nunes, G.H.: A novel analysis of utility in privacy pipelines, using Kronecker products and quantitative information flow. In: Proceedings of the SIGSAC (2023). https://doi.org/10.1145/3576915.362308
6. Alvim, M.S., Fernandes, N., Nogueira, B.D., Palamidessi, C., Silva, T.V.A.: On the duality of privacy and fairness (extended abstract). In: Proceedings of the CADE (2023). https://doi.org/10.1049/icp.2023.2563
7. Behling, O.: Employee selection: will intelligence and conscientiousness do the job? Acad. Manag. Perspect. **12**(1), 77–86 (1998)
8. Braun, C., Chatzikokolakis, K., Palamidessi, C.: Quantitative notions of leakage for one-try attacks. Electron. Notes Theor. Comput. Sci. **249**, 75–91 (2009)
9. Butz, N.T., Stratton, R., Trzebiatowski, M.E., Hillery, T.P.: Inside the hiring process: how managers assess employability based on grit, the big five, and other factors. Int. J. Bus. Environ. **10**(4), 306–328 (2019)
10. Chatzikokolakis, K., Fernandes, N., Palamidessi, C.: Comparing systems: max-case refinement orders and application to differential privacy. In: Proceedings of the CSF (2019). https://doi.org/10.1109/CSF.2019.00037
11. Dalenius, T.: Finding a needle in a haystack or identifying anonymous census records. J. Official Stat. **2**(3), 329 (1986)
12. Di Clemente, R., Luengo-Oroz, M., Travizano, M., Xu, S., Vaitla, B., González, M.C.: Sequences of purchases in credit card data reveal lifestyles in urban populations. Nat. Commun. **9**(1), 3330 (2018)
13. Fernandes, N., Dras, M., McIver, A.: Processing text for privacy: an information flow perspective. In: Proceedings of the FM (2018). https://doi.org/10.1007/978-3-319-95582-7_1
14. Freebairn, P.: Response to the farrell report into open banking. Policy (2018)
15. Gladstone, J.J., Matz, S.C., Lemaire, A.: Can psychological traits be inferred from spending? evidence from transaction data. Psychol. Sci. **30**(7), 1087–1096 (2019). https://doi.org/10.1177/0956797619849435. pMID: 31166847
16. Judge, T.A., Ilies, R.: Relationship of personality to performance motivation: a meta-analytic review. J. Appl. Psychol. **87**(4), 797 (2002)
17. Jurado, M., Palamidessi, C., Smith, G.: A formal information-theoretic leakage analysis of order-revealing encryption. In: Proceedings of the CSF (2021). https://doi.org/10.1109/CSF51468.2021.00046
18. de Montjoye, Y.A., Radaelli, L., Singh, V.K., Pentland, A.S.: Unique in the shopping mall: on the reidentifiability of credit card metadata. Science **347**(6221), 536–539 (2015). https://doi.org/10.1126/science.1256297
19. Moy, J., Lam, K.: Selection criteria and the impact of personality on getting hired. Pers. Rev. **33**(5–6), 521–535 (2004). https://doi.org/10.1108/00483480410550134

20. Narayanan, A., Shmatikov, V.: Robust de-anonymization of large sparse datasets. In: Proceedings of the of S&P, pp. 111–125 (2008). https://doi.org/10.1109/SP.2008.33
21. Rényi, A.: On measures of entropy and information. In: Proceedings of the Fourth Berkeley Symposium on Mathematical Statistics and Probability, Volume 1: Contributions to the Theory of Statistics, vol. 4, pp. 547–562. University of California Press (1961)
22. Samarati, P., Sweeney, L.: Protecting privacy when disclosing information: k-anonymity and its enforcement through generalization and suppression (1998)
23. Silva, R.M., Gomes, G.C.M., Alvim, M.S., Gonçalves, M.A.: How to build high quality L2R training data: unsupervised compression-based selective sampling for learning to rank. Inf. Sci. **601**, 90–113 (2022). https://doi.org/10.1016/j.ins.2022.04.012
24. Smith, G.: On the foundations of quantitative information flow. In: FOSSACS. LNCS, vol. 5504. Springer (2009)
25. Sweeney, L.: Simple demographics often identify people uniquely. Health (San Francisco) **671**(2000), 1–34 (2000)
26. Tovanich, N., Centellegher, S., Bennacer Seghouani, N., Gladstone, J., Matz, S., Lepri, B.: Inferring psychological traits from spending categories and dynamic consumption patterns. EPJ Data Sci. **10**(1), 24 (2021). https://doi.org/10.1140/epjds/s13688-021-00281-y, https://epjdatascience.springeropen.com/articles/10.1140/epjds/s13688-021-00281-y
27. Viegas, F., Alvim, M.S., Canuto, S.D., Rosa, T., Gonçalves, M.A., Rocha, L.: Exploiting semantic relationships for unsupervised expansion of sentiment lexicons. Inf. Syst. **94**, 101606 (2020). https://doi.org/10.1016/j.is.2020.101606

Trusted Deployer: A Tool for Safe Creation and Upgrade of Ethereum Smart Contracts

Juliandson Ferreira[1(✉)], Pedro Antonino[2], Augusto Sampaio[1], A. W. Roscoe[2,3], and Filipe Arruda[1]

[1] Centro de Informática, Universidade Federal de Pernambuco, Recife, Brazil
{jef,acas,fmca}@cin.ufpe.br
[2] The Blockhouse Technology Limited, Oxford, UK
pedro@tbtl.com
[3] University College Oxford Blockchain Research Centre, Oxford, UK

Abstract. The lack of systematic and, particularly, mechanised support to ensure a safe creation and upgrade of smart contracts has led to the deployment of instances with flaws that have been thoroughly exploited, putting digital assets at risk. Formal verification can potentially help to eliminate these high impact flaws, particularly by allowing one to check whether smart contracts obey some desired properties. We have already proposed the concept of a *trusted deployer* to address these issues. In this work we present the detailed design of a public, open-source, and off-chain tool that supports the creation and upgrade of smart contracts, ensuring that they meet corresponding formal specifications. We detail the tool's overall architecture, its usage, and its applicability to real-world smart contracts.

Keywords: Formal Verification · Smart Contracts · Ethereum · Solidity · Safe Deployment · Safe Upgrade

1 Introduction

Smart contracts are programs deployed and executed on a blockchain [1], in which their code is the one and only resort to manage digital assets automatically. Thus, a bug in the code can be exploited and result in vast asset losses [4,18]. Formal verification can help eliminate these costly flaws by checking smart contracts against their corresponding specifications and ensuring safe creation and upgrade, i.e., determining whether or not a smart contract meets its functional and non-functional requirements. By applying a rigorous mathematical process, we can prove the correctness of its behaviour with respect to a given formal specification [13].

Since smart contracts are immutable after the deployment, they cannot easily be patched when bugs or vulnerabilities are discovered, unlike other forms of software. Additionally, they must withstand years of security attacks without putting their digital assets at risk. Therefore, the most effective way to address these issues and ensure a smart contract is safe may be to formally analyze it, to identify and fix vulnerabilities before deployment. The *proxy pattern* [15], developed to overcome immutability drawbacks, is a mechanism by which one can mimic contract upgrades by splitting a contract into two instances: the *proxy instance* holds the contract's persistent state, and the *implementation instance* the code associated with its functions. This allows upgrading the code while keeping the proxy address (the one that is visible to a client) immutable.

To address the aforementioned security concerns, we have devised a *trusted deployer* [2], an off-chain service that ensures safety by allowing the deployment of smart contracts that formally meet their corresponding specifications. We use the proxy pattern to allow the safe upgrading of contract implementations. The main contribution of this paper is to detail the design of a tool that implements an instance of the trusted deployer targeting the Ethereum platform and smart contracts written in Solidity. Formal specification and verification are based on the design-by-contract [12] methodology where the behaviour of each function is given by pre- and post-conditions. We use the *solc-verify* tool [9] to mechanise the reasoning. The overall process is illustrated by an example of the creation and upgrade of the ERC20 token standard. Several other real examples of the tool usage are also discussed.

Section 2 introduces the Solidity language and *solc-verify*. Section 3 presents the architecture of the tool, detailing the characteristics of each of its design elements. Section 4 illustrates how to use the *trusted deployer tool* for safe creation and upgrade of smart contracts, and its application to a real development scenario. In Sect. 5 we make some final considerations about the work, including its limitations, and related and future work.

2 Background

To introduce Solidity and a running example to illustrate the tool in action, we present a fragment of the DigixDAO ERC20 Token implementation (Listing 1.1); in Sect. 4 we present a (data refinement) refactoring of this implementation to illustrate a safe upgrade.

The `users` attribute is a mapping from addresses (represented by a 160-bit number) to a user-defined struct `User`, which has two fields: `balance`, whose type is a 256-bit unsigned integer, that records the user account balance; and `allowed` that keeps track of the number of tokens that an address has made available to be spent by another one.

There is also a public function `transferFrom` that automates the transfer process and allows sending a given amount of tokens (`_value`) on behalf of the owner (`_from`) to a destination address (`_to`), yielding a boolean value that states whether the execution was successful. If the `condition` holds, the execution proceeds normally; otherwise, the function execution aborts, preserving the state before the function call. The condition requires that the sender must have enough balance for the transfer, that crediting the _value amount in the destination address must not generate an overflow, that the value is greater than zero and that the sender has allowance to do the transfer. The next two assignments decrease the sender's balance by _value and increment the destination by the same amount.

Listing 1.2 shows a fragment of the specification for transferFrom in the syntax of solc-verify. The first postcondition determines that the sender's balance should be decreased by the transferred amount only if the sender is not the recipient. The __verifier_old_uint clause yields the before value of the expression (at the very start of the function execution). The second postcondition states that the recipient's balance must increase by the transferred amount unless the sender is also the recipient. The third one, in turn, states that the amount allowed to be transferred is decreased, and the last one ensures that the money to be withdrawn is less than or equal to the allowed amount.

The verification strategy relies on the design-by-contract paradigm, but considers only partial correctness, as is supported by most verification tools for Solidity smart contracts, including solc-verify. Running the tool for this example, it ensures that the specification in Listing 1.2 is met by the code in Listing 1.1.

```
contract DigixDaoERC20TokenOriginal {
    struct User {
        uint256 balance;
        mapping (address => uint256) allowed;
    }
    mapping (address => User) public users;

    function transferFrom(address _from, address _to, uint256 _value) public
        returns (bool success) {
        if (users[_from].balance >= _value && users[_from].allowed[msg.sender]
            >= _value && _value > 0){
            users[_to].balance += _value;
            users[_from].balance -= _value;
            users[_from].allowed[msg.sender] -= _value;
            ...
        }
    }
    ...
}
```

Listing 1.1. Original DigixDao ERC20 implementation

```
/** @notice postcondition ((users[_from].balance == __verifier_old_uint(users[
    _from].balance) - _value && _from != _to) || (users[_from].balance ==
    __verifier_old_uint(users[_from].balance) && _from == _to) && success) ||
    !success
* @notice postcondition ((users[_to].balance == __verifier_old_uint(users[_to].
    balance) + _value && _from != _to) || (users[_to].balance ==
    __verifier_old_uint (users[_to].balance) && _from == _to) && success) ||
    !success
* @notice postcondition (users[_from].allowed[msg.sender] ==
    __verifier_old_uint (users[_from].allowed[msg.sender]) - _value || (users
    [_from].allowed[msg.sender] == __verifier_old_uint(users[_from].allowed[
    msg.sender]) && !success) || _from == msg.sender
* @notice postcondition users[_from].allowed[msg.sender] <= __verifier_old_uint
    (users[_from].allowed[msg.sender]) || _from == msg.sender */
```

Listing 1.2. Original DigixDao ERC20 specification

Another observation is that we consider only postconditions because we reason about contracts as open programs since there is hardly any control concerning the callers of a contract deployed in a blockchain, and a precondition imposes a responsibility to be obeyed by the caller, which, in this context, is not generally possible to verify. If a transaction calls a function from a (pre-)state or with input values that violate its precondition, the result is unpredictable and might not only violate the function postcondition, but also the contract invariant, which is highly undesirable. For this reason, in our verification strategy, we assume true preconditions, and that the applicable states of a function must be captured by the implementation, defining the necessary conditions in one or more require clauses. If any of these conditions does not hold, the function aborts and reverts, as previously explained. In this way, since no precondition is assumed, our verification engine is able to uncover states that violate a function postcondition (or the contract invariant) in two situations: one possibility is that the require statements might not be properly capturing the applicability states of the function, in which case the issue uncovered by the verification can be used as feedback for the developer to further constrain the conditions on the require statements; otherwise, if the applicability of the function is properly captured, the verification issue is indeed an implementation bug, which must be corrected.

3 Trusted Deployer Implementation

In the following, we present the *trusted deployer*, an off-chain service, that controls contract creation and update by checking whether a given implementation meets the expected specification. In the design-by-contract paradigm, the specification of a component includes invariants and, for each of its public functions, pre- and postconditions.

As shown in Fig. 1, the *trusted deployer tool* takes as input a contract $\mathcal{C}$ and a specification $\mathcal{S}$, which might have invariants. Each of its functions is annotated with postconditions that capture its semantic properties. Then it instruments the input $\mathcal{C}$ along with $\mathcal{S}$ which generates what we call a *merged contract* $\mathcal{M}$ - it is obtained by annotating $\mathcal{C}$ with the corresponding invariants and postconditions in $\mathcal{S}$. Firstly, the syntactic obligation imposed by Definition 1 is checked by a syntactic comparison between $\mathcal{S}$ and $\mathcal{C}$. If it holds, we rely on *solc-verify* to check whether the semantic obligation is fulfilled.

Definition 1. *$\mathcal{C}$ satisfies $\mathcal{S}$ iff $\mathcal{M}$ holds following obligations:*

- Syntactic obligation: *a member variable is declared in $\mathcal{S}$ if and only if it is declared in $\mathcal{C}$ with the same type. A public function signature is declared in $\mathcal{S}$ if and only if it is declared and implemented in $\mathcal{C}$.*
- Semantic obligation: *invariants declared in $\mathcal{S}$ must be met by $\mathcal{C}$, and the implementation of functions in $\mathcal{C}$ must meet their corresponding postconditions described in $\mathcal{S}$.*

When requested to upgrade a contract, a new pair $(\mathcal{S}, \mathcal{C})$ is given as input. In any smart contract evolution, we can change the data representation (possibly changing attributes or their types), add new functions or even new *invariants*, and *postconditions*. Every evolution must enforce the obligations imposed by Definition 1, for $\mathcal{S}$ and $\mathcal{C}$. As a part of this process, a *refinement contract* is generated capturing the proof obligation that the new specification must refine the current one. When the evolution embodies a change of the data representation, the reasoning, known as *data refinement*, also requires an *abstraction function*, which relates the data representations of two contracts: the original (or abstract) contract and a refinement (or concrete) contract. As a sophisticated

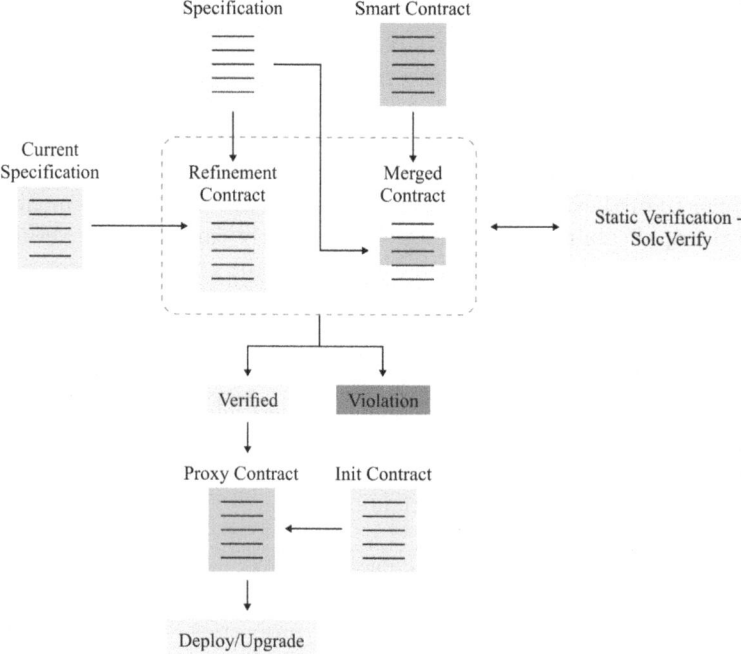

Fig. 1. Schematic workflow of trusted deployer tool

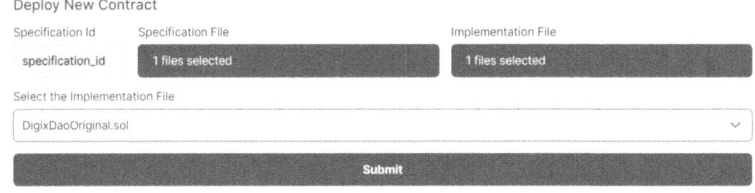

Fig. 2. Screenshot Create Smart Contract

functionality, the trusted deployer tries to automatically generate an abstraction function via an integration with the Alloy Analyzer model finder [10]. If this is successful, the specification refinement proof is fully automatic. Otherwise, the user must provide an abstraction function.

To deploy a contract, we rely on a *proxy contract*—a custom version of the diamond pattern [14] that splits the contract $\mathcal{C}$ across two instances: the *proxy instance* that holds the persistent state and upgrade logic, and the *implementation instance* that is stateless and contains all business logic. Our tool requires, for each update, an *init contract* with a single init function that carries out on chain the state migration from the original contract to the new one. The contracts that will be deployed are of version 0.6.∗. The diamond proxy relies on some Solidity primitives available only from this version onwards.

4 Tool Application Example

This section presents an example of the tool usage in a real development scenario.

4.1 Verification

To illustrate how to use our tool in a real-world scenario, we show how one can evolve an implementation and specification to match a new data representation. The snippet in Listing 1.3 shows the change in the original data representation. The original users attribute was decomposed into two new ones. The specification also needs to be updated to reflect these changes.

One of the proof obligations is to check whether the new specification is a refinement of the original one. In this case, the abstraction function (Listing 1.5) states that, for any address, the value formerly stored as primitive data directly into the users attribute now corresponds to the destructured attributes balances and allowed at the same address. The second verification ensures the implementation in Listing 1.3 conforms to the specification in Listing 1.2.

The *trusted deployer* tool itself is built on top of the modular verifier *solc-verify* and is mainly implemented in Rust and JavaScript. The implementation code as well as all instructions for its configuration and use are available at https://github.com/formalblocks/safeevolution.

Figure 2 shows a screenshot for the creation of smart contracts. According to the workflow, a user starts by providing a *specification_id*: a unique identifier which ensures that all participants interact with the smart contract instance that was created by the *trusted deployer tool*; this is formally verified and safe. The user must also provide the implementation (Listing 1.1) and specification (Listing 1.2) files. Solidity supports multiple inheritance, so multiple contracts can be inherited by a contract that is known as a derived contract. In this case, the user must inform the name of the derived contract to be verified.

In order to upgrade a contract, the *id* of a specification stored by the *trusted deployer* must be provided. The tool checks if it is a valid *id*, in which case the user must provide the new implementation and (optionally) a new specification. Listing 1.3 shows an evolution of the implementation that uses a slightly different mapping (balances) that links addresses directly to balances represented by integer values. This change in data representation is reflected in several places in the remaining (and omitted) code. In the abstract version, a balance associated with a given address, say addr, is referenced as users[addr].balance. In the concrete version, however, this is directly referenced as balances[addr]. The change of data representation is also reflected in the new specification, as illustrated in Listing 1.4.

```
contract DigixDaoERC20TokenNew {

  mapping (address => uint256) public balances;
  mapping (address => mapping (address => uint256)) public allowed;

  function transferFrom(address _from, address _to, uint256 _value) public
      returns (bool success) {
    if (balances[_from] >= _value && allowed[_from][msg.sender] >= _value &&
        _value > 0) {
      balances[_to] += _value;
      balances[_from] -= _value;
      allowed[_from][msg.sender] -= _value;
      ...
  }
  ...
}
```

Listing 1.3. New DigixDao ERC20 implementation

The tool tries to infer and suggest the abstraction function (Listing 1.5) that relates the attributes of both contracts, by using a fully automatic and sound approach we devised. The inputs to this approach are the same abstract and concrete specifications and their corresponding implementations, as depicted in Listings 1.1, 1.2, 1.3, and 1.4. From simulated executions of both implementations, we extract the concrete values of all attributes and use Alloy Analyzer to extrapolate a candidate abstraction function Af whose validity is then verified using a solc-verify. If Af is not valid, we add it as a counter-example, combined with the inputs, in a loop, until a valid Af is found or a bound limit is reached [3].

```
/** @notice postcondition ((balances[_from] == __verifier_old_uint(
        balances[_from]) - _value && _from != _to) || (balances[_from] ==
        __verifier_old_uint (balances[_from]) && _from == _to) && success) || !
        success
  * @notice postcondition ((balances[_to] == __verifier_old_uint(balances[_to]) +
        _value   &&    _from != _to) || (balances[_to] == __verifier_old_uint (
        balances[_to]) && _from == _to) && success) || !success
  * @notice postcondition (allowed[_from][msg.sender] == __verifier_old_uint(
        allowed[_from][msg.sender]) - _value) || (allowed[_from][msg.sender] ==
        __verifier_old_uint(allowed[_from][msg.sender]) && !success) || _from ==
        msg.sender
  * @notice postcondition allowed[_from][msg.sender] <= __verifier_old_uint(
        allowed[_from][msg.sender]) || _from == msg.sender */
```

Listing 1.4. New DigixDao ERC20 specification

```
forall (address x) users[x].balance == balances[x]
forall (address x, address y) users[x].allowed[y] = allowed[x][y]
```

Listing 1.5. DigixDao ERC20 abstraction function

4.2 Deployment

Since Ethereum does not have native support for upgrading smart contracts, we use the proxy pattern to split the contract into two: the proxy instance holding the persistent state and the upgrade logic; and the actual implementation instance. While the proxy instance is the one that handles all public calls, we rely on the `delegatecall` command in Solidity to dynamically execute the business logic defined in the interchangeable implementation instance.

To upgrade the implementation, we rely on our own version of this proxy pattern. We store a new address attribute called `implementation` at the proxy instance. Thus, the behaviour of the proxy's public functions can be upgraded by just changing the address of the implementation instance. However, only the trusted deployer may change the implementation instance since the upgrade logic is wrapped around a function that can only be issued by the address of the trusted deployer. It is important to mention that the upgrade creation process will be interrupted and an error message will be displayed if there is any violation of the defined rules in Definition 1.

Additionally, a difficulty regarding upgrades is the storage migration when there are changes of data representation, since the new version must import and adapt the state from the previous version of an evolution. Although there are different strategies to perform such a storage migration, this typically involves three main steps: extraction, transformation and load. In our strategy, the migration currently requires the user to provide an *init contract* that is executed by the tool. Nevertheless, this strategy has some drawbacks since it requires access to the internal state of the old contract. In addition, for migrating data stored in types such as mappings, it may require an implementation directly in the EVM.

Once the upgrade request illustrated in Fig. 3 is submitted and verified, the tool handles all the interactions with the Ethereum platform transparently to the user. It is worth mentioning, however, that the service is compatible with any network that uses EVM as its default smart contract engine like Fantom [8], Binance Smart Chain [5] and Celo [7], to mention a few.

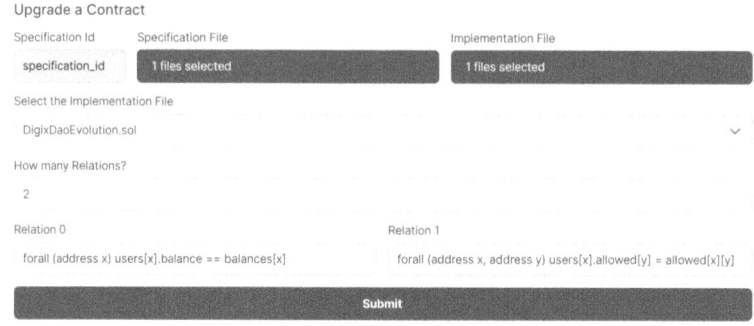

Fig. 3. Screenshot Upgrade Smart Contract

In addition to the running example, our tool was tested against public implementations of Ethereum token standards, such as ERC20, ERC3156, ERC1155, and ERC721, across 12 GitHub repositories. With more than 100 commits analysed from the chosen repositories, our tool was able to identify different types of errors, such as integer overflow or underflow; functions that do not meet a specific mandatory requirement defined in its ERC specification; contracts that do not meet the syntactic restriction defined by the standard; use of wrong relational operators; and other bugs. See [2] for a detailed report.

5 Conclusion

Creating and upgrading smart contracts are common practices in decentralized application development. Despite the increasing number of tools and techniques to boost the productivity of development teams, they do not formally verify smart contracts against a formal specification. Our framework is centred around a *trusted deployer* that prevents the creation and upgrade of non-compliant contracts. So, it guarantees both the *safe creation* and *evolution* of Ethereum smart contracts. Given that Ethereum does not even offer a built-in mechanism for contract upgrades, we offer a significant added benefit with our tool. Moreover, given that one can programmatically check whether contracts have been verified, our tool can be used to ensure that these contracts will have the desired behaviour when deployed.

Several efforts have focused on the verification of the correctness of semantic-level issues in smart contracts. Due to space limitations, we consider only a few closely related approaches. Tools operating on the level of Solidity source code such as VeriSol [21], solc-verify [9], VerX [16] and SmartPulse [19] propose automated verifiers of functional requirements for Ethereum smart contracts.

Requirements are formalized as safety properties; instrumented contracts with these properties are then fed into model checkers, which either verify the properties or indicate violations. All these tools are centred around formally verifying user-provided semantic properties. The proposed *trusted deployer* tool goes beyond and provides a service for smart contract safe deployment and upgrade. Although there is limited work on contract upgrades, we could find some closely related approaches [11,20]. The main difference between our work and theirs relates to the approach to validate patches. While they just upgrade the smart contracts, we formally verify them against a formal specification.

Our tool also shares some similar verification goals to those in [6]. Nevertheless, there are also significant differences. In particular, they proposed an on-chain solution that requires a complete change in the rules of the platform, whereas our tool involves an off-chain solution that can independently be implemented on top of Ethereum's standard infrastructure. In [17], the authors propose contract upgrades at the EVM-bytecode level, based on vulnerability reports issued by the community. Their focus is on test patches, whereas our tool is dedicated to formal verification.

Despite the promising results, our tool can be improved in some directions. The postconditions are bound to the methods that make up the contract interface so it is only possible to specify loop invariants in the body of the implementation contract functions. We are currently exploring the use of LLMs to translate from informal requirements to design-by-contract specifications. We also plan to automate the migration of the contract state when the upgrade involves a change in data representation.

References

1. Ethereum White Paper. https://github.com/ethereum/wiki/wiki/White-Paper
2. Antonino, P., Ferreira, J., Sampaio, A., Roscoe, A.W., Arruda, F.: A refinement-based approach to safe smart contract deployment and evolution. In: Software and Systems Modeling, pp. 657–693. Springer, Cham (2024). https://doi.org/10.1007/s10270-023-01143-z
3. Arruda, F., Antonino, P., Sampaio, A., Roscoe, A.W.: Solver-aided inference of abstraction invariant for the safe evolution of smart contracts. Technical report (2022)
4. Atzei, N., Bartoletti, M., Cimoli, T.: A survey of attacks on ethereum smart contracts (sok). In: POST 2017, pp. 164–186. Springer (2017). https://doi.org/10.1007/978-3-662-54455-6_8
5. Binance. Binance smart chain - a parallel blockchain to binance chain (2020). https://www.binance.org/en/smartChain
6. Thomas, D., Gazzillo, P., Herlihy, M., Saraph, V., Koskinen, E.: Proof-carrying smart contracts. In: Financial Cryptography Workshops (2018)
7. Celo Foundation. Celo - a mobile-first blockchain platform for global payments (2020). https://celo.org/
8. Fantom Foundation. Fantom - high-performance, scalable, and secure smart contract platform (2018). https://fantom.foundation/

9. Hajdu, Á., Jovanović, D.: SOLC-VERIFY: a modular verifier for solidity smart contracts. In: Chakraborty, S., Navas, J.A. (eds.) VSTTE 2019. LNCS, vol. 12031, pp. 161–179. Springer, Cham (2020). https://doi.org/10.1007/978-3-030-41600-3_11
10. Jackson, D.: Alloy: a lightweight object modelling notation. ACM Trans. Softw. Eng. Methodol. (TOSEM) **11**(2), 256–290 (2002)
11. Nomic Labs. Hardhat - ethereum development environment for professionals (2020). https://hardhat.org/
12. Meyer, B.: Applying 'design by contract'. Computer **25**(10), 40–51 (1992)
13. Misson, H.A.: Applying formal verification techniques to embedded software in UAV design (2019)
14. Mudge, N.: EIP-2535: Diamonds, Multi-Facet Proxy. https://eips.ethereum.org/EIPS/eip-2535
15. OpenZeppelin. Proxy Upgrade Pattern (2021). https://docs.openzeppelin.com/upgrades-plugins/1.x/proxies
16. Permenev, A., Dimitrov, D., Tsankov, P., Drachsler-Cohen, D., Vechev, M.: Verx: safety verification of smart contracts. In: 2020 IEEE Symposium on Security and Privacy (SP), pp. 1661–1677 (2020)
17. Rodler, M., Li, W., Karame, G.O., Davi, L.: EVMPatch: timely and automated patching of ethereum smart contracts. In: 30th USENIX Security Symposium (USENIX Security 21), pp. 1289–1306. USENIX Association (2021)
18. Siegel, D.: Understanding the dao attack. https://www.coindesk.com/understanding-dao-hack-journalists. Accessed 25 Sep 2023
19. Stephens, J., Ferles, K., Mariano, B., Lahiri, S., Dillig, I.: Smartpulse: automated checking of temporal properties in smart contracts. In: 2021 IEEE Symposium on Security and Privacy (SP), pp. 555–571 (2021)
20. Suite, T.: Truffle - a development framework for ethereum (2015). https://trufflesuite.com/
21. Wang, Y., et al.: Formal verification of workflow policies for smart contracts in azure blockchain. In: VSTTE, pp. 87–106 (2020)

Author Index

A
Alvim, Mário S.   171
Antonino, Pedro   194
Arruda, Filipe   194

B
Bu, Di   171

C
C. Soares, Luigi D.   171
Carvalho, Gustavo   86

D
Dhonthi, Akshay   35
Dihego, José   86

F
Fernandes, Natasha   171
Ferreira, Diego   49, 68
Ferreira, Juliandson   194

H
Hahn, Ernst Moritz   35
Hamid, Nadeem Abdul   139
Hashemi, Vahid   35
Herring, Jessica   139

K
Kulczynski, Mitja   22

L
Liao, Yin   171
Lima, Lucas   49, 68

L (cont.)
Lotz, Kevin   22

M
Manea, Florin   22

N
Nunes, Miguel Alfredo   120

P
Poulsen, Danny Bøgsted   22

R
Ramos, Filipe   107
Roggia, Karina Girardi   107, 120
Roscoe, A. W.   194

S
Saeedloei, Neda   3
Sampaio, Augusto   86, 194
Sarnighausen-Cahn, Paul   22
Schischka, Nicolas   35
Shankar, Subash   155
Silva, Rafael Castro G.   107

T
Torrens, Paulo Henrique   120

V
Velasquez, Bernny   139

W
Washburn, Alex J.   155

SPRINGER NATURE

GPSR Compliance

The European Union's (EU) General Product Safety Regulation (GPSR) is a set of rules that requires consumer products to be safe and our obligations to ensure this.

If you have any concerns about our products, you can contact us on ProductSafety@springernature.com

In case Publisher is established outside the EU, the EU authorized representative is:

Springer Nature Customer Service Center GmbH
Europaplatz 3
69115 Heidelberg, Germany

The manufacturer's authorised representative in the EU is Springer Nature Customer Service Centre GmbH, Europaplatz 3, 69115 Heidelberg, Germany. If you have any concerns regarding our products, please contact ProductSafety@springernature.com

Printed and bound by CPI Group (UK) Ltd, Croydon, CR0 4YY

26/03/2026

02078933-0012